Work in America Institute's National Policy Studies

With the publication in 1988 of Work in America Institute's newest national policy study, *Training—The Competitive Edge,* the Institute will have completed its seventh major study since January 1978. Previous studies are:

Job Strategies for Urban Youth: Sixteen Pilot Programs for Action
The Future of Older Workers in America
New Work Schedules for a Changing Society
Productivity Through Work Innovations
Employment Security in a Free Economy
Improving Health Care Management in the Workplace

A companion volume to *Training—The Competitive Edge* is *Successful Training Strategies: Twenty-Six Innovative Corporate Models,* edited by Jill Casner-Lotto, also published by Jossey-Bass Publishers.

About Work in America Institute

Work in America Institute, Inc., a nonprofit, nonpartisan organization, was founded in 1975 to advance productivity and quality of working life. It has a broad base of support from business, unions, government agencies, universities, and foundations, as reflected in its board of directors, academic advisory committee, and roster of sponsoring organizations.

In a series of policy studies, education and training programs, an extensive information resource, and a broad range of publications, the Institute has focused on improving the effectiveness of organizations through the use of human resources.

— Training —
The Competitive Edge

Jerome M. Rosow PRESIDENT
WORK IN AMERICA INSTITUTE

Robert Zager VICE-PRESIDENT
FOR POLICY STUDIES AND TECHNICAL ASSISTANCE
WORK IN AMERICA INSTITUTE

— Training —
The Competitive Edge

INTRODUCING
NEW TECHNOLOGY
INTO THE WORKPLACE

A WORK IN AMERICA INSTITUTE
PUBLICATION

Jossey-Bass Publishers

San Francisco • London • 1988

TRAINING—THE COMPETITIVE EDGE
Introducing New Technology into the Workplace
by Jerome M. Rosow and Robert Zager

Copyright © 1988 by: Jossey-Bass Inc., Publishers
350 Sansome Street
San Francisco, California 94104

Jossey-Bass Limited
28 Banner Street
London EC1Y 8QE

Work in America Institute
700 White Plains Road
Scarsdale, New York 10583

Library of Congress Cataloging-in-Publication Data

Rosow, Jerome M.
     Training, the competitive edge.

     (A Work in America Institute publication)
(The Jossey-Bass management series)
     Bibliography: p.
     Includes index.
     1. Employees, Training of.   2. Occupational
retraining.   3. Labor supply—Effect of techno-
logical innovations on.   4. Job security.   I. Zager,
Robert.   II. Title.   III. Series.   IV. Series:
Jossey-Bass management series.
HF5549.5.T7R64 1988   658.3'1243   88-42797
ISBN 1-55542-109-1

Manufactured in the United States of America

The paper in this book meets the guidelines for
permanence and durability of the Committee on
Production Guidelines for Book Longevity of the
Council on Library Resources.

JACKET DESIGN BY WILLI BAUM

FIRST EDITION

Code 8840

The Jossey-Bass Management Series

Published in association with
Work in America Institute

Contents

Preface

Nations everywhere are rushing toward higher technology. Even traditional low-wage countries have joined the race, having already absorbed the lessons of the industrialized West and thus solved the problems of production, quality, and marketing. If the United States is to hold its own in the era of global competition, it will have to adopt (and adapt) new technology more rapidly and successfully than ever before.

But technology is not self-implementing. Its utility depends on the skills and knowledge of the people who direct, operate, and maintain it. Skills and knowledge are the product of training.

For many years, while the United States held a clear lead, training was largely ignored. Today, as training is increasingly seen as an issue of survival or as a competitive edge, it moves toward center stage.

This report and its companion casebook, *Successful Training Strategies: Twenty-Six Innovative Corporate Models* (Jossey-Bass, 1988), grew out of a policy research study conducted by Work in America Institute from January 1985 to December 1987, following two Institute-sponsored conferences dealing with the introduction of new technology in the workplace. The topics of the study reflect areas of concern voiced by companies, unions, and public agencies.

The study was greatly assisted by a distinguished national advisory committee, composed of some twenty-five representatives of major corporations, unions, and the public sector. At each of its semiannual meetings the committee vigorously debated background papers written by experts on a single topic. In addition, the Institute commissioned five or six case studies to illustrate leading-edge practice on each topic. Most of the complete case studies have been published in *Successful Training Strategies: Twenty-Six Innovative Corporate Models;* the cases relevant to the discussions in this book are listed at the end of the individual chapters.

The committee discussions, background papers, and case studies provide the empirical base for this report, but the Institute accepts sole responsibility for the opinions expressed herein.

Readers of one or more of the interim reports that have been issued from time to time have consistently told us that the viewpoint of the study, the principal concepts developed in it, and the illustrative cases are stimulating because they present new information. In fact, few of the many books on training focus on training for new technology. What chiefly distinguishes this book, however, is its orientation. Most training books are addressed either to professionals in the field or to readers supposedly capable of influencing legislation. This one is addressed to decision makers in large companies and unions, both private and public. Politicians' interest in training comes and goes, and their actions are based on sweeping statistics whose relevance to any particular enterprise may be nil. Employers and unions, however, have to live with the consequences of the training actions they commit and omit, and they have access to information of the utmost pertinence to their situations.

The basic questions posed in the book are "What do leaders of employers and unions have to know about training for new technology?" and "How should they act on it?" Top managers and union leaders, therefore, are our primary audience. But if they adopt the views expressed here, then people throughout management ranks will want to understand them also. Most of all, managers of human resources and training will need them.

Judging again from reactions to the interim reports, this book will also be useful to academics and to members of the huge training industry that has grown up in recent years. For, although the book concentrates on training for new technology, much of it applies with equal force to training of all kinds.

Chapter One provides an overview of the issues involved in training for new technology. Chapter Two examines fundamental questions of content, budgets, and cost-effectiveness, pointing out that training needs and limitations may affect the shaping of corporate strategy. Training is essential, costly, and time-consuming—so top management must pay attention. But how? The most reliable basis for decisions about training is corporate strategy, and many companies have tried to make the linkage. Cases cited are Ebasco Services, the Travelers Corporation, Corning Glass Works, American Transtech, Motorola, and New England Telephone.

If an organization and its employees are to fulfill the continually evolving demands for new skills and knowledge imposed by corporate strategy, they need structures and mechanisms to support the effort. Chapter Three considers several of these: learning by objectives, train-the-trainer programs, continuous learning centers, work teams, and pay-for-knowledge plans.

When unions are present, they must play a part because continuous learning is bound to impinge on contracts. The chapter looks at ways in which unions and their members can become actively involved in planning and administering training. A policy of continuous learning also raises questions about the breadth of the skills and knowledge that employees need to acquire. The chapter tells how employers have added material to make job-specific knowledge more valuable to the organization.

Last, Chapter Three shows how continuous change results in a high premium being placed on employees' ability to adapt technology to new and unforeseen uses and tells how this ability can be nurtured. Cases cited are Xerox, General Electric, Joy Manufacturing Company, IBM, General Foods, Kelly/Springfield, S. B. Thomas Company, Intel, Digital Equipment Corporation, Zilog/Nampa, and FMC Corporation. Unions actively involved in several of the cases were Communications Workers of America, International Union of Bricklayers, Service Employees' International Union, United Auto Workers, and United Rubber Workers.

Insofar as successful implementation of new technology requires knowledge and skills beyond the ken of a user company, its employees should be able to obtain help from the manufacturer or vendor. Chapter Four outlines the wealth of opportunities for each side to learn from the other, a wealth that too few manufacturers and users avail themselves of. Some powerful companies get satisfactory help by making it a condition of the equipment purchase. Others obtain it from third-party organizations that combine training and manufacturing skills. New forms of manufacturer-user relationships are needed, and Chapter Four describes some suggestive experiments. Cases cited are Control Data Corporation, Ellemtel, Ford/Sharonville, General Motors/Linden, Goodyear Tire and Rubber, Caterpillar, and Miller Brewing.

Once it is determined what training is needed in order to fulfill corporate strategy, management must consider how to provide such training as cost-effectively as possible. Chapter Five focuses on a systematic approach to cost-effective management of training, already in use in a few companies on large scale and small. Cases cited are IBM; Tennessee Eastman; Manpower, Inc.; and Travenol Laboratories.

Chapter Six examines the application of a cost-effectiveness criterion to the training of employees who have nonstandard, although not uncommon, needs: engineers with bachelor's degrees who seek to earn master's degrees without leaving the workplace. It also shows how certain kinds of training can be provided more cost-effectively by a consortium of community colleges than by the in-house staff of even a very large employer. Cases cited are the National Technological University and General Motors' Automotive Services Educational Program.

Training programs especially designed for functional illiterates is the topic of Chapter Seven. Discussion centers on how cost-effective training can be tailored to the needs of functional illiterates, more accurately described as mid level literates. Examples of several programs for mid level literates are offered, including those for word-processor operators, waste water treatment workers, and electronics technicians.

Unless employees have a reasonable degree of employment security, investment in continuous learning makes no sense. Chapter Eight examines the employment security/continuous learning connection and shows how it can be made to work. In particular, the chapter focuses on retraining as a factor in employment security. It suggests a procedure by which an employer can decide whether, in any given case, it will cost more to retrain an employee or to fire and replace that person with an already-trained outsider. It illustrates how retraining can be linked to the continual forecasting of job phaseouts and job openings within or outside the firm; how even highly specialized professionals can change their specialities to meet changing technological demands within the firm; and how the effectiveness of retraining for a different work unit can be enhanced by immersing the trainee in the new work unit as early as possible. Cases cited are California Employment Training Panel, Xerox, General Electric/Fort Wayne, General Motors/Packard Electric, Pacific Bell Telephone, Pacific Northwest Bell Telephone, General Electric/Columbia, and Hewlett-Packard.

Work in America Institute wishes to express its thanks and appreciation to the countless individuals—including company and union representatives and educators—who provided extensive information in interviews and written materials. Their assistance and cooperation proved invaluable in the preparation of the case reports cited in this book. We also wish to thank the members of the National Advisory Committee, who generously shared with the Institute their ideas and insights on the issue of training, and the writers of background papers, who sparked the freewheeling discussions at committee meetings. The members of the National Advisory Committee are listed elsewhere in this volume. The writers of the background papers are Lionel V. Baldwin, president, National Technological University; Robert L. Craig, former vice-president of the American Society for Training and Development; W. Patrick Dolan, W. P. Dolan & Associates; David Felten and James C. Taylor, International Sociotechnical Systems Design Consortium; Claudia Feurey, Committee for Economic Development; Lynn Guerin, vice-president, Sandy Corporation; Paul S. Goodman, Steve

M. Miller, and Terri G. Hughson, Graduate School of Industrial Administration, Carnegie-Mellon University; Jocelyn F. Gutchess, economics consultant; Bonnie McDaniel Johnson, director, Corporate Technology Planning, Aetna Life & Casualty; Andrew O. Manzini, vice-president, Human Resources and Administration, Ebasco Services Incorporated; James F. McKenney, American Association of Community and Junior Colleges; Oscar G. Mink, director, Graduate Program in Human Resource Development, and Karen Watkins, lecturer, Adult Education and Human Resource Development, University of Texas, Austin; Richard Morano and Jeanne Leonardi, Xerox Corporation; Russell W. Scalpone, Medina and Thompson, Inc.; Thomas G. Sticht, president, Applied Behavioral & Cognitive Sciences, Inc.; Louis G. Tornatzky, director, Center for Social and Economic Issues, Industrial Technology Institute; Dan L. Ward, GTE Communications; and Kenneth N. Wexley, Department of Management, Michigan State University.

The study was made possible by the vision, financial support, and continuing confidence provided by the U.S. Postal Service. The Institute also thanks General Electric Foundation, whose generous grant assisted us in preparing and disseminating this report.

We are particularly appreciative of the contributions of Robert Zager, Work in America Institute's vice-president of policy studies and technical assistance, who was responsible for the initial planning and overall direction of the three-year policy study, which culminates in this report. He was ably assisted in this task by Jill Casner-Lotto, research editor for policy studies and editor of the companion casebook, *Successful Training Strategies: Twenty-Six Innovative Corporate Models.* In this role, she tracked down and evaluated the cases that provide the underpinning for the policy study, recruited writers, and directed the writing of the case reports.

The Institute also wishes to thank the following members of the staff, without whose editorial and production efforts the five interim reports and the final policy report and casebook could not have been published: Frances T. Harte, communications and marketing director; Carol Nardi, executive assistant

to the president; and Beatrice Walfish, former editorial director. Virginia Lentini, assistant to the vice-president for policy
studies, and the library staff were also helpful in bringing this
project to fruition.

Scarsdale, New York   Jerome M. Rosow
August 1988   President
                                 Work in America Institute, Inc.

The Authors

Jerome M. Rosow is the president and founder, in 1975, of Work in America Institute, Inc., a tripartite, nonprofit work research organization dedicated to the advancement of productivity and quality of working life in the United States. A graduate of the University of Chicago, he has had careers in both government and industry devoted to human resources, labor-management relations, and public affairs. He served in executive positions over a period of twenty-four years, as manager of employee relations for Esso Europe in London and, later, as public affairs manager for Exxon Corporation in New York City. In government service, he served as assistant secretary of labor from 1969 to 1971 under the Honorable George P. Shultz, currently Secretary of State. As chairman of the President's Advisory Committee on Federal Pay, from 1971 to 1984, he served as adviser to five presidents.

Rosow was president of the Industrial Relations Research Association in 1979. He has also acted as an adviser to the Committee for Economic Development and as director of the U.S. Business and Advisory Committee of the Organisation for Economic Cooperation and Development (OECD), Paris. He has also served as chairman of the Conference Board Council on Compensation; chairman of the European Employee Relations

xix

Council; and adviser to the International Labour Organisation, Geneva.

Author of numerous articles on management, productivity, human resources, and industrial relations, Rosow is also editor of *The Worker on the Job: Coping with Change* (1974); chairman of the American Assembly on "The Changing World of Work"; coeditor, with Clark Kerr, of *Work in America: The Decade Ahead* (1979); and editor of *Productivity: Prospects for Growth* (1981), *Views from the Top* (1985), *Teamwork: Joint Labor-Management Programs in America* (1987), and *The Global Marketplace* (1988).

Rosow has directed, with Robert Zager, the following policy studies for Work in America Institute: *Job Strategies for Urban Youth* (1979), *The Future of Older Workers in America* (1980), *New Work Schedules for a Changing Society* (1981), *Productivity Through Work Innovations* (1982), *Employment Security in a Free Economy* (1984), *Improving the Management of Health Care in the Workplace* (1985), and *Training—The Competitive Edge* (1988).

Rosow has appeared often on the television program "Good Morning, America," as well as on various network news programs. He is a frequent speaker at national conferences.

Robert Zager is vice-president for policy studies and technical assistance of Work in America Institute, Inc. He received his B.A. degree cum laude from Harvard College in 1940 and an LL.B. degree from Yale Law School in 1947. After receiving his degree from law school, he practiced law for five years in the state of New Jersey and was actively involved with official and volunteer groups dealing with city planning, housing, and education. From 1955 to 1975 he was a management consultant, about half the time in the United States and the other half in the United Kingdom, where he worked in the areas of management/organization development, labor relations, manpower planning, and long-range planning in numerous industrial companies and hospitals.

After returning to the United States in 1975, Zager served for two and a half years as consultant to the National Center for Productivity and Quality of Working Life, primarily on studies of productivity and job security. He was appointed vice-president for policy studies and technical assistance of Work in America Institute in May 1978.

Zager's writings have appeared in newspapers and professional journals in both the United Kingdom and the United States. He has directed, with Jerome M. Rosow, seven policy studies: *Job Strategies for Urban Youth* (1979), *The Future of Older Workers in America* (1980), *New Work Schedules for a Changing Society* (1981), *Productivity Through Work Innovations* (1982), *Employment Security in a Free Economy* (1984), *Improving the Management of Health Care in the Workplace* (1985), and *Training—The Competitive Edge* (1988).

National Advisory Committee for Training for New Technology

Robert M. Anderson
Manager
Technical Education
  Operation
Corporate Engineering and
  Manufacturing
General Electric Company

Paul E. Barton
NAEP Assessment Policy
  Center Liaison
National Assessment of
  Educational Progress

Moe Biller
President
American Postal Workers
  Union

Fosten A. Boyle
Vice-President, Personnel
Honeywell Inc.

**Charles E. Bravo
General Manager, Building
  Systems
Office of Maintenance
  Management
U.S. Postal Service

Owen T. Carter
Vice-President
Human Resources
Ericsson, Inc.

Dennis Chamot
Associate Director
Department for Professional
  Employees
AFL-CIO

*indicates former member
**indicates associate member

*William V. Chapp
Assistant Postmaster General
Engineering and Technical
  Support Department
U.S. Postal Service

David H. Charters
Senior Assistant Postmaster
  General
Human Resources Group
U.S. Postal Service

Donald K. Conover
General Manager
Education and Training
AT&T Corporate Education
  Center

Robert L. Craig
Editor
*Training and Development
  Handbook*
Former vice-president,
  American Society for
  Training and
  Development

Robert W. De Sio
IBM Director of University
  Relations
IBM Corporation

Donald F. Ephlin
Vice-President
Director, United Automobile
  Workers/General Motors
  Department
United Automobile Workers

Sandra Feldman
President
United Federation of Teachers

Robert S. Fenn
National Director of
  Training
The Travelers Companies

**David H. Florio
Special Representative for
  Education Policy
American Federation of
  Teachers

**Chester A. Francke
General Director
Joint Education Activities
United Automobile
  Workers–General Motors
  Human Resource Center

Robert A. Georgine
President
Building and Construction
  Trades Department,
  AFL-CIO

Leonard Glick
Organization and Employee
  Development
Corporate Personnel
Digital Equipment Company

**Richard S. Graff
Program Manager, Building
  Systems
U.S. Postal Service

Robert H. Guest
Professor Emeritus
Amos Tuck School
Dartmouth College

*Donald L. Helfer
Director of Manufacturing
  Technology
Caterpillar Inc.

**Margaret L. Hilton
Research Economist
Communications Workers of
  America

John R. Hurley
Vice-President, Director
Managerial and Professional
  Development
Chase Manhattan Bank, NA

James E. Irvine
Vice-President, American
  Telephone and Telegraph
  Communications
Communications Workers of
  America

Peter A. Jacobson
Assistant Postmaster
  General
Engineering and Technical
  Support
U.S. Postal Service

**Phil N. Jones
Manager, Technical
  Education
Manufacturing General
  Offices
Caterpillar Inc.

**Steve Komjathy
Consultant
Technical Professional
  Programs
IBM Corporation

Jeanne Leonardi
Training Project Manager
Xerox Corporation

J. Daniel Lyons
Director of Training
Goodyear Tire and Rubber
  Company

**Donald R. Mack
Manager, Technology
  Education
General Electric Company

*Samuel M. Malone
Manager, Personnel Planning
Xerox Corporation

**Stephen Margolis
Senior Instructor
The Travelers Companies

**Thomas A. Neill
Director of Industrial
  Relations
American Postal Workers
  Union

Dale Parnell
President
American Association of
  Community and Junior
  Colleges

**Jeffrey Peris
Executive Director
College Relations
Technology
Planning and Development
Merck and Company, Inc.

Richard M. Prosten
Director of Research
Industrial Union Depart-
ment, AFL-CIO

**James F. Rafferty
Senior Curriculum and
Planning Specialist
Training and Development
Department
U.S. Postal Service

*Charles J. Sherrard
Division Manager
Employment/Training
Administration
American Telephone and
Telegraph

Vincent R. Sombrotto
President
National Association of
Letter Carriers

Milan Stone
President
United Rubber, Cork,
Linoleum, and Plastic
Workers of America

**David Sutton
Principal Staff Scientist
Honeywell Inc.

**Lucille Swaim
Assistant to the President
United Federation of
Teachers

James C. Taylor
Consultant

**Don Treinen
Assistant to the
Vice-President, American
Telephone and Telegraph
Communications
Communications Workers of
America

The following members of the committee are also members of
the Work in America Board of Directors and acted as liaisons
between the board and the committee:

Irving Bluestone
University Professor of
Labor Studies
Wayne State University

James J. Renier
President and Chief
Executive Officer
Honeywell Inc.

— Training —
The Competitive Edge

1

Training:
The Competitive Edge

An almost full page advertisement in the *New York Times* of September 29, 1987, carried the headline: "Training—the Competitive Edge." The body of the ad boasted of how much the advertiser, a multinational high-tech company, had gained by intensively training its employees for new technology; it also offered training services to customers. That headline describes a notable exception to the rule in the U.S. economy, where almost all but the largest companies provide little or no training, where only a tiny fraction of the training that does take place is related to new technology, and where the take-up of new technology has been generally thin and spotty. Fortunately, however, in leading-edge companies that contend with international or domestic competition, training for new technology has moved from the periphery toward the center of managerial concern. Four reasons account for this change:

1. Constant accretion of new technology–based products and processes is an essential weapon in the competitive struggle.
2. New technology cannot be successfully acquired and implemented without training.
3. The value added by proper training and the losses incurred by inadequate training are too high to be ignored.

4. The net value of training for new technology increases with wider dissemination throughout an organization.

Strategic management of training for new technology, even in leading companies, is a new and difficult art. This report, based on a three-year study of "Training for New Technology" by Work in America Institute, seeks to extract some of the principal lessons from experience to date—lessons that will be of value not only to leading companies but to the rest of the economy as well. We are persuaded that every sizable company in the United States, in every industry, will eventually face the same challenge.

As competition intensifies and spreads, companies in all sorts of industries will find that, like it or not, they have to behave like high-tech companies because "the onrushing changes in technology and products in almost every industry have combined with increased competition to bring about shorter product lives, more products, more competitive products, more products being introduced, more products phasing out, exponentially increasing management, and operations complexity in manufacturing" (Skinner, 1985, p. 135).

For example, many manufacturing industries not yet directly exposed to international competition are suppliers to industries that are so exposed, and will have to respond to their customers' pressures. Industries outside the manufacturing sector have been insulated from international competition, but their time is approaching. Since their productivity growth in these areas has lagged far behind that of the reinvigorated manufacturing sector, the blow, when it comes, will send many of them reeling.

High-tech companies stay ahead of the competition by cramming higher value—that is, more skills and knowledge per dollar—into their products and processes. The skills and knowledge come from well-directed investments in research, development, new technology, and training. High-tech companies make these investments not because something peculiar to computers, lasers, or high-strength plastics requires it, but because they will succumb to the competition if they don't. If construction companies, banks, retailers, or fast-food specialists made similar investments, they would metamorphose into high-tech organizations. The choice open to them today is no longer whether, but when: should they begin now while the storm is gathering, or wait until it has struck? In making that decision, they will undoubtedly consider that in this instance, as in others, delaying and then trying to catch up will likely be risky.

Reaching for New Technology

In the competitive struggle, companies reach out for new technology for one or more of the following purposes:

- To turn out a product, part, or service that they could not turn out with existing technology
- To perform an operation in larger volume than before
- To perform an operation more economically than before
- To perform an operation faster than before
- To perform an operation with higher quality than before (whether quality, in the particular case, means closer adherence to specifications, better appearance, greater strength for weight, or whatever)

More and more frequently, computers play a part in achieving these purposes—and the part they play has grown. But it is erroneous to equate computers with new technology, as has become so customary in recent years. Most new-technology products and processes are not computers, although they may be computer-directed. New technology grows out of the continual advances in materials science, chemistry, mechanics, hydraulics, pneumatics, electronics, microbiology, and other sciences; it also grows out of continual advances in the art of meshing together elements based on these separate disciplines. Robots, for example, combine mechanical, hydraulic, pneumatic, and electrical features—all under the control of a computer. Computer software may draw on equally diverse disciplines, as well as on mathematics and logic.

In the field of social technology, new intellectual disciplines and better understanding of the emotional context of thinking have increased the ability of groups to solve operational problems. Finally, there are new managerial technologies—for example, the Kan Ban system of inventory control, and Statistical Process Control for quality control—that require training.

No one can know what forms of technology will dominate the economy even a few years hence. Scientific discoveries are, by definition, unpredictable; a discovery is a discovery precisely because nobody knew (although some might have guessed) that nature works in such-and-such a fashion. Economic conditions are no less elusive. Since the state of technology at any moment is a function of science and economics, only certified futurologists can make detailed predictions with confidence. The one safe prognostication—that the knowledge base of science will expand inexorably and each new wave of technology will incorporate more knowledge than its predecessor—guarantees that training for new technology will continue to grow in importance.

New Technology Demands Training

As one examines the case histories referred to in this book, it becomes clear that the amount of training required to profit from a new technology varies directly with the amount and diversity of new knowledge embodied in it. (Technology and knowledge are new insofar as they are new to the *user*.) Too often, that equation is not appreciated until after the user organization has tried to make do with insufficient training, and failed.

The failure results from the mistaken belief that "use" is synonymous with "operate." To use a piece of technology profitably, an organization must do much more than operate it—it must also design for it; power it; load and unload it (with information as well as physical material); adjust, repair, maintain, and improve it; and adapt it to new uses. In addition, the new technology may have to be coordinated with other new or existing technologies. Each of these functions is at least as difficult, technically, as operating, and each calls for its own set of skills and knowledge.

When purchasers of new process technology lack engineering backgrounds, they may be deceived by their experience with user-friendly equipment such as cars and office copiers. A modern luxury car, for all its new technology, is often easier to drive than earlier models. A high-speed copier performs all sorts of tricks at the touch of a few buttons. An advanced airliner is flown by a crew no larger than that of a less-advanced plane of similar capacity. In each case, simplicity of operation has been attained at the price of complicating other functions—but operation is visible to the untrained eye and the other functions take place behind the scenes. Repair and maintenance, in particular, require more, different, and higher skills than before. In human terms, the operator's job is made easier by making other jobs harder. In the case of process technology, "easier" often means "more boring," and "harder" means "more interesting."

Not all the cases mentioned in this report concern the use of newly acquired process technology. Several deal with the steps that precede the introduction of new technology—actions whose success also depends on technological skills and knowledge. Before hardware or software is acquired, an organization must decide what kind, in general, would suit its needs; what kinds are available; and which of the available kinds should be selected. Before reaching that stage, the organization must decide how to produce the new product or service for which the process technology will be needed. And even before that, the organization must decide what new product or service it ought to produce. Such decisions should not be made only on the basis of technology—but to make them with inadequate technological skills and knowledge is to court disaster.

It is important, therefore, to ask: In what proportion of major U.S. companies do the individuals who decide—on new products and services, on production methods, on the acquisition of new technology—have sufficient technical skills and knowledge to make reliable decisions? And what proportion of companies make organized efforts to gain the necessary skills and knowledge?

Product and process technologies do not always march in step. Companies in the semiconductor and computer industries, for example, have developed formidable products and then lost out because of their competitors' superior manufacturing techniques. Other companies with outstanding process techniques have fallen because they neglected to keep up with the competition in developing new products and services. Future survivors will have to keep running on both tracks.

Training for Everyone

The decision to adopt new technology carries with it the demand for new skills and knowledge, but it does not determine which individuals shall acquire which skills and knowledge. That determination depends on the employer's policy for making the best use of its people. If the employer asks employees simply to follow instructions and to ask for help when something goes wrong, it will give them a bare minimum of training but make sure that higher-level professionals and managers know enough to fill the gap. On the other hand, if the employer expects all employees to take responsibility for continuous improvement of quality and productivity, it will encourage and help them to learn as much about the new technology as they can. The most exciting cases noted in this report show that intensive technological training of lower-level employees boosts not only their performance but also the performance of higher-level professionals and managers.

Companies that compete on the basis of quality of product or quality of service have been most assiduous in ensuring that new skills and knowledge permeate the organization. Quality, they have found, has to be designed into the product and built in at every stage of the productive process: the longer one waits to eliminate faulty materials or work, the more costly and unsatisfactory the result. Rigorous inspection, removal of faults, and correction of fault-creating conditions must take place at every stage. Although the employer could, in theory, make these things happen by multiplying the number of quality inspectors and controllers, the cost and confusion would be fearsome. The alternative, which has been adopted with great success, has been to give workers the knowledge, skills, and opportunity to do it themselves. In such cases, the new technology often consists of software, such as Statistical Process Control, or Total Quality Control.

Similar considerations affect the repair and maintenance of new technology. When expensive, complicated equipment goes down, there is tremendous pressure to get it running again as quickly as possible. If the organization relies on higher-level professionals and managers to diagnose problems and correct them, while lower-level employees stand by, two outcomes are likely: (1) downtime will be longer than necessary, and (2) the professionals and managers will have less time to do the work they ought to be doing, work that they alone are equipped to do. The new alternative is to have hourly employees learn to troubleshoot. Training for that purpose includes a deeper understanding of the technological principles behind the equipment and the development of problem-solving skills.

The training consequences of electing to "smarten-up" the workers instead of "dumbing-down" the work stand out most starkly in the case of computer-integrated manufacturing systems:

- Since the technology is complex, draws on several disciplines (for example, electrical, electronic, hydraulic, and pneumatic), and is supplied by multiple vendors, a system requires employees who can integrate the disciplines.
- The jobs of those who run the systems have to be broader in scope than traditional jobs. Training has to match the new responsibilities.
- Operating an integrated system consists of programming, setting up, observing, testing performance, and responding to automatic "error messages"—all far from the usual image of the job.
- To keep downtime to a minimum, maintenance workers must be able to react quickly, diagnose accurately, and devise reliable solutions. They need systematic problem-solving skills and the ability to understand the flow of information as well as materials. Each worker must be capable of performing tasks in several crafts, with freedom to cross traditional craft boundary lines.
- Both operators and maintenance workers must be able to deal with computers and software.

Several of the cases discussed in this book involve quality improvement and repair and maintenance, as discussed earlier. These cases usually originate with the most common occasion for training—when the employer has decided to introduce a particular piece of hardware or software and wants to prepare employees to implement it. As previously noted, however, other occasions for initiating a training program must be considered:

- When the organization has to decide *what* new products and services to produce
- When the organization has to decide *how* to produce the new products and services
- When the organization has to select *which* new processing technology

Although training for these purposes is usually provided only to higher-level professionals and managers, a few companies have included ordinary workers, too, with remarkable results. The nonexempt employees are not expected to assume major responsibility for decisions, but they become valuable aides and advisers to the decision makers, and sometimes even share the responsibility for decisions.

When employers regard training for new technology as a central concern, fundamental questions present themselves in a new light. For example:

- Which employees need to be trained? In which skills? How much are we prepared to spend on training?
- How can we ensure that trainees apply their training in the best interests of the company?
- Are the manufacturers of our new technology doing their fair share to help us train?
- How can we ensure that training is performed in the most cost-effective way?
- Will employees be motivated to learn difficult new skills without assurance of continued employment? At what point is it more cost-effective to reassign or separate current employees and replace them with people already trained for the new technology we plan to adopt?

These questions formed the framework for Work in America Institute's three-year study of "Training for New Technology," which began in January 1985 and concludes with the publication of this report.

In conducting this study, a series of background papers by experts in the field were commissioned, and these were discussed by a national advisory committee drawn from labor, management, academia, and the field of human resource development and training. The final report—and the recommendations that follow each chapter—are based on the background papers, the deliberations of the committee, and on thirty-two case reports of training programs and policies in leading companies, unions, and institutions of learning. (The complete cases are to be found in a companion volume, *Successful Training Strategies: Twenty-Six Innovative Corporate Models,* published by Jossey-Bass in 1988.)

The paragraphs that follow seek to answer the questions we have posed. They also include summaries of the issues discussed in each of the chapters of this report.

Linking Training Strategy to Corporate Strategy

If a training program for new technology is to be managed, rather than conducted ad hoc, it must have a guiding principle for deciding who gets what training, when, how, and where. Traditionally such decisions have been shunted to the professionals of the corporate or site training department, subject to their ability to "sell" proposed programs to top management and/or the trainees' supervisors. Since these professionals had no compass other than their private vision of the company's current and future needs, and some general budgetary limits, it is not surprising that training programs proved to be irrelevant or redundant, while budgets rose and fell like women's hemlines. Conversely, programs unilaterally imposed by top management were scorned by all below.

Today a new notion has begun to take hold—that the sole objective test of relevance for a training program is whether the corporate business strategy requires it. The strategy sets forth the lines of business the company will continue, drop, or enter;

the products and services it will offer; and the new technologies it will adopt. From these flow the specifications of new skills and knowledge to be acquired. Such, at least, is the paradigm. Actual practice falls short, however, because strategic planning is much more difficult than the theory—but the force of the theory keeps companies working at it and learning as they go.

Linkages. Existence of a corporate business strategy does not automatically ensure that employees will gain requisite skills and knowledge. Top managements tend to develop strategic plans under security wraps and disclose the contents slowly, bit by bit, to one level of the organization at a time. But training, like new technology itself, needs a long lead time. Until the plan and schedule for new technology are revealed, the planning and scheduling of training programs must hang fire. Thus the lead times, which should overlap substantially, are added end-to-end.

Sometimes top management withholds information about strategic plans in order to keep competitors guessing. Often, however, secrecy reflects fear that employees and managers may resist major changes—so the firm tells them only what they must know, and only after it is too late for them to raise obstacles. Leading-edge companies find that employees try to be helpful and flexible as long as their livelihoods are not threatened, and as long as the employer provides training that will enable them to do well in a changed assignment. Training, therefore, eases the change process.

A most useful role for the training function is to help top management communicate the strategic business plan by spelling out its consequences for changed responsibilities, skills, and knowledge. The training function also can inject realism into the plan by making top management aware of those consequences while the plan is being formulated.

In some leading companies it is now customary to include in the strategy-formulating group a senior manager who is responsible for training and who plays a part in transmitting the strategy through the operation. The Saturn division of General Motors has taken a different tack: employees at every level and the unions are involved in strategy formulation (although management retains the final decision), in the needs analysis, and in the training programs thus derived.

Budgets. How much should a company spend on training for new technology? Currently, few companies know how much they actually spend on training, let alone how much they ought to spend. They may know how much is in the training department budget, but that is only the beginning of the true cost. The training profession itself is still in the process of reaching consensus on what elements of cost to include and how to measure them.

Even if measurement problems were solved, there would be no rule of thumb to tell a company how much it ought to spend. Companies vary widely on the amount of training they provide, the main variables being industry and size. "Ought" also implies that all training programs are equally effective, efficient, and necessary. Nothing could be farther from the truth.

The practical questions an employer should ask itself are: How much will it cost—in training department expenses, in facilities, in employee work time—to acquire the skills and knowledge to carry out our business strategy? Will the cost invalidate the strategy? The answers can best be constructed from the ground up, program by program.

Evaluating for Cost-Effectiveness. Techniques for designing and delivering training have proliferated to such an extent that an employer, when considering a proposed program of more than minimal scope, has to ask whether other programs would be more cost-effective. Assuming that the objectives of the program—that is, which employees are to learn what skills and knowledge—are strategically necessary, could they be attained better and/or less expensively by different means?

In the current state of knowledge, it may be easier to estimate costs than effectiveness. Few companies make systematic efforts to evaluate whether a program has actually produced the intended learning. Evaluation requires that objectives be stated in advance, but only leading-edge companies do so. The specification of objectives and the evaluation of results should involve four sets of people: (1) those who can authoritatively interpret the corporate strategy; (2) those to be trained; (3) the managers of the trainees, since they will be responsible for putting the new skills and knowledge into action; and (4) the professionals of the training department, who will be responsible for ensuring that the trainees learn what they are supposed to learn.

Toward Continuous Learning

As training for new technology moves from the periphery to center stage, companies find themselves turning into institutions of continuous learning. Continuous, both because they must contend with frequent changes in products, services, markets, and processes, and because these changes affect everyone in the organization. Learning, because employees participate more and more actively in deciding what skills and knowledge they will acquire, as well as how and when. In this new model, learning becomes an integral part of every job; employees teach and learn from each other; and interaction among workers, managers, and trainers is stimulated.

Managing this evolution raises three issues: (1) how to create and institutionalize the necessary structures and mechanisms; (2) how to involve the union, where there is one; and (3) what employees need to know beyond their own jobs.

Institutionalization. The case studies referred to in this volume highlight four types of mechanisms that have come into use, some more widespread than others:

1. Some high-tech companies that practice management by objectives have made the statement and review of *individual learning objectives* a part of the periodic negotiations between employees and supervisors. As a rule, this procedure applies only to technical, professional, and managerial employees.

2. *Train-the-trainer* is probably the most popular mechanism in use. Since every organization contains many more content experts than training experts, and since it is easier for a content expert to learn how to instruct than for a training ex-

pert to learn a new subject matter, companies have drawn the obvious conclusion: Teach content experts the rudiments of training and thus multiply the training capacity and quality of in-house resources.

3. A few companies have established *continuous learning centers,* in which junior-level employees present innovative applications they have developed for their office automation equipment to any peers or supervisors wishing to learn. Success depends on the local manager understanding the equipment, showing enthusiasm for it, encouraging free discussion of innovations, and recognizing employees who come up with outstanding solutions.

4. *Semiautonomous work teams* may be the most natural environment for continuous learning, especially under the policy of *pay-for-knowledge.* Each team comprises many skills; every member has to learn enough to cover for sick or absent members, or to accept job rotation; each additional skill learned brings a wage increment. Teaching and learning become part of the job.

Unions and Training. If employees in a continuous learning company are represented, their union must be involved, because problems with job descriptions, work rules, supervisor-employee relations, pay, and working conditions are bound to arise. The employer should regard union involvement as a plus rather than a minus; workers will feel more confident that training programs serve their interests as well as the employer's, and that their views about training will stand a better chance of breaking through organizational blockages. Workers will also be more inclined to accept the necessity for change, once the union has been persuaded.

If the union is to be involved at all, both parties benefit most when the union becomes a full partner in the training enterprise, sharing in all decisions and in responsibility for results. Union members serve as instructors as well as trainees. In some cases the partnership is symbolized by creating a separate, jointly administered fund for training purposes.

Jointly administered training programs have embraced a wide range of subject matter, from job-specific training to generic training to detailed information about the company's goals, plans, and results. Because the largest joint programs are in companies that have experienced severe job losses, they have given priority to training surplus workers for jobs with other employers.

What Employees Need to Learn. What employees need to learn, beyond their immediate assignments, depends on what the employer wants them to contribute. Leading companies want employees to consider themselves members of the organization, to recommend and implement ways of making the company more successful. Consequently, they tell them a great deal about corporate goals and plans, the operation of the job site, the jobs of peers and managers, the functions of adjacent work units, the technology in use, effective problem-solving methods, and actual costs.

A handful of companies encourage employees to learn the art of technological adaptation, an art whose importance is destined to grow. Potential new uses of flexible automation, robots, or end-user office automation are limited only by the ingenuity of the users. Continuous learning centers, mentioned above, are a good example of how to stimulate adaptation.

Manufacturers and Users

Since new technology is, by definition, new to the user, a company that purchases new technology lacks the skills and knowledge to use it profitably. In an economically rational world the purchaser would expect to obtain the skills and knowledge from the organization that presumably has them—the manufacturer. The manufacturer, in turn, would expect to learn from the user's experience in implementation. Alas, rationality seems not to prevail. A purchaser satisfied with a manufacturer's help is an exception, not the rule.

Actually, there is a rationale: manufacturers of new technology deliberately avoid training commitments and the development of training competency because they believe that, if they were to charge enough to cover the costs of training, their bids would put them at a disadvantage to competitors who do not offer training as part of the package.

In the long run everybody loses from the consequent arm's-length relationship. The purchaser takes longer to make money from the new technology. The manufacturer misses out on improving its product and on the opportunity to win both brand loyalty and an increased market share. The economy suffers because the spread of new technology is retarded.

A new form of relationship is called for—a partnership in learning, which serves a mutual set of interests. Such a partnership provides a natural setting in which companies work together productively and in which continuous learning for both manufacturer and user is the norm. The rewards for each of the partners are enormous.

Opportunities for Learning. If a purchaser and a manufacturer want to learn from each other, they can find a host of opportunities at every stage of the relationship: initial contracting, design, building/testing, formal training, installation, pilot run, start-up, steady state. Formal training, although essential, is far from the only opportunity. In addition to technical matters, the purchaser needs the manufacturer's advice about the impact of the new technology on organization structure, communications, information flows, decision making, and job design.

Examples of valuable learning opportunities include joint development of detailed training specifications at the time of contract; manufacturer training of the purchaser's engineers prior to design; attendance of purchaser's personnel at the manufacturer's work site during system integration; and supervision by a joint manufacturer-purchaser task force of final installation and debugging.

In the case of one purchaser, an automotive manufacturing plant where employee involvement is pervasive, a joint employee-management team took responsibility for designing and executing all training for a major technological changeover. Members of the team visited technology vendors' plants prior to contract; wrote training objectives for the contracts; and designated a cadre of workers who, after being trained at the chosen vendor's plant, trained the rest of the work force. Manufacturers found these interactions taxing but salutary, in that fewer demands were made on their engineers in the post-installation period. Moreover, the purchaser's workers developed more applications for the equipment.

Manufacturers Can Train Well. Some users claim to have procured satisfactory training from manufacturers (despite the odds) by demanding it as a condition of awarding the contract, and by insisting that the training meet detailed performance specifications. That is to say, the contract is not fulfilled until the trainees demonstrate agreed-upon levels of proficiency. To exact such conditions requires clout, and perhaps a buyers' market.

In one case a user obtained access for its training specialists to the manufacturer's plant, in order to prepare training materials; hands-on performance training for operators, craftsmen and managers; training content that matched technology specifications; completion of training before equipment went into operation; and dedication by the manufacturer of a full-time trainer to the project.

In another case the manufacturer accepted similar demands but was allowed to choose between train-the-trainer and total population training.

In a third case, where the technology was new even to the manufacturer, the user's engineers and craftsmen collaborated with the manufacturer's field service staff for six months to perfect the operation of the equipment.

Training Through a Third Party. Competition is driving companies to adopt more highly integrated systems of computer-controlled machines. Certain systems—those that tie together design tools, production tools, and information planning tools—intensify the problems of training for new technology for several reasons:

- Computer and software technologies are critical.
- The complexity requires multiple vendors; therefore, no single vendor has all the know-how.

- Employees of the user company must coordinate their work faster.
- Consequences of a malfunction are very costly.
- All employees of the user company are swamped with information.
- Employee displacements usually occur.

Some purchasers have solved these problems with the aid of a special kind of vendor—one that may have contributed little hardware or software to the system. What distinguishes these vendors is that they have well-developed training capabilities based on experience in manufacturing and/or installing integrated systems. Users express particular appreciation of their zest for integrated systems, their ready access to the various technological disciplines of the system, and the spirit of partnership that infuses the relationship.

Cost-Effective Design and Delivery of Training Programs: A Systems Approach

So diverse are training objectives, program designs, and techniques of delivery that employers need a systematic means of evaluating the spectrum of choices in order to choose the most appropriate training from among competitive proposals. Exciting, expensive, but not necessarily appropriate fads need to be placed in the proper perspective and considered in relation to corporate strategy and personnel requirements. Cost-effectiveness is best achieved when choices are based on a careful scrutiny of the benefits versus the costs of training.

A company widely regarded as a leader in employee training has adopted what it calls a systems approach to enhance the cost-effectiveness of programs. The approach comprises (1) detailed curriculum design that provides courses for the key stages of each employee's career, linked to people-performance requirements outlined in the corporate strategic plan; (2) instructional design, to ensure that the right lessons are learned durably and fast; (3) centralized course development by a multidisciplined team of design specialists, both in-house and consultant; (4) delivery techniques aimed at an optimum degree of decentralization, to offset the cost of professional course development; and (5) measurement and evaluation of results at each stage.

In multisite companies with broad-scale programs, one of the largest training costs is trainees' travel and lodging. Another is the amount of time trainees spend in a program. Although opinions differ on how to assign dollar values to training time, everyone agrees that if trainees can acquire the same skills and knowledge in a one-day program as in a two-day program, then, other things being equal, the one-day program is preferable. Allegedly, new design and delivery techniques can accelerate real learning to that extent.

Delivering Programs to the Geographically Dispersed: Skilled Trades, Technicians, Technologists

The new tools of design and delivery have spurred innovative solutions to training problems that are common to many employers. Two examples illustrate the potential of these new tools:

- Consortia of community colleges that maintain quality control over dispersed training operations
- Satellite communications that enable engineers and scientists to earn master's degrees without leaving the corporate work site

Community Colleges. These institutions have conducted technical training for employers in many parts of the United States, with approval ratings ranging from enthusiasm to thumbs down. As certain institutions have gained reputations for marketing, designing, and executing programs, success has brought invitations to mount large-scale programs to meet the shared needs of dispersed work sites belonging to one or more employers. The colleges have responded by banding together into consortia, and by inducing employers to contribute (sometimes with public assistance) the hardware or software for which employees are to be trained.

The largest consortium brought to our attention comprises some forty colleges all over the country, with more still to join.

Organized by a major automotive manufacturer, its object is to train technicians who will service the company's products, especially in dealers' repair shops. Since the vehicles incorporate more new technology each year, the two-year course has to stay far ahead of current technology. Quality control of the training is maintained by the company, whose national and regional co-ordinators, under the direction of a corporate vice-president, oversee the activities of the participating colleges, dealers, and trainees.

Instructional TV for Technologists. The U.S. economy needs, and will increasingly need, engineers with advanced degrees. More than 70 percent of engineers with bachelor's degrees do not continue their studies for a higher degree because they are attracted by the salaries offered by industry and repelled by the costs of further education. Although knowledge obsolescence is a clear danger, few employers are prepared to send their engineers back to school.

Now twenty-four institutions have joined in operating a satellite TV network that carries graduate-level courses to engineers at the work site. Ninety work sites, mainly belonging to large, high-tech companies, currently receive the transmissions. Nearly 1,000 engineers and scientists are enrolled. Through live broadcasts and videocassettes, students take credit courses toward a master's degree in computer engineering, computer science, engineering management, electrical engineering, or manufacturing systems engineering. Others take noncredit short courses and workshops. In all, over 450 courses are offered. Interaction between lecturers and students takes place by telephone or electronic mail.

Employers bear the cost of receiving equipment, facilities, and tuition, but most expect the students to make up for any class time taken out of normal working hours.

Designing Programs to Train "Functional Illiterates" for New Technology

Another cost-effective training design is a new method of training those who have been considered "functional illiterates."

Millions of Americans of all ages, employed and unemployed, are declared functionally illiterate and cast aside as unsuited for new technology, solely because they have limited skills in literacy and numeracy. In fact, 95 percent of these individuals can read in the sense of decoding words on a page but, for reasons unrelated to native intelligence, they have not learned to process the words into ideas that can guide action. Efforts to force-feed them into literacy by the traditional methods of textbooks, manuals, lectures, and written tests merely compound their deficiencies.

Recent experimental courses demonstrate that such individuals can increase their literacy and numeracy enough, within a fairly short time, to operate new technology competently. The courses interweave training in how to process written material with training in technical skills and knowledge. Literacy and technical components are tied closely to the requirements of the job for which trainees know they are being prepared. New technical concepts are conveyed through examples drawn from the trainees' experience.

The Continuous
Learning/Employment Security Connection

The policy of continuous learning for all is a sound investment only for employers that regard employees as permanent, and in fact those that give highest priority to training usually offer broad assurances of employment security. They rarely promise that they will never lay off or dismiss anyone, which would be unrealistic in today's world, but they do assure employees that layoffs or dismissals will occur only when there are no practical alternatives. Such assurance motivates employees to learn as much as possible in order to advance their abilities and improve their performance. This, in turn, motivates employers to protect their investment in employees.

Skeptics argue that employment security raises to uneconomic levels the cost of obtaining the continually changing mix of skills and knowledge required for global competition. When new technology is introduced, they assert, it costs less to replace current employees with already trained new hires than it does to retrain the old ones. Their claim rests on two assumptions, both unproven: (1) that retraining for new technology is too speculative and costly; and (2) that procedures for matching current employees to future job openings are practically unmanageable.

However, the displacement of career employees under the impact of new technology is a high-risk option. It destroys loyalty, increases resistance to technology, and throws the organization into turmoil. An investment in training, on the other hand, generates a stream of benefits: a smoother transition to new technology, improved morale and motivation, and more effective teamwork in the organization.

Retrain Versus Hire-Fire. The difficulties and costs of retraining have been grossly overestimated; the costs of firing employees and replacing them with outsiders have been grossly underestimated. Employers, including those who opt for retraining, have not checked the facts or made an effective cost/benefit analysis.

The case studies referred to in this volume show that new technology seldom requires employees to be retrained from scratch. On the one hand, they have to acquire certain incremental skills and knowledge, but most of their existing armory remains necessary and valuable. On the other hand, outsiders, while they may already possess the incremental skills, usually lack some of the needed existing skills (especially know-how about the way the organization operates) and, therefore, may not pull their weight on the job for several months. Even the new, better-educated employees require orientation, training, and on-the-job education.

Employers are consistently surprised by the ability of ordinary workers to learn new skills. Often the workers themselves are surprised. Even those hampered by serious deficiencies of basic skills have a remarkable capacity to grow.

On the cost side, employers rarely calculate the expense of retraining, and almost never the outlays incurred in dismissing or retiring old employees and recruiting new ones. Severance pay, unemployment insurance, "bumping" costs, and other tangible costs of firing an ordinary worker can easily amount to $8,000–$9,000. The higher the skills and knowledge required for a position, the more it costs to fire and to replace. Employers who do the arithmetic have found it economical and preferable to retrain even surplus professional employees to fill needed positions in altogether different professional disciplines.

Managing Redeployment. Planning is the sine qua non for matching surplus employees with upcoming jobs. Procedures need not be sophisticated or overintellectualized, in the manner long associated with "manpower planning." But management does need to accept responsibility for anticipating organizational change and foreseeable job closings and openings, tracking the incumbents of jobs likely to become surplus, arranging retraining programs while there is time, and then encouraging voluntary movement of employees from declining jobs to growing jobs.

Once responsibility has been accepted, managers improvise methods of fulfilling it. Refinements suggest themselves in due course. For example:

- A systematic review at corporate level disclosed that it was more economic to retool an old plant and retrain workers than to close the plant and establish a new plant in a new location.
- An employer joined with its union in planning to raise the technological level of a division, in exchange for freedom to transfer low-skill jobs to a low-wage site.
- A company issued quarterly reports of anticipated technological changes and regularly discussed with its union other kinds of changes that potentially affected the numbers and contents of jobs. Employees used this information to make decisions about their careers.
- A company developed and later computerized a system that informed employees about the kinds of vacancies that would likely occur in one or two years, for which their indicated skills and backgrounds might qualify them.

- A plant, facing unavoidable reduction of its work force, instituted training programs geared to the carefully studied opportunities of the local job market.

Context Learning. Companies that retrain employees for new technology have an interest in minimizing the number who fail. Some companies have observed that the success of retraining is greater when trainees know beforehand what jobs they will be occupying, inside or outside the firm, and when they are familiar with the new work unit, its supervisor, and its employees. Accordingly, these companies help trainees acquire this context learning as early as possible. The methods, though simple, are effective.

For example, employees in declining jobs are told as much as possible about the new opportunities arising within the company, so that they can make informed choices. Or, retrainees are assigned to "mentors" from the work units that will employ them. Or, the retrainees' current and future supervisors accept responsibility for monitoring their progress. Or, best of all, retrainees are transferred to their new work units either before or shortly after the start of the retraining process.

Having touched upon the main themes of this report, we now examine each one more closely, with evidence drawn from actual cases, and offer recommendations for action by employers and unions.

2

Linking Training Strategy
to Corporate Strategy

The problems of incorporating new technology into the workplace are as old as industry itself. Technology does not begin and end with the computer. The application of steam power 200 years ago caused as much of a stir as the application of computers is now doing—namely, anxiety and conflict, balanced by great opportunities to increase wealth. With passing years, the pace and scope of change have increased, but the basic forms of challenge to the workplace remain.

Whenever important new technology arrives on the scene, it embodies a major investment of capital by the employer and thus poses the problem of how to put it to most profitable long-term use as rapidly as possible. It must either be integrated into an existing process or become a freestanding new process. Additionally, materials must be brought in to feed it; its output must be transported; new sources of power may be required; methods of controlling the speed and quality of output must be developed; new markets may have to be found; the technology may give rise

The information in this chapter, unless otherwise referenced, is drawn from the background papers and case studies listed at the end of the chapter. Both papers and cases were commissioned by Work in America Institute in the course of its three-year policy study entitled "Training for New Technology."

24

to new products or services; new management skills are called for; and the employees in direct contact with the technology must learn to run it, maintain it, and live with it. All these changes shake the organization and affect, to one degree or another, how fast and how well the new technology comes into use.

Training has always been an essential element in adopting new technology. In previous years an organization could expect reasonable periods of technological stability between waves of change; today, however, in more and more industries, one change rapidly follows another. Accordingly, there is a premium on anticipating new technologies far in advance, so that the organization is prepared for them. The purpose of training is to help people develop skills, not only for today's technology, but for tomorrow's and the day after's.

Training for new technology is part and parcel of a broader training function. The management of technological change, for example, cannot be divorced from managing other kinds of changes, or from the rest of the management job. As a member of this study's national advisory committee said, "If your accountants aren't properly trained, they'll ruin the results of new technology." Here, too, training must deal with the needs of today, tomorrow, and the day after.

Major U.S. companies spend collectively tens of billions of dollars on training. Do they get their money's worth? There is little evidence that they seriously try to answer that question: few assess the costs of training, and fewer assess the benefits. The questions they do ask are far less to the point:

> How much ought we to spend on training?
> What subjects ought to be covered by training?
> Are we doing enough training? Are we doing too much?

Farther down in the ranks, the assessment of training is equally uncertain. Managers regard much of it as an activity of doubtful use, which consumes more time than it is worth and keeps them and their subordinates from doing the real work of the organization.

How can an employer determine whether it is doing the right kinds and amounts of training? What is the right amount to spend on training? These questions are all too reminiscent of "How much should we spend on R&D?" or "How much should we spend on national defense?" Should U.S. companies spend as much, say, as Japanese companies? Should they be guided by a percentage-of-the-payroll rule, like the French? Should underspending companies be compelled to invest more in training, as in France and Britain?

In the long run, there is no logically defensible way to answer such questions except by asking, "What is the company seeking to accomplish? What is the business's long-term strategy? What kinds and amounts of training are required to carry out that strategy and give the company a competitive edge?"

A New Role for Training

A number of interlocking social, economic, and political forces have accelerated the role of change in large organizations today and fostered a highly competitive environment. This environment calls for a new, more dynamic corporate training strategy—one that will anticipate change and help the organization maintain its equilibrium through adjustment and readjustment of its human resources. An essential element in this strategy is training people so that they can deal with change in a proactive rather than defensive manner. Among the powerful changes currently affecting corporations are the following:

1. *Business future.* Organizations are continually reshaping their futures through acquisition, divestiture, merger, diversification, and new product development. These changes realign corporate functions, programs, and resources, but do not automatically realign the capacity of people to carry them out. Since corporate strategy for change is a long-term process, and usually played close to the chest, there is a built-in time lag before the decision is revealed to the organization at large. If the organization is to avoid playing catch-up, the strategic training plan must be linked to decisions about the business's future.

2. *Technology.* Employers are reaching for new technology,

both as a competitive necessity and as a means of substituting capital for labor. Often such investment decisions are made by senior managers who lack the training or experience to plan for effective utilization of the new technology. Other managers and employees are brought into the decision only through a series of delayed rounds of information and, all too frequently, only a few days before the equipment arrives on site. Since the rate of return on a technological investment is greatly influenced by the ability of the users—managers and employees at various levels of the organization—to manage it, it is essential that they view the technology as friendly, efficient, and nonthreatening to their long-term personal interest. Technical training is indispensable for both decision makers and implementers.

3. *Work-force changes.* Today's American work force places a high value on self-development and personal growth. As the level of educational attainment and the proportion of persons with college credentials rise, so do the capacity and desire to learn. An overwhelming majority of American workers believe they have the right to participate in decisions affecting their work, but their ability to contribute depends on the training and reinforcement they receive as employees. Conversely, restrictions on self-development, personal growth, and participation feed counterproductive behavior and impair the ability of the organization to respond to change.

4. *Occupational changes.* The changing nature of the American economy, the shift from manufacturing to service, and the impact of research, development, and technology are reflected fairly rapidly in occupational obsolescence and the emergence of new occupations. The U.S. Department of Labor estimates that two out of every five people will be obliged to change occupations every five years, even if they do not change employers. If the organization fails to meet—through training—this need for flexibility, it will suffer increased turnover, lower productivity, and a widening gap between corporate investment and performance.

5. *Communications barriers.* Every large organization is plagued by communication barriers—some intentional, many unintended. Corporate strategy may be crystal clear to those

who have made decisions, but it becomes more and more blurred in the course of transmission across hierarchical and geographical boundaries. Communication gaps can be offset to some degree by a corporatewide training strategy that disseminates skills, programs, and managerial ideas, and feeds back information about what is needed by employees to achieve the corporate strategy.

6. *Resistance to change.* No matter how enlightened the organization is, or how secure the employees and managers may be, change is usually threatening. Since corporate strategy necessarily projects and anticipates change, and since most employees have no part in these decisions, messages about strategy—whether the news is good, bad, or indifferent—unsettle the organization. Training can mitigate the fear and make change more positive. It can also shorten the time between corporate decisions and organizational responses.

As the orientation of training responds to these forces and shifts toward anticipating, shaping, and preparing for a future of rapid change, top management must recast the ways training is budgeted, evaluated, and executed.

Training and Budgets

No one knows with any precision how much employers in the United States, individually or collectively, spend on training, let alone what benefits they derive from it. Nor does anyone know how much an employer ought to spend on training, although governments in Europe and the United States, along with many outside observers, believe that answers exist if one looks hard enough; most agree that more is needed.

Those who look for guidance to other companies' statistics, or to global statistics, will find little help. Most employers do not have reliable information about how much they spend on training, and there is as yet no reliable central source gathering whatever information is available. There is not even general agreement on how to measure costs.

Several years ago the American Society for Training and Development (ASTD) developed a rough figure of $30 billion as the total annual expenditure by U.S. employers for employee education and training. This number covers all private and public employers (except the military), and includes both direct and indirect (allocated) expenses; it does not include salaries or wages of those being trained—or time off the job, lost opportunity costs, and so on. The trainee population includes all employees, from entry level through top management.

Although not a precise figure, $30 billion has been widely accepted as reasonable. Various other estimates over the past ten years have ranged from $2 billion to $100 billion or more. Some of the higher numbers have taken trainees' wages into account, which obviously increases the total five, six, or more times.

The ASTD number does not include informal, on-the-job training (OJT) or coaching or normal supervision that might be perceived as training. It encompasses only formal, organized learning experiences paid for by the employer. OJT would increase that total cost many times again—assuming that there were some way of counting it.

ASTD's estimate was developed just before the economic recession of the early 1980s. True to past form, training expenditures appeared not to grow during that period. On the other hand, there did not appear to be a substantial reduction in training budgets, as so often had been the case in earlier recessions.

According to a survey of training and development executives by Psychological Associates, Inc., of St. Louis, Missouri, training budgets approved for 1983 were generally higher than for 1982, but not by much. The same survey also showed a shift to smaller increases in the numbers of trainees as well as training and development personnel.

ASTD national membership levels, another indicator of employee training activity, virtually doubled between 1975 and 1980, but stayed relatively constant during the recession. During 1984, there were signs that membership had started to grow again and strong growth signs from some of the "training industry" suppliers to the field. Sales volume from some of these firms was reported to show annualized increases of 20, 30, and even 40 percent.

ASTD developed its training-expenditure estimate by rough extrapolations from microlevel data, with allowances for the vagaries of such data. A great deal of training is highly decentralized in many companies, and records are not kept in a central location. Thus, there is no assurance that every instance of training is included in the available information. Many training expenses are never recorded as such in a company's accounting system simply because the system does not provide for effectively capturing training expenses.

There is also strong evidence that some training expenses are hidden, with varying degrees of deliberateness. Training managers, and even line managers, sometimes incur more training costs than they believe top management will approve. Training is often seen as an expense without a quick, direct payback; thus it is often postponed or dispensed with, particularly in times of economic stress.

The variables that influence employer investment in training include the rate of technological change in the business, the culture of the business or industry, the work force demographics for the industry, and the size of the company. A company that depends on the productivity of a large force of engineers at the leading edge will sense a greater need to invest in continuing education than will a trucking company in the freight business.

Training cost breakdowns vary widely, too. The share spent for full- and part-time salaries of training personnel (not trainees) ran from 16.3 percent to 81.2 percent of the total training budgets. Outside purchases for training ranged from 1.2 percent to 59.4 percent; overhead allocations, from 3.0 percent to 40.4 percent; and outside meeting expenses, from 2.6 percent to 21.7 percent. There were no particular patterns to the distribution of the numbers in between.

Some of the large differences among organizational data may well be due to the lack of consistent accounting practices for capturing training costs. Overhead costs could be a prime example. Different companies allocate their indirect, or overhead, expenses to the training function in widely divergent ways.

Another indicator of employer investment in training is reports of sales by the "training industry." The relative market share for management training is dropping. Revenues to the training industry from off-the-shelf programs, custom-designed training, and generic seminars in the areas of management development, organizational development, and supervisory training rose only 88 percent from 1977 to 1982, while, as a group, sales in seventeen other training topics went up 124 percent over the same period. Five topics jumped more than 200 percent over the five years, as compared with an average of 111 percent for all topics measured.

In 1982, the sales of instructional materials and services by the training industry reportedly totaled nearly $1.7 billion— 55 percent for off-the-shelf materials and packaged programs, 18 percent for custom-designed programs, and 27 percent for seminars.

In 1983, ASTD began a research project to develop and test a standardized data-gathering system to identify the nature and extent of employer-provided training. ASTD devised tentative standards for describing training programs and measuring their costs, designed a sampling scheme, and distributed a survey instrument. Results are not yet in.

Even if companies issued reliable and standardized data, how would one apply them? The nature of the industry, the company's size and prosperity, its personnel practices and policies, and a host of other factors influence training norms and expenditures to such an extent that little is gained from comparing the experience of one employer with that of another. For example, the public accounting firm of Arthur Andersen and Company spent about 9.5 percent of its gross revenues for professional education at its residential training center in 1982. The figures for subsequent years may be even higher. Motorola, on the other hand, plans to spend 2.0 percent of each employee's salary for training and development in 1985; the amount is budgeted as a line item in every division. The Bell System is estimated to have spent $2 billion on training in 1982, and IBM is estimated to have spent $700 million in 1984. In a group of a dozen companies chosen at random, training expense as a proportion of revenues ranged from less than 0.2 percent to 1.6 percent, and as a proportion of payroll, from 0.1 percent to 12.3 percent. The salaries of training staff ranged from 16.3 to 81.2

percent of the total training budget. In a 1981 study by Columbia University, the cost per participant among fifteen organizations was found to range from $146 to $15,914.

It may be that standardized calculation of training costs would reduce the great variations among these figures, but not necessarily. Even if it did, it would not help an employer determine on the basis of other companies' experience how much it ought to spend on training, unless the figures were linked to needs and results.

"What is the right amount to spend on training?" assumes: (1) the efficiency of the training is irrelevant or unchangeable; (2) the value of training is commensurate with expenditure; and (3) the need for training is infinite.

Linking corporate strategy directly to training makes it possible to approach training budgets in a new way. Traditionally, with training viewed purely as a staff function, whose offerings may or may not be attractive to line managers, and with line managers under no obligation to use the staff services, there is no objective basis on which to budget or even to estimate costs and benefits. Indeed, when training is seen as peripheral to the real work of the organization, trainers often try to conceal the true figures in order to present a smaller target for budget cutting in tough times.

If, on the other hand, training programs grow directly out of the business plan, then training becomes, for practical purposes, as vital as R&D, or equipment maintenance, or capital investment in new technology—which, in fact, it is. The question ceases to be "What is the right amount to spend on training?" and becomes "What will it cost to acquire the necessary skills?"

Deriving training needs from the business strategy may not provide automatic answers to the problem of budgeting, but it at least clarifies the options. At Ebasco Services, for example, what appeared to be a feasible set of business strategies was formulated; but when the costs of training employees in the necessary skills or recruiting new employees who already had these skills were computed, management decided the strategies could not be met. Instead of the usual outcome—that is, discarding the training—management chose a more affordable set of business strategies.

Another example is Travelers Insurance, where, until recently, training had been decentralized. Top management set itself the goal of changing from an old-line insurance company to a preeminent financial services company. The training implications of this goal were that (1) employees at all levels had to learn to make the best use of data-processing technology, and (2) managers had to learn to manage an organization transformed by technology. But only when the training and development division took the initiative and pointed out the needs and opportunities did it receive the authority and resources to organize the necessary programs. A new, state-of-the-art training center has been built; 5,000 employees have taken the company's custom-designed computer literacy program; and a program of management redevelopment is being prepared. In addition, the training function itself is being gradually automated, and individual computer work-stations for managers are being designed. All training materials now incorporate the leading themes of corporate strategy: creativity, innovation, productivity, customer service, low cost, fairness, and affirmative action.

Despite our comments about the futility of global training cost comparisons, there are sound reasons for measuring and comparing the costs of individual programs, as long as the measuring is consistent.

- One program can be compared with another on the same subject matter to determine which one produces a given amount of skill improvement per trainee at lower cost, or a greater amount of improvement for equal cost.
- One delivery system can be compared with another to determine which accomplishes a defined result at a lower cost per trainee. For example, is a satellite university course more cost-effective than a traditional classroom for a dispersed body of trainees?
- One company's program on a given subject matter can be compared with another company's program to determine which is the more cost-effective.

- The cost of a proposed program can be compared with the expected short-term and long-term work-unit performance gain, or the expected cost of *not* conducting the program, to determine whether it should be undertaken.

Evaluating for Cost-Effectiveness

If the primary purpose of training is to carry out corporate strategy, rather than to carry out training's proprietary objectives, and if it is assumed that training is, in fact, essential to realizing the corporate strategy, then there is no point in assessing it in terms of return on investment. Return on investment is designed for choosing between alternative uses of resources by comparing their financial outcomes.

However, there are valid and important questions about the value of training. The availability of large sums of money for training does not obviate the need for evaluation, whether the money comes from the employer alone or (as at Ford and General Motors) jointly from the employer and union. Money devoted to training is money unavailable for other purposes, such as wages and benefits. The questions are:

> How well does our training carry out the corporate strategy?
>
> Could our training carry out the strategy more cost-effectively?

To answer these questions in a useful way, each training program must be evaluated individually. Costs can be allocated to each program, and the results of each program can be assessed. Then management is in a position to ask:

> How do the results and costs of this program compare with its set objectives?
>
> Were valid objectives set for the program?
>
> Could equivalent results have been obtained at lower cost?
>
> Could the money and time devoted to this program have achieved greater results?

The implication, of course, is that a program should not be launched until objectives and a budget have been set.

The results of training can be measured at four levels:

1. *Reaction.* How well did the trainees like the program?
2. *Learning.* What principles, facts, or techniques were learned?
3. *Behavior.* What changes in job behavior resulted from the program?
4. *Results.* What were the tangible results of the program in terms of reduced costs, improved quality, quantity, and so on?

It has been argued that the first three levels count only if "Results" show improvements in the performance of the work unit that are related to the purpose of the training. This argument sounds pragmatic, but it does not stand up to examination, which may be a key reason why employers ignore it. There is no practical way to measure any but the most transient effects of any single variable upon work-unit performance, unless everything else in the situation is held unchanged; and there is no practical way to hold everything else unchanged. The larger the work unit, the more impossible to measure such effects. The best one can say is that training contributed to performance improvements, in such and such a way.

The principal client of training is not the trainee, but the trainee's supervisor (especially if training is charged against the supervisor's budget). If, as so commonly happens, employees undergo training because "management" tells them to, and without reference to whether the supervisor wants them to, the effects on work-unit performance will be infinitesimal. Supervisors cannot be compelled to make use of what their subordinates have been taught. A more accurate way of putting this is that training includes the behavior of the supervisor; any dissonance between what the supervisor actually does and what subordinates have been told elsewhere will be resolved in favor of what the supervisor does.

Evaluation of formal training comes down to a judgment of what the training department's responsibility ought to be.

Although a training program may have the ultimate purpose of improving a work unit's performance, the responsibility for the work unit's performance must rest with its manager; that is the essence of management responsibility. To hold the training department responsible for work-unit performance makes no more sense than holding line management responsible for the training department's performance.

A more reasonable allocation would hold the line manager responsible for the performance of the work unit, and the training department responsible for fulfilling the objectives of the training program, framed in terms of improvements in employee skills and knowledge.

The more closely training efforts reflect the intentions of managers and supervisors, the more likely it is that those efforts will be integrated into operations and planning. Therefore, analysis of training needs should be the joint responsibility of managers and the training department. As a corollary, the training department should help top management convey to managers a clear understanding of the corporate strategy, so that their perceptions of present and future needs are accurate. Since needs will change continually, a needs analysis should be a continuing function.

Trainees also should be involved in needs analysis. The trainee's interest in acquiring and applying new skills depends on how well he or she promotes the attainment of present and future career goals. Telling a trainee that training is ''good'' for them, or that someone higher up thinks they ought to have it, is a wasted effort.

American workers place a high value on using their capabilities to the fullest, because such use signifies higher income and status as well as more interesting work. Whether through formal career planning or other means, workers want to move ahead, inside or outside the organization. Insofar as training appears to further that end, they will grasp it.

In short, successful training has to meet simultaneously the perceived needs of the employer, the employee, and the employee's manager.

The department manager's responsibility for training the

employees in his or her work unit should be made clear by charging it to the manager's budget, whether the training is tactical or strategic in nature. At IBM, for example, all training is budgeted to the divisions and operating units, with one exception: management training and development are corporate.

As part of a needs analysis and objective setting, the training department and the work-unit manager should come to grips with two questions: (1) How much can training of any kind contribute to the desired performance improvement of the work unit? (2) How will the cost of the proposed training compare with the value of performance improvement?

At Travelers Insurance, for example, no training program is undertaken without such objectives. As a first step, the division addresses the question: "Is the problem presented to us really one that can be solved by training?" A supervisor may believe that his or her claims processors' lack of adequate keyboard skills is a drag on productivity, but closer examination may show that the obstacle lies in poor design of documents or computer screens. Or a requested training program might be shown to produce a morale boost, but without any likely impact on productivity. If the problem can genuinely be solved by training, then the need is analyzed and objectives are set by the division, working with the line department; these objectives guide all future action. The division then prepares a detailed proposal, using estimates of developmental and operational costs along with the size of the trainee population to calculate estimated cost per trainee.

A similar approach is taken in setting skill objectives and in evaluating results. Travelers' training division accepts responsibility for bringing trainees to a point where they can do something they could not do—or could not do as well—before, but is not responsible for results on the job. The trainee's supervisor is responsible for seeing to it that the training is put to good use. The training division's responsibility goes no farther than providing examples and exercises based on the job itself, or assigning projects to be performed on the job between training sessions.

In measuring the effectiveness of a training program, the employer should ask:

Were the skill objectives valid in terms of corporate strategy? How fully were the objectives attained?

Who should evaluate how well the program has achieved its skill objectives? In principle, the evaluators should be those on whose behalf the training was performed: the trainees themselves, the trainees' supervisors, and higher management. The trainees can judge whether they enjoyed the training and whether they feel they learned something valuable, but the supervisor (particularly if the costs of training are charged against his or her budget) is the individual most directly concerned with deciding whether the trainee has gained the skills for which the training was instituted. On the other hand, the validity of the objectives can properly be determined only by those who set corporate strategy. Supervisors know what they want to achieve through the training of their subordinates, but that is not necessarily what the corporate strategy calls for.

One of the few companies known to have developed advanced methods of costing and evaluating its training programs is New England Telephone (NET). NET compiles the costs of (1) developing programs (salaries and expenses of subject-matter experts as well as course-designers), (2) delivering programs (for example, trainers' salaries and expenses, purchase of classroom material, administrative support, and data-processing charges), and (3) food and accommodation at training sessions. Each "client" department is billed proportionately for the costs attributed to its trainees, and the training department's budget is credited for services rendered.

With the aid of numerous written instruments, the training department conducts evaluations of the knowledge conveyed and its relevance to the job; statistical analyses of the costs, volume, and efficiency of training; and evaluations of outside training vendors.

NET's evaluations consistently point up the importance of involving "client" managers in the training process to give them a sense of "ownership." They find, for example, that the likelihood of a trainee applying newly learned skills to the job is strongly linked to the interest the manager shows in having that happen. This finding reflects the existence of the traditional relationship between training departments and their clients; that is, training is viewed as a quasi contractor, which designs programs and then tries to induce managers to send employees to be trained and to encourage the trainees to use their new skills on the job.

It is noteworthy, however, that when NET's training department reversed roles in one particular program, managers no longer had to be ''sold'' on the value of training for their subordinates. In that case, managers themselves were the trainees in a one-day course on effective listening; they then went back to the field and instructed their subordinates on effective listening. The subsequent evaluation report stated, ''The positive results to the company were both humanistic, in helping people develop better boss-subordinate relationships and teams, and financial, in producing (documented) annual cost savings of $2,280,000 due to improved productivity occurring as a result of Directory Assistance operators' more effective listening.''

Experts distinguish between tactical training, to meet current needs, and strategic training, addressed to future needs. Tactical training is accepted and managed reasonably well, they say, at major companies. Strategic training encounters resistance, in part because the needs are hard to define and the benefits are hard to predict. Insofar as training is regarded as tactical, budgets go up and down with the business cycle. Strategic training demands long-term financial commitments, which are unlikely to be given unless top management sees them as an essential cost of carrying out the corporate business strategy.

When training is driven by corporate strategy, the support of top management is assured. And when the organization as a whole understands the thrust of the strategy and accepts its validity, training moves from the periphery to near the center of corporate activity.

Mechanisms for Linkage

To ensure that training is aligned with corporate strategy, certain communications and relationships are required:

- The corporate business strategy must be transmitted to those who plan and provide and to those who receive training.
- Strategy must be formulated in the light of reliable information about the capacity of the organization to train and be trained.

A study of ten major companies, drawn at random from a wide variety of product and service industries, found different mechanisms for conveying business strategy to the providers of training. In most cases the providers received the information in attenuated form and too late to have any say in it. Anecdotal information suggests that this is the norm.

The exceptions are usually found in high-tech companies or those with ambitions to become high-tech. For example, the vice-president for human resources of Ebasco Services sits on the strategy committee. At Motorola, the CEO is a member of the committee that sets policy for technical training. At Caterpillar, the manager of technical education is a member of the group that determines manufacturing strategy for the company. IBM has established a vice-president for technical personnel development (separate from the personnel function), who reports to the highest corporate level but who, surprisingly, has no direct participation in strategy. At Travelers, the corporate strategy planning group includes the vice-president for administration, to whom the training function reports.

When the training function is not represented in strategy formulation, the strategists miss two important pieces of advice: (1) they may set their sights too high because they cannot be sure that the organization has, or will have at the right time, the skills required to carry out their plans; (2) they may set their sights too low because they do not know what new skills the organization might acquire through training within the strategic time period. Such information is as relevant as a cash-flow projection.

Companies usually see the desirability of training people at all levels for day-to-day needs, and of training others for future needs: since those who are not on the fast track have less employment security and are more vulnerable to turnover, such training seems wasteful. But the success of an enterprise depends on how well everyone in an organization performs. Corporate strategy and training, therefore, both rest on certain assumptions about the permanence of people in the firm. Companies that invest most heavily in training, it turns out, also provide strong assurances of employment continuity.

Investment in training (and in R&D) is highest among companies at the leading edge of technology. For example, at IBM, a systems engineer or marketing representative spends 20 days per year in training; employees in programming and software development, 7.5 days per year; the typical engineer, 5.5 days per year; and employees who service IBM hardware and software, 20 days per year.

Motorola set a mandatory guideline of 24 hours of training per year for every employee in 1984, with the average to rise to 40 hours per year by 1986. At Corning Glass, many work units devote 5 percent of annual work time (90–100 hours per year) to training for quality improvement, and by 1991 that percentage is scheduled to become a companywide average.

These examples are generally interpreted to mean that high tech requires and justifies training. The opposite interpretation is equally valid: intensive training, in conjunction with R&D applied to both processes and products, helps propel a company to the leading edge. Industries are not inherently low-tech or high-tech. Railways, steel, and autos once represented the state of the art, and their economic declines paralleled the declines in their technical progress. Nothing inherent prevents the U.S. Postal Service, for example, from becoming a high-tech enterprise.

Even in a currently low-tech company, it is valuable to the employer to have employees learn more than just enough to operate the new technology to which they are assigned. Broader knowledge enables them to see:

- Additional, new, or better ways of operating the technology
- Other profitable applications of the technology
- Ways of improving the technology itself
- The possibility of technological advances that will enable the employer to develop new products or processes, or to produce current products/services more economically

In other words, the role of training is both to carry out strategy and to influence it. But only if the individual who represents the training function views the role in that light can he or she hope to persuade top management to see it that way.

Early, reliable, and detailed knowledge of corporate strategy is important to training because equipping employees with skills for future needs is more demanding—for both provider and trainees—than equipping them with skills for current activities. Corporate strategy, of itself, does not identify needed training programs. Strategy must be translated into more detailed business plans; the business plans, into people and skill requirements. Who will need what skills, when?

The longer the time frame of the business strategy, the longer the time frame available for responsive training; ideally, the two should coincide, as in Ebasco Services, where both look ten years ahead. Caterpillar also uses a ten-year horizon, with key tasks and milestones. Clearly, however, training, like strategy, does not consider the time period an undifferentiated unit. A series of events and substrategies articulate the period. Plans are made for a year or two at a time, but the long-term strategy should be kept in mind.

Ebasco Services. One key objective of training is to prepare managers for succession. This is no easy matter, even when the organizational environment is stable or slowly changing. It becomes a serious challenge under today's conditions, as society, markets, products, and technology evolve faster and faster. Under stable conditions, the organization could hold up its successful managers as role models for the coming generation. But now the organization must project future needs, which may differ quite radically from those of the past, and if it finds that none of its available models will be appropriate to the future, it must design and institute training radically different from the past.

Ebasco Services, Inc., found itself in such a situation in 1983, when the impact of the downturn in the nuclear and utility engineering construction industry became most severe. For some years prior to that time, the company had practiced a sophisticated form of corporate planning, based on environmental scanning, internal data analysis, and the development of primary and alternate strategies. But in 1983, prospects for the industry looked so dark that the company decided it must move vigorously into nontraditional lines of business. Therefore the skills of the management group, whose careers had been spent almost entirely in the old industry, would have to be considerably augmented.

First, two dozen of the company's most senior managers put themselves through a special twenty-six-day Wharton School training program, spread over thirteen months. Courses concentrated on longer-range strategic planning, marketing, entrepreneurship, management of technology for the diversification program, government relations, financial management, economics, forecasting, decision making, and human-resource management. The outcome was a thoroughgoing revision of the company's goals, objectives, and plans, and the selection of several new businesses to replace much of its involvement in nuclear engineering.

A new strategic planning process was set up. Strategic plans were developed with a ten-year horizon, to take account of numerous contingencies; these led to operational plans, with eighteen-month horizons, and associated tactical plans and budgets. The human-resources plan also has a ten-year horizon, to match that of the strategic plan; it deals separately with managers and supervisors, professionals, and clericals.

To meet the new strategic planning needs, the company established a parallel management structure consisting of a top-level corporate strategy group; seven business-family planning groups to develop and monitor group operating plans; and seventeen business program planning teams, to develop and monitor individual strategic programs.

Plans were also made for the financial and human resources to implement the individual strategic programs. The vice-president for human resources, having been involved in the entire process (including the Wharton School program), fully understood the profound changes under way and was in tune with them. He was charged to ensure that there would be people available to fill the new skill requirements by hiring and/or training. It was up to the program planning teams to specify those requirements in sufficient detail for him to follow through.

Ebasco's human-resources group estimates the internal supply from its data base of individual skills, talents, qualifications, and career paths. Management and employees jointly develop employee career paths. The career path leads to a development plan specifying the training each employee needs in order to improve performance in the present position and also to prepare for the next position in the career path. The organization is obliged to do the training. When employees realize that their career paths are directly linked to strategic objectives— that is, that the positions they are aiming at will be genuinely needed by the employer in future years—they become more committed to career planning.

Career paths are based on two kinds of appraisal. *Performance appraisal* gauges the capabilities of the existing managerial and technical staff on the basis of past performance. *Potential appraisal* assesses how well these individuals might do in higher jobs, which require different managerial and technical skills. The criteria for both appraisal systems are developed on the basis of foreseeable specific needs; for example, if the company foresees that a growing number of managers with well-defined technical backgrounds and the ability to delegate authority in managing complex, multidisciplinary projects will be needed, those criteria will be built into the evaluation instruments. This procedure gives rise to an administrative burden so vast that a special computer system has been created to handle it.

The resulting data base thus enables Ebasco to determine where each individual stands with respect to specific technical skills at present and where he or she will stand at various times in the future, taking account of existing training and development, career paths, attrition, and other factors. It can also forecast gaps between demand and supply of staff for any given strategy and estimate the cost of going outside for talent. If the gap is too wide, the company may decide that a given strategy must be abandoned.

The computer identifies what training—both managerial and technical—each employee needs in order to improve performance on the present job and to prepare for the next. Since individuals' names are linked to departments and completion targets, the training department can schedule training to meet each person's needs. Thus the strategic plan literally determines what training is done, by whom, when, where, and how.

Desiring to move rapidly into new fields without recruiting more outsiders than absolutely necessary, Ebasco has devised the method of "leveraging" technology, analogous to training residents in a teaching hospital. The center of such training is an expert who is actually carrying out one of the firm's engineering projects. Management assigns to that expert a group of competent fast-learning engineers or scientists with sufficient background to learn the technology. These individuals perform real work assignments on the job, under the expert's tutelage, and rapidly absorb the new field; some later become technical leaders.

Ebasco believes that the new approach is a success: the company has maintained staffing levels and profitability over the past four years, while its competitors have suffered cutbacks and losses.

Corning Glass Works. Corning Glass Works has long led the fine glass industry in technological innovation and product quality, and has, in fact, based its competitive strategy on quality. In recent years, however, competitors in Japan and Europe have stepped up their technology far enough to rival Corning on both quality and price. In October 1983, the chairman announced that the company, in response, would begin a long-term effort to improve quality, not only in its products and services, but in every aspect of the way it runs its business. Underlying this strategic impulse was the concept that higher quality leads to higher market share and, at the same time, to lower unit costs.

The company stated its quality objective was to deliver error-free products and services, on time, that meet internal and external customer requirements every time. A corporate director of quality was appointed, and each corporate group appointed a quality executive. The chairman and the management committee agreed to provide the necessary resources and to review progress quarterly. The education and training department was given responsibility for disseminating the new strategy throughout the organization.

New skills and habits of mind were to be communicated: to prevent errors by removing their sources in events or processes; to emphasize teamwork, education, communication, and recognition, as the social context of quality improvement; to institute key processes—getting agreement on customer requirements, measuring quality, measuring the cost of failure to meet requirements, setting up corrective systems, and setting realistic goals for improvement.

At every level of the organization, committees were established to focus the effort. The training and education department then undertook the job of exposing all 28,000 worldwide employees of the company to basic education in "total quality."

The department, in collaboration with the Corporate Quality Council and outside consultants, developed a textbook using Corning case material. Six midlevel managers were selected as core faculty and trained to teach. Multilingual print and videotape materials were made available. Although each class was limited to twenty-five employees, with two instructors, 600 to 800 employees have been trained per month. The chairman and his immediate subordinates attended the initial classes.

The emphasis on teamwork and the educational effort have generated needs for further training in interpersonal skills, problem-solving skills, and statistics, which have now been slated for the next phase. Many work units are aiming to devote 5 percent of their total annual work time to quality training; a few factories have been devoting 7 percent. To meet these demands, Corning has trained over 100 employees from all levels of the organization to serve as quality instructors.

As a result of the organization's enthusiastic response to quality education, the Training and Educational Department is taking stock of its other programs, with the aim of making the strategy-training linkage still more pervasive.

American Transtech. American Transtech was formed by AT&T in 1983 for the specific purpose of handling stock transfers for AT&T's 3.2 million accounts, a function previously performed by AT&T's Stock and Bond Division. The AT&T divestiture of 1984, by raising the number of accounts to 22 million, placed an unexpectedly huge demand on Transtech to increase productivity. The goal was achieved so successfully that the company began to diversify into shareowner services for corporations outside the Bell System. Thirty-five percent of its business came from outside the Bell System in 1987. Recently Transtech has focused on financial services and direct marketing services.

Transtech's 2,400 employees are young (average age thirty-four), predominantly white-collar clericals and professionals, who are inclined toward self-management. The managerial style is nonhierarchical and participative, including profit sharing. Work is computer-centered and organized into teams, with the team manager as facilitator. Open bidding allows ambitious team members to move up the ladder.

Training contributed directly to these accomplishments in several ways:

- Managers were trained to seek and identify qualities of self-management in people they interviewed for employment.
- Early employees were formed into pilot teams, which then served as models for the rest of the organization.
- Training was carried out on a team basis. Computer-based programs, specifically designed for Transtech, cut learning time in half. Team members were encouraged to learn from one another, as well as from the coaches.
- In preparation for the massive sudden increase in work load caused by divestiture, the teams held "dress rehearsals" to ensure that their methods were free of snags.
- Managers and team members were trained to deal with business problems, not as occasions for fault finding, but as items to be solved by the group concerned.

By the end of 1984 Transtech's productivity in processing shareholder stock accounts was 60 to 80 percent higher than in the old AT&T Stock and Bond Division.

With the 1985 decision to expand and diversify its services, the company saw a need to redesign the work teams.

Originally each team was organized to handle a particular function (for example, shareowner contact, stock transfer, stock purchase plan, and so on). Now each team performs the entire range of services for a single corporate customer. The first new team to provide shareowner services to BellSouth was designed by a group of 18 employees, drawn from 150 volunteers. The design group met daily for six weeks to study BellSouth's requirements; many of them became part of the eventual work team, carrying with them a breadth of understanding which is rare among nonmanagerial employees anywhere. Meanwhile, pilot teams in other departments have been experimenting with methods of raising productivity further.

Ford Motor Company. As demand for V-8 engines dried up in the late 1970s, Ford Motor Company, working under forced draft, developed a state-of-the-art, four-cylinder engine with 1.6-liter displacement. In 1978 the company decided to build the engine at the obsolete Dearborn Engine Plant (DEP). The decision meant that plant conversion and employee retraining would take place almost simultaneously, and quickly. To add to the problem, the engine was of a type unfamiliar to DEP employees, requiring quality control beyond that of any previous Ford mass-manufactured product; and the manufacturing technology was just as new to them. The situation called for a training strategy that likewise departed from Ford traditions.

Five key subject areas were chosen, based on a needs analysis:

1. *Product familiarization and quality awareness,* a four-hour orientation for all employees, to explain the importance of the new product, its technology, the technology that would be used to build it, and the cars in which it would be used.
2. *Technical training,* much of it supplied by the technology vendors, in either packaged or customized programs.
3. *Human resources training for supervisors,* to pave the way for employee involvement.
4. *Versatility training,* to familiarize workers with tasks related to, but outside, their normal range of duties. This led to

an agreement with the UAW local to introduce flexible work assignments, such as adding setup to a machine-tool operator's job.

5.   *Pre-recall training* for a large number of workers who had been laid off while V-8 production was running down. Ordinarily, Ford workers would be recalled to their jobs and then given training, if needed. This time they were called back to update skills *before* starting their new jobs.

Gilroy Foods, Inc. At the main processing plant of Gilroy Foods, Inc., in Gilroy, California, which specializes in high-quality food products such as dehydrated onion, garlic, and capsicums, quality has to be monitored, controlled, and graded with great care at every stage—from growing through harvesting, processing, packaging, and final delivery. With the steady introduction of new technologies at the plant, management felt that a more structured and focused approach to technical training for employees in maintenance and quality control was needed. A second motive was the shared desire of the local union and maintenance managers to improve career progression for apprentices, journeymen, and supervisors. Plant management, realizing how much a large-scale training project would cost in time and money, decided that, rather than try to cover everything trainees might conceivably use, they should concentrate on subjects demonstrably vital to the future success of the plant.

In selecting subject matter for maintenance supervisors and workers, Gilroy singled out the most costly repair categories in each area of the plant by checking maintenance records, comparing the frequencies of different categories of repair jobs, measuring each category's total cost in parts and labor, and ranking the categories according to their costs.

Gilroy then conducted a staffing analysis to determine how many apprentices to appoint, and to schedule training so that each level of maintenance workers would advance in parallel with the plant's needs. Staffing demand was calculated on the basis of expected plant capacity, capital plans, projected work load, and so forth. Supply was calculated by applying turnover and attrition forecasts to current staff levels. Comparing supply and demand yielded the net number required for each job level in coming years.

Continuing evaluation of the training program was based on the following criteria: overall maintenance department costs; frequency of high-cost repairs in each area, by category; frequency of production stoppages due to maintenance-related problems; completion of training in accordance with schedule; and advancement of trainees.

Gilroy took an analogous approach in identifying the test procedures in which quality-control training would have the greatest payoff. First, the company measured "appraisal cost" by counting the frequency of the various tests performed in the laboratories; it then multiplied each frequency by its cost in labor and materials, and ranked the tests in order of total costs. Second, they measured "failure costs," that is, costs incurred when a product is returned, reworked, recycled, or scrapped because of quality. Here again, the sources of cost were ranked from greatest to least. Comparison of appraisal costs and failure costs not only highlighted procedures to be featured in the training program but also showed how and where quality-control testing, data collection, and problem solving might be more effectively carried out by other departments, such as production.

Management by Objectives as a Strategy-Training Link. Another, less direct, way of linking corporate strategy to training is via a management-by-objectives (MBO) process. For example, at IBM, "training and education are an integral part of the job. The company and the individual are directly tied to every individual's development and overall performance plan. The job the individual does, how he or she performs that job, and the individual's overall development are worked out with the individual on a contractual basis each year."

In some areas of Xerox a similar approach is taken. At regular intervals, supervisor and subordinate meet and reach written agreement concerning job performance goals, subjects for special improvement efforts, measures of improvement, assessment of performance in regard to previous goals, training needed to reach job goals, and training needed for professional development. Individual training needs are compiled and form the basis of the curriculum.

Insofar as the agreements result from a genuine meeting of the minds rather than from supervisory domination, they should both motivate the subordinate to learn and ensure the supervisor's willingness to accept the cost of training. But it does not necessarily follow that the training would promote corporate strategy; that depends on how well the supervisor understands corporate strategy and its implications.

Another Route. In most companies, corporate strategy is formulated by a small, select group of top officers; it is then transmitted less and less fully to successively lower levels of management and, perhaps ultimately, to the rank and file. With each step in the diminishing communication, the ability to translate strategy into training needs is diminished.

A few companies distinguish between strategy formulation and strategy decision. Although top management can never delegate the responsibility for decision, it can, if it chooses, involve every level of the firm in formulating strategy. For example, the strategy for developing and producing the Saturn car was worked out by a joint General Motors/United Auto Workers team of 100, with equal membership from management and workers. Arguably, GM's top management would not have considered such a committee if it had not been at least open to the possibility of attacking the small-car market in the United States, but it would almost surely not have committed $5 billion to the project without the benefit of the committee's study, creative solutions, and enthusiasm.

The joint committee had two valuable side effects on the nature of training: (1) it provided the committee members with a hard-to-duplicate year of intensive training in management skills, technology, manufacturing, sociotechnical organization, marketing, and problem solving; and (2) it developed a basis for widespread understanding of the strategy at all levels of the firm, upon which strategic training can readily be built.

Recommendations

Recommendation 1. The chief executive officer (CEO) and senior associates should include a training plan as a critical component of the corporate strategic plan, to ensure that all levels of the organization will have the knowledge and skills to carry out the strategic plan. The training plan should distinguish clearly between (1) tactical programs designed to meet current needs, and (2) strategic programs designed to keep up with—and even anticipate—changes in technology, competition, and work-force standards, as well as with the rapid obsolescence of occupations.

Recommendation 2. The vice-president responsible for the training function should be actively involved in formulating corporate strategy, to ensure that:

- Strategic goals are realistically ambitious with respect to the reservoir of skills that will be available to meet them
- The training function will be able to help top management communicate corporate strategy throughout the organization and to help managers translate the strategy into training needs

Recommendation 3. The vice-president for the training function should ensure that all training programs (1) are necessary to the corporate strategy; (2) are recommended by (and, if possible, budgeted to) the managers whose employees are to be trained; and (3) help the trainees progress along the career paths jointly set by them and their managers.

Recommendation 4. The CEO should regularly monitor the training function to ascertain that (1) program priorities match those of the corporate strategy, (2) program cost and skill objectives are valid, and (3) program cost and skill objectives are met.

Background Papers

Craig, R. L. (American Society for Training and Development). "Measuring Employee Training." Feb. 1985.

DeSio, R. W. (IBM). Oral presentation on training for product support. Feb. 1985.

Manzini, A. O. (Ebasco Services, Inc.). "Integrating Management and Technical Training with Corporate Strategy." Feb. 1985.

Wexley, K. L. (Michigan State University). "Training for a New Technology: How Companies Make the Strategic Plan/ Technical Training Linkage." Feb. 1985.

Case Studies

Casner-Lotto, J. "Keeping Track of the Training Dollar: New England Telephone." June 1985.

Hickey, J. V. "Corning Glass Works: Strategic Response Through Total Quality." June 1985.

Hickey, J. V. "The Travelers Corporation: Expanding Computer Literacy in the Organization." June 1985.

Plous, F. K., Jr. "The Motorola Training and Education Center." June 1985.

Plous, F. K., Jr. "Training for a Change in Production Technology at Ford Motor Company." June 1985.

Rubin, N. "American Transtech: Training as Part of the Job." June 1985.

3

Continuous Learning:
A Strategy
for Ongoing Change

An evolution in training is now under way in our leading companies, moving clearly in the direction of continuous learning. The steps have been hesitant, tentative, partial, often uncoordinated, and pushed by economic imperatives rather than pulled by preconceived goals. However, the shift from "training" to "learning" is more than semantic. Training puts the emphasis on what someone does to employees; employees are regarded as passive recipients of ideas and information. Learning implies that employees actively participate in expanding their own skills. Moreover, with growing frequency, employees are learning from one another.

Learning has to be continuous because organizations face continual change of products, services, processes, markets, and competition, as well as technology. Since everyone in the organization is caught up in change, everyone must be involved in learning.

The information in this chapter, unless otherwise referenced, is drawn from the background papers and case studies listed at the end of the chapter. Both papers and cases were commissioned by Work in America Institute in the course of its three-year policy study entitled "Training for New Technology."

The need for a redefinition of training and learning within industry is dictated by the work environment. The operative forces include:

- The unending search for the competitive edge in a world economy
- The need for sustained, high-level quality of products and services, requiring a responsive, qualified work force
- The burst of technology and its constant impact upon organization
- The information age, which changes the flow and speed of transfers of knowledge and requires different and changing skills
- The need for flexibility and interchangeability of skills and knowledge, with an adaptable, responsive work force
- The rapid change in occupations and the need for employees to adapt and learn new occupations within their career employment
- Better educated, more capable workers, who can participate effectively in decisions affecting their jobs

Continuous learning exists as a policy when everyone is in a permanent state of learning, through a conscious collaboration between organization and employee. In this interchange, the organization also learns. Individual employees come and go, but their knowledge and accumulated experience must be preserved and applied by those who remain; such transfer enables the organization to maintain equilibrium in the face of continual change, both within and without.

The Continuous Learning Model

Although individual companies have put into practice one or more pieces of the continuous learning model, none known to us have adopted it completely. We are confident, nevertheless, that it is only a matter of time before continuous learning establishes itself as an indispensable policy for survival in a highly competitive economy. The essentials of the model are these:

- Learning is an everyday part of every job. The line between job performance and learning disappears.
- Employees, in addition to mastering the skills specific to their immediate tasks, are required to learn the skills of others in their work unit. They are also required to understand the relationship between their work unit and the organization as a whole, and to be familiar with the operation and goals of the business.
- Active, free-form interaction among employees, teams, trainers, and managers is encouraged and institutionalized.
- Employees are required to transmit their job knowledge to, as well as learn from, co-workers.

Continuous learning presents a new and challenging response to the changing nature of the economy and the workplace. It addresses the threat of obsolescence through a forward-looking, in-service educational policy, which supports the concept of learning rather than the force-feeding of training. It is entirely different from conventional training in industry, and it opens an exciting vista for education within the context of changing organizational needs.

Corporate training strategy gains unprecedented strength when recast in terms of continuous learning. The state of the art of knowledge transfer is integrated with employee-machine compatibility. Corporate investment and commitment are deeper and more penetrating.

Some of the principal characteristics of continuous learning discussed and documented in this chapter include:

- Establishing appropriate structures and mechanisms.
- Achieving top-management commitment on a long-term basis.
- Committing adequate resources and recognizing the opportunity factors.
- Employing train-the-trainer programs, which engage the expertise and talents of "content experts" in organizations. Content experts provide needs analysis, design, teaching, assurance of relevance, evaluation, and adaptability of content.

- Ensuring maximum employee involvement, with the free flow of ideas to identify knowledge gaps and to inspire voluntary interactive teaching and learning within peer groups.
- Integrating learning within advanced organizational design in semiautonomous teams, where the members regularly train and are trained by one another.
- Delegating training, from staff to line and from the line organization to the involvement of all levels and subdivisions, so that training is the operating manager's responsibility.
- Offering recognition, through intrinsic and extrinsic rewards, to reinforce participation, achievement, and reward.

This chapter concentrates on three aspects of continuous learning:

1. Institutionalizing the structures and mechanisms that make continuous learning feasible
2. The effect of union presence on the evolution of continuous learning
3. The subject matter of continuous learning, beyond the job-specific

Institutionalizing Continuous Learning

Continuous learning can be sustained only if it is institutionalized in appropriate structures and mechanisms. The forms taken depend on which segment of the work force is concerned, the depth of its involvement, and the subject matter to be learned.

For example, there is a modest degree of involvement when professionals and managers negotiate training goals with their bosses, as part of management by objectives or in connection with a periodic performance appraisal. A greater degree of involvement marks train-the-trainer programs, whose object is to give content experts in the organization the skills to deliver, and sometimes also to design, courses which would otherwise require professional trainers. Still greater involvement is found in continuous learning centers, where employees on a voluntary basis teach and learn from one another more productive ways of using a particular technology to which all are assigned. The deepest involvement probably takes place in certain semi-autonomous work teams, whose members, as a regular part of the job, train and are trained by one another.

Institutionalization also implies a system of extrinsic, as well as intrinsic, rewards to reinforce continuous learning. Learning by objectives, for example, ties training and development directly to performance appraisal. Train-the-trainer programs and continuous learning centers offer peer recognition, and sometimes a career boost, to those who make outstanding contributions. Members of work teams receive pay for knowledge as they master each additional set of skills.

A different sort of institutionalization occurs when funds for training are jointly administered by an employer and its unions (see section on unions and continuous learning later in this chapter). Joint administration may also lead to union involvement in other phases of the training process, such as needs analysis, course design, instruction, and evaluation.

Learning by Objectives

Companies in high-tech businesses have evolved a variant of management by objectives as the vehicle for involving technical, professional, and managerial employees in the analysis of their own training and development needs. Usually as part of a formal MBO system, manager and employee sit down together and negotiate a written agreement on the technical and professional training the subordinate will undertake in the coming six months or year. At the end of the period they review the outcome and decide what further training is called for. Both of them understand that the subordinate's career will be shaped by these decisions.

Trainees' involvement in needs analysis reduces wasted effort by eliminating the teaching of what is already known, by getting quickly to questions that engage the trainees, and by affording them a chance to ask questions that help them acquire skills.

Xerox Corporation's Business Products & Systems Group. The Business Products & Systems Group (BP&SG) is the segment of the Xerox Corporation that develops, engineers, and manufactures photocopying machines and supplies. Most of its activities are carried out in Webster, New York, by a force of 8,500 employees, about half of whom are directly involved in manufacturing and half in product engineering and support services. To meet the demands of intense competition and rapid technological change, BP&SG in 1984 developed a linkage between training and its system of Performance Feedback & Development (PF&D).

The system requires that each employee and his or her manager jointly write down the objectives the employee is to reach over the coming year. Objectives are stated in specific—preferably numerical—terms, to minimize the likelihood of subsequent disagreement. At the end of the year, they jointly measure accomplishments against objectives, and a summary of the findings goes into the employee's permanent record. Employee and manager meet at least once during the year to review progress and, if necessary, revise objectives. The company has taken extraordinary care to ensure that the procedure is clearly understood by everyone concerned.

Although training at BP&SG is not compulsory, an increasing percentage of objectives statements call for employees to enroll in one or more training courses. The proportion is expected to grow as managers become more adept at identifying educational needs and coaching employees to deal with them.

Nevertheless, because training is readily available and is considered important to career advancement, about 40 to 50 percent of BP&SG employees enroll in courses or workshops each year. The Human Resources Research and Technical Education Department offers 324 technical courses in its Day/Evening Training Program—not to mention those in tuition aid programs, learning centers, and special programs and workshops. Day/Evening courses are taught by 120 BP&SG employees of all levels, who volunteer to share their knowledge; some have taken courses in the art of teaching as part of the Day/Evening program.

Curricula are developed by a ten-member Technical Education Committee and by ten Curriculum Advisory Committees (one for each major occupational group at BP&SG), which revise the curricula each year. In addition to the many Xerox-specific courses, the Day/Evening program offers refresher courses for long-service technologists as well as "broadening" courses, such as learning about customer reactions from Xerox sales representatives and service technicians, or examining how the Japanese mounted their strong challenge to the company.

General Electric Company's Aerospace Electronic Systems Department. The Continuing Engineering Education Program (CEEP) at General Electric Company's Aerospace Electronic Systems Department (AESD) keeps engineers ahead of the competition through courses conceived and devised by the department's most expert technologists and marketers. CEEP was launched in the spring of 1982, based on lessons learned from an anxiety-producing catch-up effort a few years earlier, "to keep our engineers abreast of emerging technologies and to introduce them to what is brand new and not available anywhere else." Its courses are directly linked to performance appraisal and development.

With annual sales of $400 million, AESD has only one customer: the U.S. Department of Defense. Its products are airborne electronics at the leading edge of technology. Of its 3,500 employees, 1,000 are in engineering, but engineering training accounts for half of the local training budget. Local trainers have discretion in developing and administering courses for specific needs, within broad guidelines set by the corporate education department.

In 1976, AESD projected that the ratio of analog to digital technologies in its products would decline from the then-current 2:1 to 1:2 by 1980—a fourfold decline in four years. The change would entail massive application of digital and very-large-scale-integration techniques, in which only a handful of its engineers were expert. The penalty for failure would be severe.

A two-year program of mandatory training in these subjects was quickly put together and successfully carried out, but not without highlighting some clear warnings for the future. First of all, catch-up and coercion were unproductive ways to deal with training on such a scale. The sale of a new product to the U.S. Department of Defense is a long, competitive process, starting with concept, then proceeding to prototype, to pilot model, and finally to approval for full-scale production; in effect, a sale has to be made at each stage. As AESD says, "If we haven't done at least two years of homework on a potential customer need, we'll never win that contract. Training has to prepare engineers for that kind of role."

AESD resolved to take a more proactive approach, with the following characteristics:

- Strong top-management support
- A training administrator with solid technical background
- Clear goals, directions, and budgets
- Strong, positive motivation for trainees

Accordingly, CEEP has a full-time, technically qualified administrator who develops training plans, chooses and trains instructors, and helps in developing and scheduling courses. An Engineering Education Advisory Council, composed of the administrator and nineteen other members, reports trends and changes of technology, and evaluates proposed and existing courses. The members include senior engineers and managers from each major technical area plus representatives of planning and marketing.

Most course instructors are drawn from within AESD and receive train-the-trainer support. Occasionally, someone from academic life is brought in.

CEEP administrators constantly evaluate and review new methods and techniques of instruction, seeking higher cost-effectiveness. However, they make little use of computer-based or videotaped materials for two reasons: (1) such materials cannot be prepared fast enough to meet AESD's schedules, and (2) the cost would not be justified, inasmuch as each course is given only once or twice.

Equally important are the feedback mechanisms through

which CEEP continually improves its performance. Each student fills out an anonymous questionnaire for the administrator, rating the course and instructor and suggesting changes, improvements, and additional courses. A different questionnaire is filled out by each student who drops a course. Students receive feedback on their own efforts through scores on homework, quizzes, and exams.

At year's end, managers receive printouts showing which of their employees have taken which courses. They note this information on performance appraisals and may recommend further courses. Employees, although not forced to take courses, understand that not taking them may weaken their credentials for advancement.

As a result of such prodding, four or five times as many courses are now offered as before CEEP, and enrollments have risen from 300 a year to 2,000. Enrollees come from all age groups; indeed, employees aged fifty-one to sixty make up 25 percent of the students.

Another advantage of CEEP has been its attractiveness in recruiting and retaining the most desirable engineering graduates. It has also helped to bring back to the fold some engineers who were hired away by other companies.

AESD has concluded that training its own engineers to fill knowledge gaps is more effective, more motivating, and faster than hiring qualified outsiders. CEEP is also given part of the credit for the fact that AESD's business has increased 45 percent while its staff has risen only 20 percent.

Training the Trainer

If learning is to be truly continuous, an organization must look to its own resources for more and more of the teaching. Sole reliance on professional trainers, whether internal or external, is expensive and, in many instances, redundant. As Andrew Carnegie said, the only irreplaceable capital an enterprise possesses is the knowledge stored in the brains of its people. But the productivity of intellectual capital depends on how effectively the owners share it with those who can use it.

Skill at teaching comes naturally to a few; most of us have to acquire it the hard way. Leading companies in the United States have therefore adopted the practice of training the trainer, and their experience confirms that content experts learn the art of training more readily than training experts can master unfamiliar technical content. As a bonus, they find, the ad hoc trainers gain new insights and reinforce their own knowledge as they transmit it to others.

Joy Manufacturing Company. At Joy Manufacturing Company, it became necessary to consolidate three overlapping and sometimes competing marketing units into a single regional structure and to add the support functions of manufacturing and warehousing to each regional structure. A management steering committee in charge of the reorganization determined that before selecting and training current employees as new first-line regional managers, they should first identify the critical competencies and levels of proficiency the new positions would require. Having identified the needs, the committee developed a catalog of courses, one for each major area of skill. Next, they invited line managers, most of them at levels above the regional, to instruct in their special skills.

Since managers were unfamiliar with instructional design or delivery, a train-the-trainer program, consisting of (1) an introduction to designing competency-based units of instruction and (2) basic presentation of skills, was developed with the aid of external consultants. In the design sessions each manager drafted the course materials he or she would use in the form of written units or modules. The consultants fine-tuned the modules to ensure a reasonable degree of consistency among diverse subjects and instructor styles. Modular structure also made it easier to alter courses incrementally, as needed.

The presentation sessions stressed conveying information in a natural style, with an eye to the needs and sensitivities of adult learners. With the consultants as role models, the managers were encouraged to think of their students as already motivated to learn, willing to participate actively in the training process, having much expertise of their own to offer, and as problem-oriented. Each manager was filmed by a video camera as he or she presented part of the proposed course to the other managers; then the manager watched the replay, listened to the comments of the audience, and presented a revised version.

Initially, thirty-two courses were designed and twenty-five managers were trained as instructors. The courses, given several times over the subsequent two years, were improved by students' suggestions. Additional instructors joined the program. In the judgment of the external consultant, about two-thirds of the instructors attained professional training proficiency within a year.

Success of the train-the-trainer program induced Joy Manufacturing to engage line managers in other forms of employee development as well, such as identifying training needs for themselves and others.

General Foods. Personnel Department staff at General Foods often share responsibility with line managers for design of training programs and for teaching. The managers' principal problem with this is making the time required for their role in training. They are given primary responsibility for identifying training needs in their work units and bringing them to the attention of Personnel. Each plant absorbs its own training costs. Seventeen of General Foods' twenty-two plants coordinate their activities through a training network, which meets formally twice a year but maintains informal contacts throughout the year.

Corporate personnel keep abreast of training needs through a steering committee of five plant managers, who also recommend the names of line managers to act as trainers or as facilitators in training exercises. In addition, top-level manufacturing managers hold an annual round table to discuss the latest technological developments, exchange ideas, and describe new projects under way at their plants. The round-table agenda is set by a volunteer task force.

IBM's Federal System Division. This IBM division, which has 2,600 employees in computer programming, determined a few years ago that a uniform strategy for software development was needed. Software users and developers were therefore assigned to organize and conduct a three-week training course which everyone in the division, from president on down, attended over an eighteen-month period. Later, the course was extended to the commercial divisions, and attendance has now exceeded 10,000. The project has produced "alumni" and a "fraternity." Instructors convene once a year to review changes in technology, new methods of teaching, and new content needs.

General Foods, Dover, Delaware. At this multiproduct plant, with 900 hourly and 325 salaried employees, management and the United Food & Commercial Workers carry out training jointly. When a new training manual is needed, the department manager selects a team of employees and managers representing the affected areas or functions; operators, supervisors, professionals, and managers may take part. The team, usually with about five members, spends three days in learning-task analysis, and two days in train-the-trainer sessions.

One team member selected by the department manager is given two to three weeks to do the actual writing of the manual, with access to team members, other employees, and outside experts. When manuals are prepared for technical positions involving the operation of high-tech equipment, engineers and R&D staff help in the design and execution. The manual's writer may be either a supervisor or an hourly employee. Team members are relieved of regular responsibilities while working on the manual. The twenty manuals produced in this way have won strong approval from line managers, workers, and union, who believe that the manuals contribute to improved efficiency and quality.

Train-the-trainer classes drawn from several plants are formed into small teams to go through intensive exercises, such as task analysis, development of objectives, identification of specific segments for training, design of a segment, testing of the design by presenting it to another team, revision of design, a test presentation of the revised design to experienced employees at the "home" plant, and the final evaluation.

Kelly/Springfield, Tyler, Texas. At this tire plant, some ninety members of the United Rubber Workers took part in a train-the-trainer program and then served as trainers in a massive technological conversion from bias-ply to radial tire manufacture (see section on unions and continuous learning later in this chapter).

S. B. Thomas, Inc. At Thomas's English muffin plant, in Schaumburg, Illinois, shop-floor workers are paid a bonus to take on supervisory responsibilities for training new members of the work teams. All shop-floor workers are expected to pass their skills on to other team members in the course of day-to-day work (see section on work teams later in this chapter).

Intel. Although Intel's operational plan for training secretaries to use personal computers called for extensive use of "peer trainers," only six people qualified to teach even basic levels. It took six months of remedial work with 200 secretaries before 15 could be selected to start a train-the-trainer program. Peer trainers were specially trained and received special recognition; their training and support efforts were officially recognized in their quarterly objectives. Eventually "train-the-trainer" became a cornerstone of the project, as managers perceived that peer trainers bring an organic approach to learning. The more peer trainers there are in a given area, the closer and more relevant the assistance they can provide.

Corning Glass Works. In this company, as part of a Total Quality Program, over 100 regular employees of all levels have been trained to train others in quality skills. In some cases, hourly workers are training plant managers!

The examples above suggest, as a realistic goal, that everyone—or almost everyone—in the organization should be trained to teach his or her skills to other employees and thus move the organization a long step toward becoming a learning body. And if ordinary employees can learn to teach, why should they not also learn to impart their know-how through less formal methods, such as coaching, guiding, and developing—the whole panoply encompassed by the work training?

Continuous Learning Centers

A continuous learning center (CLC) is an arrangement whereby a group of employees who operate similar equipment come together to learn from one another how to achieve higher performance from their equipment. Unlike a work team, the members of the CLC do not share responsibility for output, although they may, on occasion, help one another out. Management initiates the center, offers guidance and support, and provides the time and place for meetings. Employees take part on a strictly voluntary basis, on company time.

For example, a CLC was established in one division of Intel to help secretaries learn to use and adapt their new personal computers. A representative council, composed of secretaries who had participated for years in departmental decisions, became the board of directors of the CLC. Secretaries became ''members'' instead of signing up for one course at a time. Membership committed the individual to attend classes and share knowledge with others; it committed the organization to help individual development. To encourage participation, members were publicly identified as such. Meetings were held regularly, with feedback conducted through surveys and evaluations of CLC services. Managers constantly communicated with members about adaptations developed in other parts of the organization and about the importance of experimenting and sharing ideas.

A CLC in another Intel division was designed to support employees at all levels in learning to use and adapt PCs. It began by helping secretaries install their equipment and deal with problems of reliability. Those who developed interesting new uses demonstrated them before large groups. Those who ran into trouble with equipment could call a hot line for immediate help. This CLC also had a board of directors, and the members were trained to advise management on how to make the center increasingly useful.

Work Teams and Pay-for-Knowledge

As consultative and participative work innovations spread across the United States in the 1980s, many factories and offices adopted the work-team form of organization. As with any new design, there have been successes and failures, but enough is now known to load the odds in favor of success. From the standpoint of this report, interest lies in the fact that the work-team mechanism is particularly conducive to continuous learning (see also the American Transtech case study in Chapter Two).

A work team consists of a small, permanent group of employees who combine their different work assignments to produce a shared output; the output may be a product, a service, or a component of either. For example, at the S. B. Thomas Company's English muffin baking plant in Schaumburg, Illinois, with just over fifty shop-floor employees, one team is responsible for production, one for packaging, and one for maintenance and sanitation. Each Thomas team is responsible for the quality, quantity, and cost of its output.

At many companies, a team member's job may integrate related skills. For example, machinists might be trained to perform not only the usual setup and operating tasks but also quality inspection and minor maintenance, because combining the knowledge and the means of controlling problems at their source can prevent costly errors. Managerial as well as operating responsibilities may be included. Teams having the broadest range of responsibilities are known as "semiautonomous" ("semi" because no one can have full autonomy in an organization).

In early experiments with team organization, companies often bestowed a full range of duties and authority on teams at their inception—basic operation, self-supervision, discipline, and training. Before long, they discovered that such a broad assignment exceeded the capacity of any new team. Today, the normal approach is to start with a set of basic operating duties and to expand them as the team's competency and cohesiveness grow.

Central to the concept of work teams is that each job should contain a reasonable amount of variety and self-direction, and that each employee should have the opportunity to learn and to add responsibilities. At a minimum, each member learns some of the tasks of other members. At a maximum, the member learns all of the assignments of all other members. This breadth of know-how enables members to rotate jobs and keep the team functioning in emergencies. It also implies a heavy dose of continuous learning and flexibility in work design.

S. B. Thomas, Inc., Schaumburg, Illinois. At this S. B. Thomas plant, each team trains itself. Training is viewed as one of the many supervisory duties shared by team members. Other supervisory responsibilities include costs, attendance, work assignment, counseling, safety, and communications. The team selects one member to assume each of these responsibilities for a period of weeks or months, with a bonus of ten cents an hour for each. (Increased knowledge of the operation and heightened self-esteem are additional bonuses.) The member responsible for training is designated "training facilitator" during that period.

A newly hired employee spends the first weeks or months learning the job under the tutelage of the training facilitator. The latter is familiar with all jobs performed by members of the team but does not necessarily conduct all the training; parts may be conducted by other team members skilled in the task at hand. However, the facilitator is expected to praise, criticize, or suggest concrete improvements. The facilitator decides when the new hire is up to speed and can safely start working on his or her own.

As a rule, several team members are simultaneously training and being trained. For example, member A, whose regular task is to monitor the final product inspection before packaging, may be training member B to do that inspection, while at the same time member A is being trained by member C to, say, monitor the packaging machines.

Recently, a group of Thomas team members developed training films to explain and illustrate the teams' tasks; an activity list accompanying each film describes the particular task in detail. One training facilitator has written a manual on the plant's cooling system to help new workers pace themselves during the production cycle.

The training system is still evolving, having passed through three stages since the plant opened in 1983. In stage 1, employees learned the rudiments of making English muffins through a formal companywide program of demonstrations, videotapes, files, and on-the-job training. During stage 2, delegates from the teams met with managers over a five-month period and solved some of the principal operating and training problems that had surfaced during stage 1. Now, in stage 3, a committee of nine employees has been assigned to develop a standard training approach for all teams, starting from the first day of hire to completion of skills.

Digital Equipment Corporation. At Digital's plant in Enfield, Connecticut, when a member asks to learn more about an indirectly related skill, such as accounting or purchasing, it is up to the team to approve, because the team has to keep up production while the training goes on. Team-based operation can broaden the members' understanding of how the workplace functions as a whole. This enables them to make better judgments on where their attention should be focused.

Zilog/Nampa. Shop-floor workers at Zilog/Nampa do business daily with engineers, maintenance workers, plant managers, supply/material clerks, and others. In a traditional plant, it would be supervisors or technical specialists, rather than workers, who took part. Since these contacts are work-centered rather than social, they impel the participants to try to understand and help one another to coordinate efforts, to learn from one another. Team members thus learn more about future business plans and strategies than they would in a traditional organization.

In return, Zilog team members are expected to share their knowledge and skills with others. For this purpose, management carefully trains all employees to know the manufacturing process from beginning to end and to understand what happens to the product at each stage. Thus, everyone in the organization—operatives, managers, engineers, maintenance crew—speaks the same language.

For example, in the manufacture of semiconductors a major source of product contamination is the "dust" produced by an oxide machine, which is part of the process. Dust removal in most plants is regarded as too unpredictable for routine maintenance and too complex to be identified by shop-floor workers; so the dust accumulates until an engineer, in the course of in-process electrical tests, spots it and directs maintenance or operation employees to remove it. At Zilog/Nampa, the team in charge of this stage of production is responsible for routine cleaning and maintenance of the oxide machine. The team monitors the quality of semiconductor wafer surfaces and metal-poly "shorts" for evidence that contamination is under control. The duty of operating the oxide machine is rotated among several members, who discuss methods of keeping the dust down and train the other members to operate the machine. The engineering department trains the team to inspect the wafer surface. The process maintenance department trains team members to do routine maintenance, which frees the maintenance experts to "hot rod" the equipment so that it performs above the original design specifications. As a result of this pooling of expertise, not only is the oxide machine utilized more effectively, but its life is extended well beyond industry norms.

Continuous technical learning at Zilog/Nampa is also fostered by posting diagrams, tables, and charts to illustrate complex parts or procedures at a central point where members can easily refer to them and discuss them with co-workers. When new products or processes are introduced, managers display a Key Factor Identification Chart, showing the technical factors with greatest impact on quality, quantity, or cost of the product.

When new technology is to be purchased, a whole team or a few of its members may be sent to the manufacturers to learn about it and explore the options. The team as a whole decides which equipment to buy and which members should return to the manufacturer for operating instructions.

FMC Corporation. This company has applied the work-team approach at a much higher level of task complexity—namely, to chemical research and development. At the company's R&D Center, chemists and chemical engineers have shared responsibility for every step from the laboratory through start-up of new full-scale plants (by contrast with the traditional system in which each profession did its own thing and problems fell through the cracks).

The sharing of responsibility requires and encourages the two groups to teach and learn from each other. For example:

- After the chemists complete their detailed laboratory work for a new or modified process, they do not, as in the old days, merely pass their results along to the engineers. They join with the engineers in challenging their own lab findings and in evaluating the economic implications.
- To obtain a permit to construct a pilot plant, the two groups jointly examine safety, toxicity, operational compatibility, and environmental controls.
- During construction of the pilot plant, the two groups jointly pinpoint potential safety hazards, design failure, and uneconomic decisions that might prevent their obtaining a permit to operate.
- The two groups jointly prepare a report recommending construction of a full-scale plant; and when construction is approved, they share in its design.

In addition to the economic benefits of the team approach, FMC claims that the increased responsibility of the team members sharply improves staff morale, efficiency, and recruitment. Working and learning on a team basis also improve overall communications between chemists and engineers and, as a result, lead to increased innovation in the R&D process. In fact, using teams of chemists and engineers proved so successful that FMC applied the approach in six different large-scale projects over a five-year period. Managerial coaching and support— especially in the initial stages to help chemists and engineers overcome reluctance in shedding their traditional professional roles—are critical elements in this team approach.

In another part of FMC, a manager within the Group Technology division of the Industrial Chemical Group (ICG) has been applying a similar strategy to the broadening of technologists by challenging them with assignments that require business skills outside their normal range (for example, marketing and strategic planning). In this approach, technologists work in informal ad hoc teams. The strategy directly supports ICG's long-term business goals: To continue as the company's largest profit contributor by supporting its established businesses and, at the same time, adding new businesses that are strategically compatible with its established ones. Once chemists and engineers are knowledgeable in the company's basic technology, they are given assignments in new product and market analysis in order to stretch their horizons and help them to better understand the fit of technology with the whole business.

In one instance, when a manager sent an engineer to be trained in a specialty of chemical engineering at the company's Material Research Lab, he assigned as backup a technician who was studying for a master's degree in that specialty (working three days a week, attending school the other two). As a result, when the engineer moved on to a new assignment, the backup was ready to take his place. In another instance, a chemical engineer formerly in charge of process and engineering development is now handling the evaluation of acquisition candidates from both a business and a technical perspective. Acting both as role model and as mentor, the Group Technology manager works closely with both individuals who moved into new positions, assigning projects that specifically encourage learning, providing advice and general direction, and creating a work environment where the learning of new material becomes a natural part of the job rather than being confined to the classroom. As a result, employees have become increasingly adept at formulating their own training experiences, often through informal methods such as self-selected readings and one-on-one sessions with other company experts.

The manager has restricted this approach to a few employees whom he identifies as having potential for broadening and willingness to devote extra time and effort. Other managers in the division, however, are encouraged to provide—at least to some degree—this type of broadening job experience to their subordinates as well. The eventual goal is to build teams of engineers, chemists, and other technical personnel who understand business and marketing issues and who are thus in a better position to communicate and work with the company's strategic planners.

Thus, work teams are learning machines by design, especially when introduced into a preexisting workplace, where employees have to unlearn habits they were taught in the past. During the early learning period, any team needs the help of a guide, or facilitator. At an older site, the organization as a whole needs guidance in retraining supervisors and middle managers for their new responsibilities.

For all their virtues, teams are subject to drawbacks. They may, if allowed, become ingrown and "territorial." Teams on shift A may consider their counterparts on shift B as opponents rather than colleagues; or they may come to believe they have nothing more to learn from the outside world. When an organization develops such blinders, it may have to be shocked into rethinking its mission from square one. In this respect, there is little to choose between team-organized and traditional workplaces.

In a growing number of companies, team members receive a wage increment for each new skill they master (pay-for-knowledge), whether or not the new skill is actually applied on the job. For example, at the Zilog plant in Nampa, Idaho, employees who apply for a pay-for-knowledge increase have to be certified under a system designed by a plantwide task force. Claimants must perform the new tasks on the job for several months and then pass a test. Each work team certifies, and decides the amount of salary increase for, its members' new skills. A similar pattern is followed at Thomas/Schaumburg, at several plants of General Motors, and elsewhere.

Unions and Continuous Learning

A unionized workplace can conduct a policy of continuous learning only if the union is involved. Continuous learning means widespread participation by individual employees in many stages of the training process, including the transmission of their own skills to others, and such a policy would inevitably have an impact on job descriptions, work rules, and other collective bargaining issues. On the other hand, union involvement in training does not necessarily lead to continuous learning.

Experience to date indicates that union involvement in continuous learning is most effective when it displays the following characteristics:

- Management policy actively invites and supports an important partnership role for the union.
- The collective agreement between management and labor defines their respective roles and establishes the lasting basis for cooperation.
- The parties act jointly in program control, planning, design, and direction of learning programs—at national, regional, and plant levels.
- Unions and workers participate fully in needs analysis and course-content decisions, and they share the responsibility for successful results.
- Instructors are selected from the regular work force. They are assigned equal status and full-time duties to develop content, deliver courses, and evaluate results.
- A jointly administered fund finances training programs and assures a long-term commitment to goals and objectives.

These joint programs benefit management, union, and the worker. Management benefits by raising the level of worker competence and by increasing the motivation, commitment, and performance of the work force as a whole. These changes are reflected in improved quality and productivity and a more flexible work force, with interchangeable skills and a faster response to change. Unions gain a deeper role in advancing the careers and performance of their members, causing them to be viewed as a major factor in employment security and in the sustained improvement of wages, benefits, and working conditions. Employees gain self-improvement, self-esteem, greater employment security, and increased participation.

Traditionally, employers have involved unions in training only insofar as the collective bargaining agreement prescribed when and where training might take place and how wages and benefits would be protected during training. In industries characterized by many small employers, such as graphic arts, a multi-employer joint fund might conduct job-specific skill training. In a few cases, joint apprenticeship programs were developed.

For example, the International Union of Bricklayers and Allied Crafts, with 100,000 members, has conducted a strong joint apprenticeship program with the Masons Contractors for over twenty-five years. The parties jointly set standards and administer the program, which is funded by employer contributions of six cents per hour to a jointly administered trust.

As advances came about in welding, insulating, restoration, anchoring, and tunnelization, many new and more technical (but not especially theoretical) skills have been required. Employers provide most of the training content. Although programs are usually on a short response time, tied to local ups and downs of the construction industry, the union feels that cooperation on even such a limited scope of training has improved relations between the parties, including at the negotiating table. As competitive threats to the union bricklayer sector have mounted, so have the membership's concern about and interest in training and retraining. Response to their concern will depend on the availability of additional funds.

In recent years employers and unions have collaborated on joint training programs, not only to provide job-specific skills but to keep up with new technology or to provide educational background for job change or for the long-term future. Some programs enlarge the concept of the worker's job to encompass problem solving and business partnership (junior level). More often the purpose has been to retrain displaced union members for outside jobs.

An ambitious and imaginative approach to joint training in a multiemployer setting has been evolved by the Service Employees' International Union (SEIU), whose membership includes many employees of hospitals and hospital-like institutions. SEIU's Lifelong Education and Development (LEAD) program trains and upgrades hospital workers to fill vacancies for licensed practical nurses and registered nurses, and it provides basic skills and computer training to help service workers move up the ladder into jobs other than nursing. The union works with institutions to ensure that training meets their needs without disrupting employee schedules.

Active union involvement contributes both symbolically and substantively to the outcome of the training process. The symbolic significance is that the program will not be solely at the whim of the employer, and that employee interests will be considered along with the employer's.

The practical significance is even greater, particularly when a jointly administered fund is established to finance the training. Employees have much know-how to add to the content of training for themselves and for their managers, but often their ideas are blocked for unwarranted reasons by supervisors and middle managers. A strong union can break through such barriers in instances where an individual employee cannot.

Conversely, when the employer wants to ensure that corporate information and ideas filter through to all employees, especially when major changes in organizational behavior and training are contemplated, a cooperative, involved union can penetrate the normal employee skepticism.

The Learning Agenda in Joint Programs. Once training is elevated to a joint program and participation is in effect, the program expands in many useful ways to reflect the needs of the organization and its employees. Leading-edge programs develop an agenda which is multidimensional and compatible with corporate strategy and employee expectations. The agenda includes the following:

- Job-specific skills
- Generic training to provide a head start for new careers
- Problem-solving training to improve quality and performance
- Keeping up with new technology
- Learning and education for upgrading or promotion
- Training for multiskills and job enlargement, to increase flexibility
- Retraining for new jobs or occupational shifts in the company
- Retraining for outside placement

- Training for teamwork, participation in decision making, and/or semiautonomous team assignment
- Detailed information about the business, its goals, and its plans

Kelly-Springfield/United Rubber Workers. Not long ago Kelly-Springfield (a subsidiary of Goodyear Rubber) had to make a decision about its big, old bias-tire plant in Tyler, Texas. Either the plant had to be converted to an entirely new technology to make radial tires, or it had to be shut down and a new radials plant built elsewhere. In either event the company would have to install radically new machines, processes, skills, and methods. Ultimately, the company agreed to convert Tyler in exchange for acceptance by the United Rubber Workers local of sizable concessions in pay and work hours.

The employer characterizes the changeover process as management-driven but with a high degree of union participation. The participation provides for joint managers of organization development—one union, one management.

During the eighteen-month transition to continuous-process manufacture of radial tires, the plant's veteran tire builders were totally retrained. The job-specific training program, called Program Development Instruction, was jointly designed and executed by employer and union. All Program Development Instructors (PDIs) were drawn from the hourly work force and classified as such during the instruction period.

Joint management-union committees in each department invited applications for PDI, interviewed applicants, and made final selections by consensus. Departmental choices were checked by a plantwide joint committee for compliance with equal-employment regulations and other systemwide requirements.

PDIs were trained to develop and deliver objective-based training programs. They spent eighty hours learning how to write such programs, and an additional twenty-eight hours working on computer terminals. Returning to their home departments, the PDIs were assigned to new job areas, machines, methods, and processes involved in the transition to radial production. These instructors visited other Goodyear plants, Japanese tire plants, and U.S. equipment vendors with similar machinery. (They became so well versed, in fact, that management now depends on their knowledge, to the chagrin of supervisors.) Next, they drafted the training programs they intended to use and submitted them for critique by other PDIs, training staff, and department managers. When a program was approved, the PDI would teach the course to machine operators and others as they began radial operation. Finally, PDIs collected data on the quality of their operators' training and performance and met weekly to review progress and consider improvements. Thus, they trained themselves along with the operators.

As of 1986, the Tyler plant had 1,300 employees, of whom about 100 were full-time trainers (about 7.5 percent of the work force). Ninety of these trainers were PDIs. The number of PDIs will diminish as the plant reaches a steady state, but PDI is expected to remain a permanent employee classification.

John Deere/United Auto Workers. John Deere & Company, like the rest of the agricultural machinery industry, has been passing through hard times and has had to make severe, permanent cuts. Aside from that, its relations with the United Auto Workers (UAW) have always been satisfactory. In the early 1980s, the company and union signed agreements to work jointly on improving quality, productivity, and quality of working life at several levels of the organization. A joint national committee with six members sets guidelines, controls the pace, and gives general direction to the effort. In addition, there are joint committees at most plants.

At four major plants, where programs of participation have been under way since 1981, the parties set out deliberately to develop new technical skills in the work force: not skills in the narrow sense but the ability to identify, discuss, and solve technical problems through work teams. Every natural work group in these plants has been trained in the art of solving problems, starting with the simple and proceeding to the complex. Hourly employees, UAW stewards, and first- and second-level supervisors have been trained to facilitate the groups.

This problem-solving training takes place within a broader framework, which includes:

- Thorough sharing of current, concrete information about the business
- Problem-solving teams at every level, from corporate engineering to shop floor
- Joint "listening" committees within major manufacturing areas in each plant and within corporate-support departments, to maintain contacts and ensure that information flows up as well as down
- Seminars for union leaders and middle managers, to help them develop new roles suitable to the emphasis on worker participation and joint problem solving

Programs similar to John Deere's are also under way at several other large companies, in cooperation with locals of the UAW, the United Steelworkers of America, or the International Association of Machinists.

Most intriguing are the handful of cases where large corporations (for example, Bell System, General Motors, Ford) set aside large sums of money annually from the wage/benefit package into training funds that are controlled jointly by employer and union. These quasi-independent administrative boards run a broad scope of training programs for active and/or separated employees. The benefit to the union is assurance that the employer will meet its commitment to train employees for new technologies. The dangers are (1) that the boards may accept responsibility for programs not germane to the fund's strategic objectives, and (2) that the boards may try to conduct programs beyond their current capacity to manage, with the results that union members begin to feel that the diverted wages and benefits are being wasted.

Jointly administered training funds symbolize dramatically that training is a continuing need, regardless of economic fluctuations, and that training is linked to employment security financed by company prosperity. Since money for the fund is diverted from the wage-benefit package, employees have a visible stake in it and a measure of control over the content and form of training. A fund's separate bookkeeping makes clear how much money the employer is investing in training. This helps to focus attention on cost-effectiveness, which, in turn, should incline the parties to think more objectively about purposes and methods.

With respect to new technology, the fund gives the parties more opportunities to reach a common understanding about the nature and timing of changes long before the actual changes take place. Since the impacts of technological change on the organization and individuals are so often disregarded until it is too late to plan for them, this may prove to be the greatest advantage of all.

Joint funding creates shared responsibility for the management of training and its results. Thus, the employees have a sense of investing in training, and the union has a responsibility with management for delivery of results.

Lastly, joint funding, as a permanent embodiment of employer-union agreement on shared goals, can serve to keep communications open and cooperation alive whenever the going gets rough.

AT&T/Communications Workers of America. The telecommunications industry's investment of time and money for training has grown so large that AT&T and its competitors increasingly require employees to be pretested to qualify for new jobs, and job-specific training is given only to those who meet qualifying standards. Divestiture quickened the already rapid pace of technological change and forced the Bell companies to develop new products and services. These demanded new and higher skills, while calling into question the survival of many current jobs.

In 1980, the Communications Workers of America (CWA) began to pay close attention to the changes in qualifying standards. The 1983 contract committed $36 million for training and retraining workers and stated that the actual programs would be carried out by joint union-management Training Advisory Boards (TABs) at AT&T and at each of the seven new holding companies. The TABs were not meant to duplicate job-specific training, but to help active workers and those whose jobs were being phased out to broaden their skills and general background to qualify for new jobs. Such "generic" training was to take place after hours, on a voluntary basis: trainees were not paid, but they received support for tuition and materials.

TABs are now in action at several of the holding companies. Some have built on and expanded established training programs; others have moved into new fields, such as computer literacy and basic accounting, in addition to basic math, English, and vocabulary. Support staff and mechanisms are still sketchy.

The Northwestern Bell/CWA TAB has contracted with local community colleges in five states for aptitude testing and continuing guidance as well as courses. Job-displacement training has not yet taken shape, because it presumes more advance communication than now prevails concerning business plans, job changes, and new technology.

The Bell Labs/CWA TAB has contracted with Rutgers to furnish courses in English as a second language and to provide an individualized learning center for reading improvement.

The Chesapeake & Potomac Bell/CWA TAB allows members to take free self-paced courses in basic skills.

Pacific Bell/Communications Workers of America. Since divestiture, the employee population of Pacific Bell—the operating unit of Pacific Telesis that services the state of California—has declined from 111,000 to 67,000. Of these, 40,000 are CWA members in clerical, operator, sales, and technical positions, and 27,000 are exempt staff.

By 1990 the work force will shrink to 60,000. Pursuant to its long-standing policy of employment security, the company managed the reduction until 1986 with only 500 layoffs. Since 1986, when a new Pacific Bell/CWA contract established employment security for the three-year term, there have been no layoffs. The contract provides a broad range of jointly administered measures to help surplus employees obtain new jobs within or outside the company. One such measure is generic training, which, as noted in the AT&T/Communications Workers of America case cited earlier, provides a head start for jobs both within and outside the company.

Because of the predivestiture tradition of "cradle-to-grave" employment, the company has had a hard time persuading employees that the future really is insecure and that they should seek retraining for their own safety. Union involvement has lent credibility to the message.

Rapid technological change has eliminated many traditional clerical, typist, and operator jobs at Pacific Bell, but it has increased the demand for technically knowledgeable service representatives and for technicians skilled in fiber-optic splicing, computer-aided diagnosis of equipment problems, and similar work.

Generic training helps both employer and employees. Under the contract, CWA members who transfer to new jobs in the company have the right to return to their original positions within six months. Generic training, by increasing the ability of workers to master job-specific training, has reduced the rate of return to original jobs from 40 percent to 5 percent, representing a large cut in job-specific training costs. New skills in electronics, computer technology, mathematics, and logic also can help qualify people who cannot be placed at Pacific Bell for job-specific training elsewhere in the telecommunications field. Employers can be assured that applicants will master the specific training for the jobs they seek and that, once placed, they will remain.

Retraining of CWA members at Pacific Bell is regulated by a joint TAB made up of three management and three labor representatives. The board projects future job trends, reviews and approves curriculum, selects training sites, and discusses key issues affecting training.

Courses are developed collaboratively by the TAB with community college officials and company department heads. The two most active current courses are for electronic technicians and service representatives. Both were developed with, and carried out by, two California community college districts, with state and local financial assistance.

The electronics training course covers basic electronics, digital techniques, transmission fundamentals, logic, and numbering systems. The service representatives' generic pretraining course offers a combination of technological and "people" skills that reflects the versatility needed on the job: computer keyboarding, selling, customer interaction, handling stress in the workplace, clerical overview. This 120-hour course has increased the success rate of those who subsequently take the job-specific program for service representatives from the previous 55 percent to 85 percent.

The electronics technical training course has succeeded in steering 750 employees (including many women) out of nontechnical jobs such as telephone operator, secretary, and clerk—which pay about $9 per hour—into ten highly skilled kinds of jobs, such as communications technician and splicer, at about $17 per hour.

Participants in the generic courses are volunteers. They attend on their own time, before or after work, but the only cost to them is $50 for the purchase of books. The self-paced course takes three to twelve months. It employs computer-interactive instruction, with much homework; students can consult instructors when necessary.

To cope with the expected volume of employee transfers, Pacific Bell and CWA have systematized job placement. An employee's right to transfer is based on both seniority and qualifications. Those who want to be trained for new jobs place their names in a transfer file containing three categories. In category 3 are those who are eligible for pretraining, either because they already have the minimum skills required or because they have passed a test. In category 2 are those who, having successfully completed the pretraining, are considered qualified for the job. In category 1 are the job incumbents. The files of potential transferees for upcoming jobs are kept well stocked, so the company rarely has to hire off the street except for entry-level jobs. First preference goes to laid-off employees with recall rights and to current employees whose jobs may be displaced by new technology. The TAB notifies employees whose jobs are in jeopardy at least sixty days before layoff. Despite the difficulty of forecasting job surpluses accurately, layoffs have been kept to a minimum.

Through a regularly issued pamphlet, the company publicizes retraining programs, job trends, career workshops, and registration dates for courses. The union does its part through its own network of letters to locals, stories in the union newspaper, and oral transmission by stewards.

Ford Motor Company/United Auto Workers. The most fully developed of the joint union/employer training approaches is the Ford/UAW Employee Development and Training Program (EDTP), inaugurated in 1982 and expanded by the 1984 contract. EDTP is supported by corporate funds (about $40 million a year), which are maintained as separate book accounts under the control of a Joint Governing Body (JGB).

In accordance with the contract, EDTP provides training, retraining, and developmental opportunities for active and displaced employees, supports other local and national joint activities, and provides opportunities for exchanging ideas and innovations about development and training needs. The 1984 agreement increased funding to support (1) certain aspects of the employee involvement process (today a dominant feature in the life of the company), (2) the "mutual growth forums" by which top management and the international union leadership exchange information vital to the progress of the company, and (3) the training of employees whose jobs are in jeopardy. In addition, EDTP was charged (and funded) to operate a new business development group, an employee-assistance program, a child-care program, health and safety training and research, and joint labor studies.

Separate funds are raised locally for local training in job skills, interpersonal skills, and employee involvement, within guidelines and controls set by the JGB.

The sources of funds deserve special mention. JGB receives ten cents for each straight-time hour worked in the company, plus fifty cents for each overtime hour in excess of 5 percent of straight time. Another two cents per hour straight time goes to the National Health & Safety Committee. Each local committee receives five cents for each hour of straight time worked at the site.

The funds are considered part of the wage/benefit package. Should the EDTP be discontinued, accrued national funds would be subject to negotiation or allocation to employees, but local money would not be.

The JGB, which has equal numbers of union and management representatives, headed by a vice-president from each party, establishes program policy and overall guidance, authorizes expenditures, and directs administration through a not-for-profit agency, the National Development and Training Center (NDTC). The NDTC's bipartisan staff of twenty-two persons actually plans, designs, and coordinates training efforts and provides on-site assistance for local committee programs; but it does not directly train anyone except local committee members and program coordinators. All employee participation is voluntary.

Due to the depression in the auto industry, EDTP gave first priority to displaced employees. The training of active workers, which began in 1984, allows UAW employees to choose from the following menus:

- Life/education planning
- Prepaid tuition assistance for formal education and training
- Basic skills enhancement
- College and university options
- Targeted education, training, or counseling
- Retirement planning

The objective was to provide something of value to as many employees as possible.

Targeted programs, a growing area of utilization, aim at the needs of particular locations or work-force segments. Local committees identify the needs, assess potential responses, locate providers, develop proposals for funding, carry out approved projects, and evaluate their effectiveness. Often they concentrate on vocational and technical training, such as computer programming, word processing, and communication skills. They also include on-site group delivery of courses under tuition assistance and individual development plans.

As the previous cases show, union involvement in training can embrace few or many steps in the process. It may be limited to fund administration and the setting of goals; it may extend to selecting courses and contracting with outside institutions to conduct them; and it may include detailed development of course content and delivery and the selection and training of trainers from the union ranks. The broader the involvement, the deeper the learning and the more durable the policy of joint training.

Union leaders warn, however, that employers may dissipate the gains of joint training if they portray union collaboration as weakness and concession. Since joint programs usually cause members to worry that the union is getting into bed with the employer, union leaders cannot afford to have the employer aggravate that suspicion.

A different and greater potential danger faces union leaders, even where employers play straight. Joint funds, as previously noted, contain scores of millions of dollars that could have been allocated to wages or benefits. Union members looking at the figures are bound to ask before long, "What are we getting for our money?" If the funds are spent on financing the construction of buildings or installing a new class of officeholders while the substance of training remains much as before, union leaders will begin to feel the heat. Membership support will wane and participation will decline. The future of the program itself may come into question.

Content of Training

How much discretion should employees have in deciding the subject matter to be covered by training for which the employer pays? Policies vary widely from one organization to the next; experts hold widely divergent and heated opinions, based on different philosophies.

In most companies the question does not arise: it is simply assumed that content should be job specific, that is, directly applicable to the job today or in the near future.

But sometimes content goes well beyond the job specific. Companies in the Bell System, as previously noted, provide job-generic training to help employees qualify for training for more technical jobs within the company or elsewhere in the industry. In certain companies, employees are trained to operate a set of related jobs rather than just one. Elsewhere, employees are trained to understand all operations at the work site.

Further afield, some employers provide training in general problem solving. In a pilot program, General Foods trains hourly and salaried workers in leadership and management skills, in order to develop production-line leaders, enable employees to supervise themselves, and encourage involvement in production decisions. A few companies regularly inform employees in detail about the state of the business and its plans for the future. Some allow employees to take any courses that interest them, whether visibly related to the job or not.

How valuable is it to the employer, aside from social responsibility or morale, to provide these broader opportunities for learning? Most employers would probably accept that detailed knowledge about the business and its plan can help managers (and perhaps supervisors) do a better job. Only a handful deem it useful to give such information to rank-and-file employees, except perhaps when they are about to be asked to make sacrifices. Many more employers might do so if they believed that thinking about the job is a legitimate function of low-level as well as high-level jobs.

It does not follow, however, that any and all training and development, regardless of subject matter, contributes to an employee's ability to think about the business. One can reasonably argue that if a course in income taxation or gemology is all right for managers to take, whether visibly relevant to the business or not, then it is equally all right for other employees; but evidence has yet to be adduced that such courses *are* all right for managers, from the employer's standpoint.

One skill whose importance is steadily growing, but which is rarely considered a subject for training, is technological adaptation.

The knack of adapting tools and machines to all sorts of unexpected uses has been a hallmark of American culture since frontier days. It is so pervasive that even though large corporations have tried to squelch it, under the misapprehension that "scientific management" demands technocratic uniformity, workers have found ways to "bootleg" their improvements into the workplace. (A notable exception is Lincoln Electric, which rewards employees for improving on the industrial engineers.)

Today, adaptiveness in the workplace is more necessary than ever. As single-purpose machinery gives way to flexible automation, robots, and end-user office automation, the potential for new uses is limited only by the ingenuity of the users.

To innovate successfully, employees must first have a solid grasp of the equipment they run; but they must also know where to look for profitable opportunities for adaptation and they must be encouraged to seize them. For example, at Travelers Insurance every manager takes a course in computer literacy to learn what the machine can do. If he or she completes the course and asks for a computer, the request goes to a special committee for approval. If the committee finds the manager is in a position to control his or her own work and that the proposed applications are valid, approval is granted. The cost is assessed to the manager over a ten-year period at about $1,000 a year.

Today, large companies ensure that factory workers are properly trained to use their equipment. Surprisingly, few companies take such pains with office workers. And when it comes to training in equipment adaptation, factory and office workers are in the same leaky boat.

In particular, office technology is too often introduced with no clear idea of what it is to be used for, beyond the hope that it will somehow improve productivity. Some companies train executives to use office technology more creatively and assume that it will rub off on subordinates. They have been disappointed, because it does not suffice to ask employees to be creative; the work environment itself must encourage creativity.

Wherever one finds employees innovating with above-average frequency and success, one can count on finding the following conditions:

1. The introduction of new technology is led by a high-status manager, whether in a line or staff capacity, who has a proven record of success and has faith that the equipment will upgrade the work unit's performance. Sometimes the manager's faith is so strong that he or she has persuaded the company to buy new technology without hard evidence to justify it. Such managers may put in long hours of overtime to prove what the equipment can really do, and enthusiasm spills over to subordinates. In the case of office technology, reliable technical support helps to maintain enthusiasm when local managers or subordinates run into operating difficulties.

2. The people who actually operate the new equipment

have a say in deciding the application and the uses it will be put to. Even better, they may have helped decide that the equipment should be introduced in the first place, because they shared in visualizing its potential uses.

3. The operators are constantly exchanging information about how to get the best out of the equipment. Formal training programs are probably needed at first, but eventually people are carried along by their own interest.

If employees work in view of each other, exchange comes naturally. If they are dispersed, special meetings and specific places and times may have to be provided. For example, in one company a group of secretaries from various areas were brought together at frequent intervals to "show and tell" about their innovations with their desktop computers. On one occasion, a group of ten users presented the adaptation they had developed to an audience of 100, with extensive use of computer graphics.

4. The manager's words and actions demonstrate that all operators are expected to innovate in order to raise the performance of the work unit. Although creativity is unevenly distributed among the members of any organization, everyone— guru or apprentice—has something to contribute. For example, if one wishes to innovate, one must experiment, and experimentation takes time from the employee's regular duties. The manager makes a special effort to provide the time.

A frequent obstacle to employee innovativeness is the manager who remains silent, because he or she does not use— or is uninformed about—new equipment. Employees devote effort to what they believe their manager considers important. If the manager is silent and withdrawn, they infer that he or she doesn't care.

A pro-innovation manager is also careful not to standardize the uses of the new equipment too soon. Between confusion due to excessive innovation on the one hand and dullness on the other, it is better to err a little on the side of confusion.

5. Employees are encouraged to communicate with one another about new uses and procedures, in both formal and informal settings. Innovation becomes a regular subject at staff meetings. Often rank-and-file employees eagerly discuss experi-

ments, while professionals hold back. Indications are that this reticence reflects the corporate culture rather than occupational characteristics. When the culture encourages communication, professionals communicate. For example, if professionals have no time to help others, the employer can provide staff support to help make the time.

6. The manager systematically gathers information on the progress of the innovation effort and its paybacks, and conveys the information to employees. Employees can then assess past practices and visualize new opportunities. Success in improving the quality of one's output is a potent reinforcer of further adaptation. For example, employees in a manufacturing unit got a "lift" when a computer program they had devised enabled them to determine sooner and more accurately that machinery needed repair, with the result that product quality gained and equipment downtime was reduced.

However, feedback does not mean blanket acceptance of whatever employees do. The manager has the duty to reject unacceptable innovations as well as praise and disseminate good ones, so that employees continually sharpen their sense of what the organization needs.

One caveat needs to be borne in mind, however: Even though the elements of an innovation-friendly workplace are understood, there are no off-the-shelf solutions for creating one. Solutions must grow organically from each particular situation.

Recommendations

Recommendation 5. Employers should think of their organizations as, in a sense, institutions for continuous learning, and should make them function as such. They should, therefore, aim to involve all employees in all stages of training, from needs analysis through evaluation.

Recommendation 6. Where employees are represented by unions, employers should invite the unions to share in the design and administration of training for their members. Unions should press for and accept such joint programs, but they should be careful to take on responsibility no faster than they acquire the skills and experience to discharge it.

Recommendation 7. To institutionalize continuous learning throughout the organization, the employer should encourage employees to make special efforts to learn—and/or to help other employees learn—skills valuable to the employer. Encouragement should take such forms as:

- A clear declaration that continuous learning and helping other employees to learn are integral parts of every job and every employee's responsibility
- Favorable structures and mechanisms, for example, learning by objectives, train-the-trainer programs, continuous learning centers, semiautonomous work teams
- Appropriate rewards, for example, pay raises, eligibility for promotion, recognition by peers
- Where a union is present, a jointly administered training program and fund

Background Papers

Dolan, W. P. (W. P. Dolan & Associates). "Training for New Technology: The Union's Role." Sept. 1985.

Felten, D. F., and Taylor, J. C. (International Sociotechnical Systems Design Consortium). "Involving Teams in the Design and Implementation of Technical Training." Sept. 1985.

Johnson, B. M. (Director, Corporate Technology Planning, Aetna Life & Casualty). "Growing Productive Information Systems: The Case for Participative Learning Environments." Sept. 1985.

Mink, O. G. (Director, Graduate Program in Human Resources Development, University of Texas at Austin), and Watkins, K. (Lecturer, Adult Education and Human Resources Development, University of Texas at Austin). "Extending Training's Impact." Sept. 1985.

Case Studies

Casner-Lotto, J. "Pacific Bell and Communications Workers of America: Retraining for the Computer Age." Dec. 1985.

Casner-Lotto, J. "Training and Development at General Foods: A Participative Process." Dec. 1985.

Hickey, J. V. "A Participative Approach to a Technological Challenge: General Electric Company's Aerospace Electronic Systems Department." Dec. 1985.

Plous, F. K., Jr. "Advanced Employee Training in High Technology at Xerox Corporation." Dec. 1985.

Rubin, N. "Training in the Team Environment: S. B. Thomas, Inc." Dec. 1985.

4

Manufacturers and Users
of New Technology:
Partners in Learning

Today, the weakest link in the chain of technology transfer is the most obvious and least noted: the transfer from technology manufacturer (or vendor) to user. A new link must be forged to create a strong connection between the economic interests of both parties in response to technological innovation.

The manufacturer and the user cannot function without each other. Any distance between them diminishes the outcome for both. The manufacturer-user link carries implications far beyond the well-being of the parties immediately involved. Although no single factor can be pinpointed as the cause of the disappointingly slow spread of new technology, a large measure of the problem is surely related to the way manufacturers and users deal (or fail to deal) with each other.

As long as design remains something the manufacturer does, and implementation something the user does, a knowledge gap exists and the resurgence of the U.S. economy will be delayed. This standard arm's-length relationship, which works

The information in this chapter, unless otherwise referenced, is drawn from the background papers and case studies listed at the end of the chapter. Both papers and cases were commissioned by Work in America Institute in the course of its three-year policy study entitled "Training for New Technology."

against the interests of both parties and the economy at large, should be replaced by a partnership in learning, with shared responsibility for profitable implementation. The benefits of partnership are many: for the user, faster implementation, more uptime, and more flexible application and adaptation; for the manufacturer, customer satisfaction, improvements to the product, and ideas for marketable new hardware and software; for both, the opportunity to gain a competitive edge.

Manufacturer and User: Forging a New Link

When new technology is purchased for production or office work, the very fact that the technology is new requires the purchaser to look outside for the knowledge and skills with which to run it. Logically, the best source to turn to would seem to be the manufacturer (the use of the word "manufacturer" here includes "technology vendor"), whose knowledge enabled it to create the equipment in the first place.

Indeed, every stage of the user-manufacturer relationship, from specification of functions to steady-state operation, presents opportunities for learning, and most are relatively inexpensive for both sides. Formal training is only one among many opportunities, albeit an essential and expensive one.

From all indications, however, the opportunities are seldom offered and seldom requested. Informal surveys of large companies that have purchased new technology disclose widespread dissatisfaction—cynicism might be a better word—with the training provided by manufacturers. They describe it as cursory (sometimes little more than a detailed technical manual), non-user-friendly, hard to apply, vendor-specific, inattentive to the practical needs of the workplace, and unavailable when most needed during the postinstallation period.

Explanations for these deficiencies spring readily to mind:

- Vendor sales engineering personnel are often dedicated more to sales and estimating activity than to customer support. They are better equipped to talk about competitive product features, design parameters, or suitability to a particular application than about training. Moreover, the incentive compensation under which they work encourages them to spend as little time as possible with any one customer, especially after the sale is concluded.

- The vendor's sales and customer support staff usually deal only with the customer's buying staff, engineers, and technicians. They assume that the customer knows what it needs and is capable of, and responsible for, training its own employees.

- The manufacturer usually lacks expertise in analyzing training needs, setting training objectives, developing customized programs, or producing programs or materials for the customer's organization—although the manufacturer may be well supplied with expertise for training its *own* employees.

Such explanations carry weight only if one accepts both parts of the implicit underlying policy: (1) that a manufacturer should undertake no obligation, legal or moral, to provide training or customer service beyond that offered by the contract, and (2) that the package should include no more than the customer asks for, since training is costly and might make the manufacturer's bid look less attractive than a competitor's.

No doubt, this policy is legally and ethically correct; it will stand up in court. The question is, how well does it serve manufacturers' long-term interests? In our opinion, it has severely damaged them: directly, by undermining the credibility of their performance claims; indirectly, by retarding the spread of new technology in general.

Arm's-length dealing between purchasers and manufacturers of new technology is a delusion. A manufacturer simply cannot afford to disregard what happens after the equipment is installed (Beam and Lewis, 1987). Proof that the equipment is capable of meeting specifications may win a case in court; but if the customer cannot make a profit with it, what does it do for the manufacturer's sales? A vast amount of new technology—especially office automation—is currently unemployed or underemployed (Uchitelle, 1987). As major suppliers have discovered, neither former customers nor new ones will buy additional equipment as long as those conditions prevail.

In order to use new technology profitably, the purchaser and its employees need to know how to operate and maintain it. They also must understand as much as possible about the range of its potential applications and be able to adapt it to company-specific conditions. Ideally, they should have learned—before the manufacturer considers its contract fulfilled—how to get better performance from the new technology than the manufacturer envisaged.

In helping the purchaser learn, the manufacturer itself can learn much of value. For example, it can pick up a great deal of information that will help it modify and market current technology as well as design and market newer models. Also, it can collect innovative applications devised by end users and market them as software or offer them as advice to prospective purchasers. As the technology is brought to optimum levels by the user, the user staff become a new source of knowledge for the manufacturer. For example, the head of advanced fabrication systems for Grumman Aircraft has asserted, with respect to robot installation: "In many cases, we can get a piece of equipment to do things the salesman and manufacturer didn't know it could do" (Feder, 1987, sec. 3, p. 1). In this cooperative relationship, there is continuing feedback of information from the user to the manufacturer.

The emergence of adaptations, and their value to the technology manufacturer, are graphically depicted by Charles F. Sabel in a description of high-tech cottage industry in northeastern Italy:

The production of ever-new parts and machines requires constant experimentation with the production equipment. To make a new machine at a reasonable price or produce a new weave with an existing loom, it is frequently necessary to modify an existing machine tool or to jimmy rig the loom. The necessity for making this kind of adjustment is completely independent of the sophistication of the equipment. An innovative artisan with a numerically controlled lathe or grinding machine is just as likely to tinker with it—

inventing new tools, finding new ways to cut oddshaped pieces—as an artisan with traditional equipment.

This tinkering, furthermore, constantly spurs and jostles suppliers of machine tools to improve *their* products. By listening to the reports of the men who service his machines in the shops, a maker of machine tools quickly learns what needs to be done and how to do it; and if he does not learn quickly enough, his servicemen will take what they have discovered and go into business for themselves. In this way Italy has become a leading manufacturer of wood-cutting, ceramic, and metal-cutting machinery [Sabel, 1982, p. 225].

Control Data. An interesting case in point is the Training and Education Group (TEG), a unit of Control Data Corporation, in Minneapolis. In addition to the computer hardware for which it is best known, Control Data produces many kinds of software. TEG develops and markets a series of computer-based training courses known as the Industrial Automation Training Program (IATP). In addition, TEG provides consulting services in support of automated production equipment and systems for manufacturers of automobiles, aircraft, petroleum, chemicals, and foods and beverages.

Most of the courses, whether standard or customized, teach generic skills to maintenance workers, whose needs in connection with new technology are most acute. The objective of each course is to raise the technical skills of maintenance workers to the level required for them to benefit from equipment-specific training. Subjects include electronics, microprocessors, computers, data processing, hydraulics, pneumatics, more advanced courses in programmable controllers and robotics, as well as remedial mathematics, blueprint reading, learning techniques, and maintenance skills.

Also, TEG offers an "authoring" package, containing software, texts, videotapes, and lab simulation procedures, which enable a customer to design and develop its own courses.

To market its courses more effectively in this highly competitive arena, TEG seeks detailed information about its customers' experience with IATP products and about their other needs relating to training for new technology. It employs two vehicles: (1) a TAB, comprising representatives of major Control Data customers, and (2) visits to customers' workplaces by TEG's professional consultants, many of whom have technical backgrounds.

The TAB grew out of lengthy discussions among TEG, Control Data salespeople, and customers who wanted a forum where training problems could be talked through. It meets semi-annually at Control Data headquarters with an agenda, formed by consensus, that facilitates the desired give-and-take about technical and training matters. Members say they benefit from the interchange with people from different industries and corporate cultures as well as from having to develop more active communications within their own companies so they can report accurately. The discussions have stimulated TEG to find more flexible ways of delivering courses—for example, disks that can be run on a personal computer (PC) at the workplace and a system that allows courses to be given on a local area network that connects multiple IBM-PC-compatible microcomputers within a plant. TEG has also learned how to eliminate redundant sections of generic courses and thus allow students to proceed more quickly to equipment-specific training.

In their site visits, the TEG consultants spend a full day on the shop floor. They interview maintenance workers, trainers, supervisors, engineers, and managers, and sometimes accompany maintenance workers on troubleshooting and problem-solving assignments to get a firsthand view. Also, they conduct on-site evaluations of IATP courses by sampling the opinions of employees who have taken them and of others who are concerned with their application. From these they gain insight into the relevance, applicability, and weaknesses of the courses.

Through the TAB and the site visits, TEG hears frequent comments on the need to put high-quality, equipment-specific training into a computer-based format. Customers allege that most equipment manufacturers slant their training packages toward engineers rather than toward the people who actually maintain and repair equipment, that essential information lies buried in thick manuals or baffling diagrams, and that the problems that cause a large part of machine downtime usually arise from faulty training or lack of information.

Developing the desired courses, however, is very expensive; few have attempted it. Members of the TAB have considered the possibility of a three-way effort involving an equipment manufacturer, a customer, and Control Data (which would have the right to market to other users of the equipment). Although no three-way consortia have materialized, a less ambitious variant has worked well. Control Data and Allen-Bradley jointly developed computer-based courses on two subjects in which Allen-Bradley has special expertise—programmable logic controllers and variable-frequency drives. The courses are applicable to controllers of any brand. With that experience under its belt, Allen-Bradley has now begun to develop computer-based courses on its own and has agreed to let Control Data market some of them.

Self-interest, therefore, instructs manufacturers to seize every available opportunity to develop their customers' know-how. It does not necessarily follow that manufacturers themselves should provide formal training; they may not be equipped to do it well. At a minimum, however, they should ensure that the customer receives appropriate training, whether from a division, subsidiary, or affiliate of the manufacturer, or from a subcontractor for whose performance the manufacturer accepts responsibility. Two recent news items suggest the potential for such third-party arrangements in the office automation field:

1. IBM, perceiving that sales have been hurt by insufficient training of office workers on minicomputers, has engaged Manpower, Inc., to train end users at customers' workplaces. Manpower, Inc., was chosen for its experience in the development of software for training the temporary workers it supplies to client offices (Harris, 1987).

2. A small Dallas-based consulting firm, Corporate Information Group (CIG), develops training materials tailored to the precise needs of value-added resellers (VARs), "dealers who market specialized computer systems to narrow markets such as medicine or law" and to the needs of VARs' customers.

"Since VARs sell hardware and software in a combined package, they compete for customers on the basis of expertise and service rather than price." CIG also rewrites VARs' documentation to make it more understandable, and responds to service calls from VARs' customers (Cook, 1987, pp. 74–75).

It also behooves manufacturers, as a group, to level with purchasers and make them understand that the costs of training and implementation are equal to the costs of hardware, software, and modifications combined. "Implementation includes meetings, information gathering, planning, and task restructuring—the labor-intensive steps involved in fitting technology to work functions and vice versa" (Bikson, Stasz, and Mankin, 1985, p. 25).

It would be useful at this point to describe an example of a manufacturer and a purchaser acting in the fullest sense as partners in learning, sharing the responsibility for profitable implementation of a piece of new technology. The closest approximation we have found is Ellemtel, a Swedish corporation created for the express purpose of managing the long-term relationship between a manufacturer and its prime customer. The manufacturer—L. M. Ericsson, a large (sales $5.5 billion in 1986) multinational based in Stockholm—plans, designs, makes, and installs world-class telecommunications equipment and systems. The customer is the Swedish Telecommunications Administration (STA), a state-owned telecommunications service.

Until the 1960s, STA did its own development work and even some manufacturing, but when it saw that electromechanical telephone switching was about to give way to digital, STA entered into a gentleman's agreement with Ericsson to cooperate in preparing for future technological needs. Cooperation-by-committee proved to be clumsy, expensive, and incapable of producing agreement on major projects. So in 1970, the parties formed Ellemtel, with ownership divided equally between them but with operating control (and 70 percent of the costs) assigned to Ericsson. The joint company's revenues come entirely from the two parents. Its staff of 600, including 50 on loan from Ericsson and/or STA, devote most of their effort to developments of benefit to Ericsson and/or STA—for example, the AXE modular digital exchange system, sold worldwide by Ericsson, which can incorporate technological advances as they occur.

A complex web of training arrangements also binds the parties together. Although STA has a training school for operators, it sends senior people to Ericsson to learn about newly developed telecommunication products. Ericsson has a center that trains other customers (mainly Swedish), with assistance from Ellemtel on courses and materials for new technology. In addition, Ericsson's field training and maintenance staff feed their findings back to the center. Ellemtel educates and reeducates its own staff to keep up with technology, yet it also sends employees to take courses at Ericsson.

Occasionally, Ericsson customers do their own training, using Ericsson materials. For example, when some Bell operating companies in the United States bought Ericsson equipment, the contract specified that Ericsson staff would train Bell employees in the beginning, but that eventually Bell would train its own employees. Ericsson hired several former Bell employees to assist in the preparation of the training materials, tailoring them to Bell's needs. These people were also brought to Stockholm to become familiar with the Ericsson equipment.

Opportunities for Learning

Without formal training of some kind, prospective users of new technology will not learn to operate and maintain it successfully, but formal training alone does not suffice. The more complex the equipment, the more the user has to know about (1) how to get it working again when it stops, (2) how to prevent it from stopping, and (3) how to get it to produce up to and beyond its capabilities. Such know-how is absorbed through diverse formal and informal experiences, many of which can be provided inexpensively in the course of the relationship between user and manufacturer.

A fully developed relationship between user and manufacturer is long and complex, passing through a series of discrete phases:

- *Initial contracting.* The purchaser states the functional specifications to be met, the manufacturer offers to meet them, they negotiate, and a formal agreement is signed.
- *Design of equipment.* The vendor translates the specifications into an operational design.
- *Building and testing.* The technology is fabricated and assembled at the vendor's workplace.
- *Plant visits.* The user visits other workplaces, where the technology is already in operation.
- *Formal training.* Classroom training is conducted by the user and/or the vendor in either the vendor's or the user's plant. Usually the training combines classroom and hands-on experience.
- *Installation.* The new technology is placed in the user's workplace by the vendor and/or the user.
- *Pilot and start-up.* The new technology is given a pilot run or planned start-up, buffered from the regular production environment.
- *Steady state.* The new technology is brought up to speed and goes into regular use.

Although formal training constitutes an essential stage of the relationship, opportunities for valuable learning arise at every stage, waiting for users and vendors to seize them. The effectiveness of vendor-user cooperation in training reflects the quality of the overall relationship. The more cooperative, flexible, and productive the relationship, the more cooperative, flexible, and productive the training.

To aid conceptualization, the range of learning opportunities may be diagrammed as follows:

	Formal	*Informal*
Structured	Classroom	Resident expert
Less Structured	Working in a build shop	Observation
	Pilot run	Hands-on experience
	Start-up	Talking with peers

Classroom training epitomizes the formally initiated and structured occasion. A formally initiated but less structured opportunity occurs when the user firm sends employees to the vendor's plant to help build and maintain the new equipment. What the employees learn there is directly transferable to the home base. For example, General Motors Corporation, in preparing a plant to manufacture the new Quad 4 engine near Lansing, Michigan, ''dispatched dozens of skilled tradespeople for weeks at a time to help its selected equipment suppliers build the plant's machinery'' (Hampton, 1987, p. 88).

By contrast, a skilled tradesperson may learn to manage the new technology by working out a structured but informal arrangement with a resident expert from the vendor. A tradesperson may also learn by just talking with co-workers and experimenting with the equipment. (Talking with one's supervisor, however, does not increase understanding—in fact, it may diminish confidence—unless the supervisor knows a lot about the equipment and knows how to impart this information.)

In a recent study of three plants where computer-integrated manufacturing technology was being introduced, researchers from Carnegie-Mellon University turned up a wide variety of activities that directly or indirectly facilitated learning. (The research omits opportunities during the steady state because, in the cases studied, the technology had only recently passed the start-up phase.)

Employees reported that conditions such as the following proved helpful to learning:

Initial Contracting

- The user's corporate staff involves representatives from the plants early on, to establish the relationship with the vendor and help in working out the terms of the contract.
- The parties reach a common understanding of what will constitute acceptable performance under the contract.
- User and vendor agree on detailed specifications of what the user's employees are to learn through training and other means.

- If the equipment vendor agrees to provide training, it has the necessary resources.

Design of Equipment

- User and vendor jointly develop and refine clear functional specifications for the new technology. For example, the vendor trains the user company's engineers one-on-one concerning the real capabilities of the technology.
- The vendor simulates design options that help both parties to validate the concept and refine the details of the design.

Building and Testing

- In the case of an integrated system, the lead vendor accepts responsibility to integrate it fully so that the system's capabilities can be tested and demonstrated at the vendor's workplace. The vendor gets the subcontractors to cooperate in that effort.
- The user's hourly workers spend a few weeks at the vendor's workplace getting hands-on experience with the new system while all elements of the system are present. Tradespeople practice assembling, troubleshooting, repairing, and maintaining. Production workers practice programming for specific applications.
- The user's engineers and tradespeople observe the final stages of system integration at the vendor's workplace.

Formal Training

- All members of the user organization who have been identified as end users of the new technology take part in the training.
- Training occurs close to start-up time so that end users can go straight from classroom to workplace without forgetting.
- Installation of the new technology is completed in time to allow formal training in class and in the workplace.
- The lead vendor thoroughly understands the subcontractor's equipment and can train on it.

- Instructors know enough about the system to earn the respect of skilled students.
- Classes provide suitable amounts of hands-on and problem-solving experience.
- The user keeps production and training priorities in balance.
- When the technology requires training across trades, all the trades involved take classes together.
- Training materials are well documented.
- If multiple subcontractors contribute to the system, a single coordinator manages the training, using a single information system.

Installation

- The user forms a start-up team to oversee installation and debugging of the system. The team comprises a member of the vendor's on-site support staff, the user plant's project engineering leader, and key people from the user's production and maintenance group. An engineer from the user's central staff joins the team regularly and keeps it informed of what has been learned elsewhere in the user company. The team meets daily, systematically records equipment functioning problems, and uses the records to identify and assign priorities to problems for joint solution. (Such a team could make important contributions even at the design stage.)
- The user's tradespeople have a hand in installing the equipment, under the vendor's supervision. The user dedicates enough people to ensure that some are on hand whenever the vendor needs help or wants to bring something of importance to their attention.
- The user has decided on specific job assignments for its people; they know which aspects of the system they will have to work with and what they need to learn.
- The user's management and union have agreed on (1) the vendor's right to work in the plant, and (2) modifications of job classifications, if necessary, to permit cross-learning.
- The vendor has enough support staff on site to meet installation deadlines without turning aside questions from user employees.

- The vendor's support staff knows as much about subcontractors' components as about its own, and thus can answer user questions about the operation of the whole system.

Pilot and Start-Up

- The vendor has finished installing the system so that it can be operated in fully automated condition during the pilot run.
- The user has enough available material that meets specifications to allow fully automated operation.
- The vendor has technical support staff at the user's facility on a nearly full-time basis to help supervise operation, maintenance, and repair of the system. User personnel begin to adjust the system and experiment with it under vendor supervision. Vendor and user personnel work together to prove the system is operating reliably.
- With the vendor's active encouragement, the end users modify and refine the system on their own. As they do so, the mystique that usually attaches to integrated systems gives way to familiarity and a sense of being in control.
- The user's resident experts gradually take over supervisory duties from the vendor's on-site staff.
- Members of the user staff, with expertise in different parts of the equipment and system, work together on problem-solving teams.
- User employees assigned to work with the vendor during the pilot and start-up phases complete their classroom training before going on to that assignment.

Ford Motor Company at Sharonville, Ohio. The experience of Ford Motor Company's transmission plant at Sharonville, Ohio, is consistent with the findings of the Carnegie-Mellon study. In 1987 the plant converted to manufacture a sophisticated new four-speed, electronically controlled automatic truck transmission, with the first product scheduled to come off the line in 1988. In Ford plants undergoing a major changeover, a corporate group often controls the installation of and training for new equipment. At Sharonville, where employee involvement has become a way of life, the Launch Training Team, formed in 1986 and consisting of seven salaried and five hourly employees from the plant, is responsible for all training in connection with the changeover. When 119 machines needed to produce the new transmission were purchased from 40 vendors, the Launch Training Team designated 19 as high-priority for equipment-specific training.

The Launch Training Team shaped training programs to accommodate the form of organization on the shop floor— Natural Work Teams—which is part of the new manufacturing system. All members of Natural Work Teams are volunteers, bear the manufacturing technician (MT) classification, receive pay-for-knowledge, and agree to share their skills and information. The Launch Training Team, therefore, has designed two curricula for MTs: an eighty-hour course in non-vendor-specific machine skills and a forty-hour course in group-working skills. Methods include stand-up teaching, hands-on learning, and interactive skills. The actual training of MTs in machine skills is conducted by any skilled tradesperson or other hourly worker who is considered an expert on a particular subject.

Equipment-specific training is organized as follows. First, members of the Launch Training Team visit the vendor's plant to "find out what they don't know." Upon returning, they write training objectives for the equipment and designate workers to specialize on it from a pool of skilled tradespeople and MTs whose knowledge and skills are most relevant to the equipment. The specialist tradespeople go to the vendor's plant for extensive training and train their fellow employees to meet the objectives set by the Launch Training Team. Attainment of the objectives is tested by means of procedures designed by the team, often using equipment built by members of the team.

Sharonville's representatives say their experience has taught them:

- To involve the vendor as early as possible in developing the training
- To visit the vendor early to "find out what you don't know," because that cannot be known in advance
- To specify training in the purchase contract, if possible (When

that has not been done, which is most of the time, they have regretted it; once a contract has been written, it is very difficult to bulldoze training into it. The division's purchase engineers must be made to understand the need.)

• to specify the intended behavioral outcomes of the training and to establish certification procedures that will demonstrate accomplishment

Dealings between Sharonville and two of the new equipment vendors are illustrative. For example, since placing the order for a transmission case-line with Lamb Technicon of Warren, Michigan, Ford production and manufacturing engineers have met biweekly with Lamb and have contributed to the design of the equipment. Lamb offers formal training courses (at a fee) and encourages user technicians to visit its plant (without fee) during the building phase, because the resultant familiarity with the equipment helps in troubleshooting and also helps to bring design problems to light. Sharonville's Launch Training Team did not accept Lamb's standard training package but did arrange to send skilled tradespeople and MTs to the plant, where they operated the equipment. This enabled them to identify operating problems before the equipment was installed at Sharonville.

Gould Inc., the other example, is supplying 200 programmable logic controllers for the new product line. Before developing training on the controllers, Sharonville sent two electricians to observe the Gould training program in progress at another Ford plant. The Launch Training Team worked with Gould to tailor its standard training package more closely to Sharonville's needs and objectives. It also modified the training schedule and Gould's choice of instructors, and determined which employees should be trained in which order (all had taken the eighty-hour curriculum beforehand).

Gould representatives say that although 98 percent of the training they supply is standard, they now want to make it better known that they are prepared to tailor training to customer needs. Customizing, they say, is not a problem, so long as the customer is willing to pay for it. The advantage to the customer is that only the customer can know what is important to it. The advantages to Gould are, first, that user employees get such good training that they do not have to ask Gould engineers to run the equipment and, second, that the users attain greater skill in developing applications for the equipment.

Manufacturers Can Train Well

In our informal survey of companies that were major purchasers of new technology, only two—General Motors (GM) and Goodyear—reported instances in which suppliers of equipment had provided satisfactory help in training the purchaser's employees; and in both cases, seemingly by coincidence, satisfaction had been achieved by making each supplier enter into a written agreement to provide training as a condition of obtaining the equipment contract. By a further coincidence, the forms of agreement used by both companies require the supplier to meet a detailed set of training specifications, with demonstrated performance of tasks by trainees as the test of the compliance.

The purchasers spoke well of their suppliers' ''cooperation'' in these agreements. Neither GM nor Goodyear simply tosses the ball to the supplier and walks off the court. Purchaser and supplier work closely together in developing, executing, and following through on the training programs. Whether suppliers would agree to such demands from less powerful customers remains to be seen.

In another interesting comparison, Goodyear training agreements call on the supplier to ''train the trainers,'' that is, to train a relatively small proportion of those who will be operating and maintaining the equipment and to prepare them to train the remainder. GM allows the vendor to choose between train-the-trainer and training everyone.

Goodyear Tire & Rubber Company. Goodyear has integrated training so fully into the regular operations of the company that when a new plant is to be built or an old plant modernized, training staff join in the planning from the start. Together with plant managers, they assess the skills, experience, and knowledge of the current or proposed work force; with the help of the vendors, they analyze the skills and knowledge that will be needed to operate and maintain the new equipment; and, based on this information, they prepare a training plan.

As each contract for new equipment is awarded, the supplier signs an agreement to provide training for operators and maintenance workers. A typical training agreement, which is not part of the purchase order but is coordinated with it, requires:

- Access to the supplier's manufacturing plant by Goodyear training specialists for the purpose of preparing detailed task analyses and training materials
- Hands-on performance training for operators, maintenance workers, and managers (Learners must (1) be told how to do a task, (2) be shown how to do it, and (3) demonstrate the ability to perform it. The process uses specific learning objectives for each task, simulators, classroom work, diverse media, actual equipment, and sequenced instruction. Performance is certified against a checklist.)
- Training content that matches specifications
- Completion of training before the vendor's equipment goes into operation
- Conduct of training by a representative of the supplier who is dedicated full time to training

Usually training takes place at a Goodyear site, unless so few employees are to be trained that it is more practical to send them to the vendor. Sessions run as long as necessary to meet the training objectives and may take as long as forty days. Occasionally, the sessions are conducted on an intermittent basis.

The training agreement does not require the vendor to train all employees involved with the new equipment, because Goodyear assiduously follows a train-the-trainer policy. For example, in preparation for the opening of a radial-tire wire-cord plant in Asheboro, North Carolina, in 1984, the company sent a small group of managers and technicians to its then only wire-cord plant, located in Luxembourg, for nine months of training with major vendors. Later it sent another group for five months. Today, out of a work force of 460, Asheboro has 110 labor trainers, trained by the original two groups. The principal European vendors continue to support training at Asheboro.

Each employee selected to become a labor trainer must have had work experience in Goodyear and be certified as having met all performance objectives for the job in which he or she gives training. The policy is facilitated by the practice of subjecting every job to a thorough task analysis.

Despite this rigorous agreement, Goodyear does not refuse to pay a vendor if a trainee fails to perform for reasons beyond the vendor's control. However, the vendor is expected to bring the problem to the attention of Goodyear for corrective action.

In a typical plant modernization, thirty or forty vendors may be involved, and training agreements are entered into with most of them. At Tyler, Texas, there were over fifty. As an example, the training representative of one of them, which made solid-state motor controls for the Tyler production line, collaborated with Goodyear's training expert to decide exactly what an employee needed to know to operate and maintain the equipment. Task statements, written training objectives, and selection of training aids followed. The vendor then developed the training materials. Employees who completed the training were certified to handle and troubleshoot the equipment.

Goodyear also calls upon a few vendors for help in recertifying maintenance workers to keep up with changes in technology. Suppliers have carried out the required periodic updating of performance checklists, but with little enthusiasm.

The need for vendor assistance does not end with the plant start-up. Downtime is so costly, especially for a computer-integrated system, that someone must always be at hand to get the system up and running again quickly. To train and retrain Goodyear employees as such troubleshooters, either a vendor representative is brought in or employees are sent to the vendor.

General Motors at Linden, New Jersey. Through a series of carefully analyzed experiences of training for high technology over the past six years, GM's auto assembly plant at Linden,

New Jersey (now part of the Chevrolet-Pontiac-Canada Group), has evolved a prescription for working relationships that yields satisfying results for itself and its technology vendors. The core of the relationship is the vendor's explicit commitment to develop "effective training as an ongoing part of doing business with GM."

The series began in 1979, when the plant's paint shop acquired a new automated conveyor system. Although the vendor taught the Linden electricians the electronics of the programmable logic system, it did not teach them how to solve hookup and synchronization problems on the job. Linden's plant engineer and chief electrician, besieged by calls for help on the line, joined with top electricians to design and conduct a supplementary, in-house course to rectify the omission.

From this experience the engineering staff discovered that many of the electricians felt uneasy with the new electronic equipment and with the concepts needed to understand and repair it. In 1981, therefore, Linden engaged the local branch of a nationwide technical institute to deliver an in-house course in basic industrial electronics to twenty electricians. When the plant's training staff reviewed the proposed curriculum and found that it, like the 1979 course, devoted very little attention to problem diagnosis and solution, they realized there had to be a "hands-on" component to balance classroom training. So they set aside a programmable logic machine, on which electricians could simulate maintenance problems and practice solving them. A noticeable gain in skill development resulted.

The success of the revised electronics course was marred somewhat by the difficulty of accommodating it to the schedules of very busy electricians. Seizing on computer-based learning as a key to more flexible delivery, the Linden staff employed it, from 1982 to 1984, to teach not only basic electronics but also pneumatics and hydraulics. Once again they found that formal training alone could not do the trick. The trainees needed opportunities to solve production problems on actual equipment away from the shop floor, followed by application on the shop floor.

In 1984, Linden was designated to build the new Chevrolet Beretta and Corsica, for which it received a host of new automated production systems. An immense job faced the in-house training staff. In conjunction with the union, they decided that it could be done only by instructors familiar with automobile assembly, and that the way to obtain them was to train an in-house corps of instructor-experts. The corps would design the courses; teach co-workers to operate, maintain, and repair the new systems; and later provide "hot line" assistance when a system failed. Nine tradesmen, handpicked to form the corps, were split into teams and sent to equipment vendor schools for lengthy train-the-trainer courses. Other equipment vendors trained the teams in teaching techniques and provided free instructional texts.

The teams then developed job-specific, shop-floor-oriented courses, combining classroom and hands-on work, and with these they trained 400 workers to operate and troubleshoot the new systems.

This design achieved six key goals of the training staff: (1) it ensured hotline assistance beyond that which any one manufacturer could provide; (2) it allowed training to be synchronized with production and maintenance schedules; (3) it cost much less than having the vendor do all the training; (4) it allowed great flexibility in matching training to skill levels and in digressing to consider actual shop-floor problems; (5) it made it easy for trainees and instructors to deal candidly with their uncertainties; and (6) it enabled the staff to provide introductory training before equipment was installed in the plant.

On the basis of these cumulative experiences, Linden eventually spelled out, in a brief document, a set of training specifications that are now incorporated in its contracts with equipment vendors. For example:

- Prior to the award, the vendor assigns a coordinator to work with Linden's training coordinator.
- Thirty days after the award, the vendor proposes a detailed training plan.
- The plan may provide for either train-the-trainer or total population training; in either case, scheduling must be flexible.

- Different levels of training are specified for different levels of employees.
- Specifications emphasize diagnostics, troubleshooting, and so on, with a substantial amount of hands-on experience.
- Trainees must demonstrate competent performance.

Most important, the document puts training specifications on an equal footing with equipment and system specifications and declares that "the equipment vendor will be responsible for the development of effective training as an ongoing part of doing business with GM."

The training specifications have now been carried out in two contracts, with pronounced success: first, for a system in which robots apply urethane coatings to windshields and back lights (rear windows) in the glass installation area of the plant; second, for an automated system in which a robot, using a vision sensor, seals strategic points in the car body against water, fumes, or fire.

The second contract introduced a new element that added to the training's effectiveness. Because the technology was so new that its documentation and manuals were still being written as the system was being installed, Linden engineers and electricians worked in tandem with the vendor's field-service staff, perfecting the operation of the system over a period of six months. Both parties affirm that this joint hands-on experience contributed the most to developing Linden's in-house ability to diagnose and remedy malfunctions of the system.

Training Through a Third Party

In the effort to regain lost markets and win new ones, companies are turning not merely toward computer-driven machines but toward more and more highly integrated systems of computer-driven machines in the shop and in the office. The integration of systems, particularly in manufacturing, raises new problems for those who must learn to operate and maintain them—problems that make it more necessary but also more dif-

ficult for the systems suppliers to help them learn. Some purchasers have therefore turned to third-party specialists who combine technological and training expertise.

Integrated systems tie together elements of three major
families of technology:

- computer-aided design tools
- computer-aided manufacturing tools (e.g., robots, numerically
  controlled (NC) machine tools, flexible manufacturing systems
  (FMS), and automated materials handling)
- computer-aided techniques for management (e.g., management
  information systems and computer-aided planning)

Integration of systems is simple in concept but extremely difficult
in practice. Companies have pursued the challenge because "the
greatest benefits of automation occur when the computers used by
design engineers, order clerks, inventory planners, production
schedulers, and production machines all speak the same computer
language and refer to the same data bases. The laborious work of
generating paper production documents such as routings, parts lists,
schedules, and so forth, is eliminated. Customer requests are scheduled and executed in a timely manner. Parts and tooling are available to make the product, the chances for error are reduced, and
customer commitments are met" [Scalpone, 1987, p.3].

As far as training is concerned, the critical attributes of
integrated systems are these:

- Computer and software technology is the driving force. Each
  machine is controlled by a microprocessor or a programmable
  logic controller, linked to larger computers via communication networks. In the larger companies, software controls
  many aspects of system operations.
- The technology is inherently complex. Because individual
  machines on the factory floor must operate at high levels
  of precision and be flexible enough to process a range of products, they require the integration of mechanical, electrical,
  and software functions. Because multiple vendors supply the

machines, computers, and software, the complexity is compounded.

- Better, faster coordination of human activities is needed. People in functions such as production, quality control, and maintenance have to work together more closely to achieve output and quality goals simultaneously. The speed of automation forces people to coordinate quickly.
- Malfunctions are more costly. Automated systems must be working most of the time to meet payback criteria, but with highly integrated systems, a malfunction in one part of the workplace can shut down operations in other parts.
- All employees must contend with a major explosion of information. As a result of greater computer control, information on the performance of the operation is automatically generated and easily collected, aggregated, reformatted, and distributed. Employees are inundated with more information at all levels of the operation.
- Computer-based systems usually replace some human activities at all levels of the organization.

The new technology differs fundamentally from the old, and the differences have important consequences for training. First, employees must acquire knowledge in what is for most of them a new area—computers and software. Many workers, especially those who are older and/or have not used computers during their education, view the technology as not just a new version of what they have worked with in the past but as qualitatively different. Their anxiety inhibits learning.

Second, since the technology is complex, and since different vendors may supply different parts of it, knowledge about the components will come from different areas of expertise. Training must integrate these diverse disciplines so that an employee or group of employees can run the total system.

Third, the greater coordination demanded by integrated systems tends to smudge traditional boundaries between work areas. The consequence for training is that maintenance workers in particular need to be multiskilled: they need to know adjacent jobs as well as their own. On the other hand, tradition reinforces the boundaries. The issue becomes whether to train people in a given trade (for example, electricians or millwrights) separately or together with people in other trades.

Fourth, the job of the machine operator changes profoundly. "Operating" a machine becomes the task of programming, setting up, observing, testing to see that it is working properly, and responding to various automatic "error messages." Thus, the line between operation and maintenance work also blurs.

Fifth, the newness of the technology precludes clear job descriptions, particularly in new facilities. The dilemma is that it is hard to train people for jobs that are not well defined.

Sixth, since the new technology requires sizable capital investment, downtime must be kept to the minimum, which puts a premium on fast reaction time, accurate diagnoses, and reliable solutions. Maintenance people must be good at isolating faults in a complicated system (that is, troubleshooting). This requires both a systematic problem-solving approach and the ability to conceptualize the system in terms of logical flow of information as well as physical flow of material. Training must produce these skills.

Satisfactory solutions to many of the problems of training for integrated systems were found by Caterpillar Inc. and by Miller Brewing Company, but in neither case did the solution come from a lead vendor. At Caterpillar Inc., training was provided by one of the system's component suppliers; at Miller Brewing, by a training vendor that had contributed neither hardware nor software to the system. What the two training organizations had in common were: (1) the possession of well-developed training resources that had emerged as offshoots of high-tech manufacturing operations; (2) familiarity with most, if not all, of the specialized fields of knowledge embodied in the components of each system; (3) a strong belief in the value of integrated systems and a solid body of experience in working with them; and (4) commitment to the successful implementation of the new technology, not merely to the success of the training program.

The two cases clearly demonstrate that manufacturers of new technology can, if they wish, develop strong training capabilities. Recent straws in the wind—still too early to report—suggest that others have begun to do so. The U.S. economy urgently needs many, many more.

Caterpillar Inc./Allen-Bradley. Caterpillar Inc. designs, manufactures, and markets a wide variety of heavy equipment and vehicles in many parts of the world, with 50,000 employees and sales of $7.3 billion in 1986. It has fifteen plants in the United States and fifteen overseas. After three disastrous years, from 1982 to 1984, the company resolved never to let itself be edged out again by foreign competition or changing markets.

In 1985 Caterpillar committed itself to the "Plant with a Future" (PWAF) plan, aimed at reducing manufacturing cost without losing the company's position as the highest quality producer in its markets. PWAF lays down a detailed guide to upgrade manufacturing facilities through four steps:

1. Simplify and streamline operations.
2. Consolidate related manufacturing operations into cells, each embodying a particular product or process (for example, machining, assembly, engine making, transmission housing). Make the employees of a cell responsible for controlling their own process and inventory.
3. Automate cells with state-of-the-art computer-guided equipment.
4. Tie the cells together with a computerized planning and control network, all using a common data base. Link day-to-day operations to product planning, process planning, business planning, and production planning; execute customer orders through just-in-time scheduling.

Recognizing that PWAF implied profound organizational and individual changes, Caterpillar developed a human resources plan to support it. The plan dealt with such matters as: corporate human resource philosophy, job design, qualification of people for newly designed jobs, reward systems, management climate and communications, and training.

A schedule for training in computer-integrated manufacturing (CIM) theory and practice was drawn up on the basis that timing for each group of participants should coincide with their first contact with actual CIM applications on their jobs. The first contact took place earliest for salaried people in plant management, engineering, and planning—those who were developing the systems, software, and standards, and who were purchasing the equipment. Supervisory and hourly groups were scheduled for late 1987, when CIM applications were expected to reach the plant floor. Local union officials took part in an overview course in November 1986.

In mid-1985 a corporate technical training team outlined an eight-session survey course, designed to enable plant managers, engineers, and planners to recognize and experience at first hand various components (especially manufacturing hardware) of a CIM installation. Major topics included: hierarchical design of CIM systems; computer-aided engineering and its linkage to production control; sensors and coding systems that track products through successive stages of production; logic systems, controls, and computerized controllers; programming and operation of robots; data-flow systems; flexible manufacturing; and the business-planning aspects of CIM. The team specified precisely what the participants were expected to be able to do after each session. For example, after the session on flexible manufacturing participants should be able to use a selected group of electrical and electronic terms relative to flexible manufacturing systems and CIM; identify advantages and disadvantages of various coding methods; list the advantages of flexible manufacturing; describe the components of a typical flexible system; and explain cell and process-simulation capabilities at Caterpillar.

Given that the CIM technology was new to Caterpillar, the training team realized it would have to look outside for subject-matter experts in a wide variety of techniques. The team's search led to the Allen-Bradley Corporation, one of the company's many vendors (by no means the lead vendor) of CIM components. Allen-Bradley, a Milwaukee subsidiary of Rockwell International, has a long-established reputation in controls, communications networks, and integrative software. Moreover,

Allen-Bradley actively markets training as part of its customer-support services. It maintains a training course production studio, technical writers, videotaping facilities, and a catalog of over fifty multiday training sessions in CIM-related topics, for which continuing education credit is available.

Not surprisingly, therefore, Allen-Bradley responded with enthusiasm: seven of its customer support staff, from groups making products or components of the kinds featured in the course sessions, served as instructors; and its technical writers and support staff supplied training materials, videotapes, product information and specifications, equipment setups, and demonstrations for the hands-on portion of the course.

More important, perhaps, Allen-Bradley supplied its own conceptual model of how CIM is planned, organized, and managed—a model derived from (1) the organization of responsibility for CIM-related products within Allen-Bradley and (2) experience with CIM products in its own facilities.

In addition, the sales engineer (customer coordinator) who permanently represented Allen-Bradley to Caterpillar had a working knowledge of each of his company's component product groups. Whenever additional technical support was needed for the course, he could get hold of a knowledgeable product engineer or product service center to fill the gap. A lead vendor trying to perform a similar function in a multivendor contract would have to call on assistance from numerous subcontractors, a much more challenging situation to manage.

The course was tested in October 1985 on two groups of twenty-four Caterpillar managers—manufacturing systems engineers, planning supervisors and staff, training staff, and corporate staff involved in developing PWAF standards and documentation—from facilities throughout the United States. At its conclusion, the participants registered strong approval but recommended a number of ways to make the course more directly relevant to their needs and easier to absorb. As of this writing, the revised course has been presented to 450 managers and staff people, and a shortened version has been presented to 160 managers.

Interviews with training managers and participants confirmed that the training has facilitated the implementation of PWAF and CIM. The participants reported that experimenting with hardware during the sessions had put them at ease with the equipment. They now understood how their own work and the work of others would affect and be affected by CIM, and they were more ready to accept and work with the equipment slated to be installed in their plants. In addition, they no longer regarded the system as a "black box," but as a graspable collection of components and controls.

Miller Brewing Company/Amatrol. At Miller Brewing Company, the selection of a training source for a multivendor manufacturing system took a fascinating twist. The choice fell on none of the component manufacturers; it fell on a vendor of bench-training equipment and courses named Amatrol, Inc. Amatrol's strength derives from its evolution as the training arm of Dynafluid Systems, Inc., a small but well-regarded manufacturer of industrial automated machines and fluid-power equipment.

Miller Brewing in 1986 had sales of $3 billion, a 20 percent share of the intensely competitive U.S. beer market, 11,000 employees, six container-making plants, and six breweries. In recent years new technology has been introduced into the company's beer-making process, not least in the packaging production line, with a great increase in speed and labor saving. The line is driven either by electricity or by hydraulic or pneumatic pressure. Machinery is controlled by microprocessors with specially designed electronic systems.

Two detailed needs-analysis surveys, in 1982 and 1984, revealed that the workers who maintained the packaging production lines were receiving excessively narrow training from the equipment suppliers. Because the training provided by each supplier was highly specific to its own equipment, flexibility was sacrificed. When a line went down for repairs, the skilled tradespeople had a Hobson's choice: either replace parts by trial and error, or go back to the manufacturer for advice and help. Management decided on a corporatewide training program for maintenance workers and supervisors, to include hydraulics, pneumatics, electronics, microprocessors, welding, centrifuges, filtration, Sankey CO_2 systems (to fill beer kegs), continental seamers (to seal the cans), and microbiology—the whole panoply of technical skills required to maintain the lines.

It was also determined that the training should follow these guidelines:

- Supervisors should be enabled to do the in-house training, so as not to be permanently reliant on equipment suppliers.
- Hands-on training should be part of every course.
- All courses should be systems-oriented. For example, hydraulics should be taught in a way that gives the trainee a sound basic knowledge of hydraulics theory as well as application, so that the trainee can troubleshoot any type of hydraulic system.

The first courses chosen to inaugurate the new program were hydraulics and pneumatics. Two decisions followed: first, the company would develop its own curriculum and training materials; second, the company would seek help from a trainer capable of providing both the theoretical and hands-on aspects of the training. The consultant would train Miller supervisors, who would then be responsible for passing the knowledge on to the people under their supervision.

After looking at ten or so manufacturers of hydraulic bench training equipment, Miller selected Amatrol, Inc., for several reasons:

- The training equipment was well designed and built and provided an acceptable simulation of Miller's production units.
- Amatrol was able to perform realistic industrial systems training.
- Training materials and programs were of high quality.
- Amatrol's managers demonstrated the desire to work with Miller in developing a complete training program tailored to Miller's specifications.

Amatrol had come into being because its founder and CEO realized, soon after launching the parent manufacturing company, Dynafluid Systems, Inc., that sales of Dynafluid's dedicated industrial automated systems depended on the ability of its customers to operate them profitably, and that this implied training as part of the total package. He was dissatisfied, however, with the training offered his customers by educational institutions of all types. He therefore added an education division to Dynafluid. As demand grew, the division was spun off into a freestanding company, called Amatrol, Inc., dedicated entirely to technological training and education.

Amatrol courses feature:

- Opportunities for trainees to be involved in their own training, with plenty of hands-on experience
- Changes of programs at twenty- to thirty-minute intervals, to prevent attention from dropping off
- Diagnosis and troubleshooting as the core elements
- Industry-experienced trainers, well versed in theory, application, and training techniques

Amatrol's repertoire includes courses in microprocessor control, air logic control, servo control, robotics, and CIM, in addition to hydraulics and pneumatics.

As of early 1987, three cycles of Miller supervisors, with fifteen or sixteen in each, had completed their train-the-trainer hydraulics sessions, and one cycle had completed pneumatics, at the Amatrol facility. Each session lasts a week—a very intensive week of long days at the facility plus required homework. The high trainee-instructor ratios permit individualized instruction. Trainees are encouraged to develop rapport with the Amatrol staff and to keep in touch afterward, when tough problems arise on the shop floor.

Miller and Amatrol have cooperated in developing a leader's guide that is used by Amatrol trainers at the facility and by Miller supervisors when they train their maintenance workers back at the Miller plants. The supervisors have, in fact, helped to set up second-generation training programs at the plants.

Miller and Amatrol are now cooperating on a new course in microprocessor control. Miller is also working with an analogous vendor, Energy Concepts, Inc., to create a train-the-trainer course in electrical technology, a subject not offered by Amatrol.

Aside from the technical implications, which present the most urgent and evident training needs, integrated systems transform jobs and organizations. Implementation of computer-assisted technologies on the shop floor or in the office alters organizational structure, communication patterns, and the nature of jobs—permanently. Work rules and job classifications are among the most frequent problems encountered in implementation. Robot systems, for example, inundate skilled trades workers with information and thus stimulate more informal and interunit communication. Administrative practices change in parallel with the technology. Integrated data-exchange networks overturn hierarchical and functional barriers.

The process of adopting and implementing integrated systems normally takes months, sometimes years, and usually upsets the organization. The process, therefore, needs to be planned and managed. User participation and planning have been found to be strong predictors of success in implementation—and their absence, a predictor of failure.

Should technology vendors try to help purchasers deal with these sensitive areas? One major vendor, with extensive experience in applying the sociotechnical approach to its own organization, is known to have begun offering such services to customers, but it does not yet feel ready to report results. In principle, there seems to be no reason why vendors could not develop the necessary resources, or link up with subcontractors that have them.

The Case for Manufacturer-User Cooperation

The two key players in the race for new technology are the technology manufacturer and the user. Both parties have a strong incentive to succeed, but neither can optimize results independently of the other. The complexity of technological systems calls for continuing efforts on the part of both actors and their respective employees.

New technology is expensive. It can be disruptive rather than productive in its early period of use. It can be intimidating, even hostile, to employees who are unprepared. We need to recognize, however, that machines depend on their users, not vice versa, and that we should capitalize on the creativity of people in developing a training strategy. In the same way that machines expand the capacity of production or services, creative employees expand the capacity of the machines they work with. But to do so, they require multifaceted training that transcends the conventional on-the-job training programs of the past— and these programs must be as dynamic and complex as the technology itself.

The reputation of the technology manufacturer and its future sales to current and potential users depend upon customer satisfaction. A manufacturer of new technology systems, unlike a manufacturer of consumer goods or even a manufacturer of low-tech producer goods, cannot leave it up to the user to install, apply, maintain, and adapt the technology at arm's length or even with a cordial but elementary transfer of know-how.

When the user is left to "sink or swim," the technological investment becomes a painful burden. The incidence of failure, costly start-ups, unacceptable downtime, and employee resistance, not to mention management frustration, rises sharply. This counterproductive pattern can be eliminated when the manufacturer works hand-in-glove with its customers.

As a working partnership between maker and user matures, the behavior of the parties changes from adversarial to cooperative. The results enrich both parties and enhance the value of the technology. The user as an active partner shares its solutions and innovations with the manufacturer and learns to respect and trust the manufacturer's employees as teachers and peers. The manufacturer, moving into a learning mode, gains the opportunity to improve the design and performance of its own systems (hardware and software). The potential benefits—in costs of production, versatility of equipment, improved design, more efficient installation and start-up, reduced downtime, and competitive edge in the marketplace—are enormous.

The essence of these new relationships is linked learning, on a continuing basis. Both parties must broaden the base of participation to include each other's employees in learning, teaching, and adapting new ideas. Neither party should wait for the other to make the first move.

Recommendations

Recommendation 8. The manufacturer of new technology should, in its own self-interest, take responsibility for ensuring that the user becomes capable of operating the new technology profitably. Such a relationship is advantageous to the manufacturer because (1) it binds the user to the manufacturer in goodwill; (2) it gives the manufacturer a competitive edge in acquiring marketable innovations and adaptations developed by the user; (3) it helps the manufacturer develop improvements in current technology and designs for newer technology; and (4) it minimizes the possibility of user disappointment, which acts as a drag on sales.

Recommendation 9. Since formal training is an indispensable part of implementing new technology, manufacturer and user should jointly develop a training strategy that will ensure profitable operation by the user. The manufacturer should act either directly or through a third party for whose performance it accepts responsibility.

Recommendation 10. The manufacturer should adopt a formal business plan that establishes the function of user training as a critical element of long-term business survival and growth.

Recommendation 11. Training needs and costs should be included as an explicit part of the investment in new technology. Hopes of accomplishing training cheaply and by improvisation are doomed to failure.

Recommendation 12. Manufacturer and user should jointly ensure that the user's employees learn not only the technical aspects of operating, troubleshooting, and maintaining a system, but also the scientific and technological principles on which it is based. This will enable the user's employees to solve problems on equipment of all kinds.

Recommendation 13. Manufacturer and user should pay early attention to how the new technology will affect organization, decision-making patterns, work rules, job design, communications, and learning systems. These issues require advance planning and may determine the success of the organization. Ad hoc or ex post facto decisions are often too little, too late, and too costly.

Recommendation 14. When an integrated system is assembled from components supplied by multiple vendors, the user should seek the assistance of an organization whose expertise encompasses both training and most or all of the technologies involved.

Background Papers

Goodman, P. S. (Carnegie-Mellon University, Graduate School of Business Administration). "Designing Effective Vendor-User Training." Feb. 1987.
*Gutchess, J. F. (Consultant). "Miller Brewing Company and Amatrol: A Successful Partnership in Training for New Technology." Feb. 1987.
*Scalpone, R. W. (Medina and Thompson, Inc.). "The Vendor's Role in Training to Support Computer-Integrated Manufacturing at Caterpillar Inc." Feb. 1987.
Tornatzky, L. G. (Director, Center for Social and Economic Issues, Industrial Technology Institute). "Computer-Assisted Manufacturing Technology: Training in What, by Whom and for Whom?" Feb. 1987.

Note: Background papers marked with an asterisk can be found as case studies in the companion volume *Successful Training Strategies: Twenty-Six Innovative Corporate Models,* edited by J. Casner-Lotto (San Francisco: Jossey-Bass, 1988).

Case Studies

Casner-Lotto, J. "Learning from Customers: Control Data Corporation's Training Advisory Board." June 1987.

Gutchess, J. F. "Telecommunications Technology Training in Sweden: A Successful Public/Private Partnership." June 1987.

Gutchess, J. F. "The Goodyear Tire and Rubber Company: A Commitment to Training." June 1987.

Hamburg, S. K. "Manpower Temporary Services: Keeping Ahead of the Competition." June 1987.

Hemmens, K. C. "A Proactive Approach Toward High-Technology Training: General Motors' Linden, New Jersey, Plant." June 1987.

Sickler, J. L. "The User-Vendor Relationship at Ford Sharonville: Employee Involvement in Training Design and Delivery." June 1987.

5

Cost-Effective Design and Delivery of Training Programs: A Systems Approach

In Chapter Two we recommended that "the CEO and senior associates should include a training plan as a critical component of the corporate strategic plan, to ensure that all levels of the organization will have the knowledge and skills to carry out the strategic plan."

When an overall training plan is presented for approval, the CEO and his associates should ask:

> How well does the plan carry out the corporate strategy?
> Could the plan carry out the corporate strategy more cost-effectively?

Looking at the plan as a monolith can only yield crude answers to these questions. A plan is composed of many and diverse programs, each with its own specific objectives and "target groups," and each program can be constructed in many

The information in this chapter, unless otherwise referenced, is drawn from the background paper and case studies listed at the end of the chapter. Both paper and cases were commissioned by Work in America Institute in the course of its three-year policy study entitled "Training for New Technology."

different ways. Therefore, the questions should be focused on one program at a time, allocating costs to each program and assessing the results of each. Since there is at present no one best method of measuring cost-effectiveness, we recommend only that the measurement be consistent.

In this chapter, we assume that senior management has already agreed on the strategic necessity of the objectives that a proposed program is to meet. Similar questions now must be asked regarding the proposed program: Is this particular program the most cost-effective way to meet these objectives? Could a different program do it more cost-effectively?

Innovative designs and delivery systems that multiply the options for cost-effective training are available in the United States today. The review and analysis of leading-edge developments presented in this report reveal more systematic methods for determining training needs in industry, which, in turn, make it feasible to design programs that are tailor-made, responsive, fast, and economical.

This process enables managers to optimize their training investments and more reliably predict the outcomes. Key decisions typically concern the selection of project manager, goals and timetables, in-house versus outside talent, instructional systems, and methods for measuring and evaluating results. Comparative costs and benefits and the penalties of not training can also be assessed.

A vast spectrum of training and educational solutions has been devised to meet industry's diverse and ever-changing needs. As companies in the forefront of technological change explore these possibilities and find that they must put more and more resources into training, they grow increasingly concerned about the cost-effectiveness of that expenditure.

The concept of training's cost-effectiveness has been raised in two quite different decision-making contexts. The first involves deciding whether to spend money on training as against spending it on other forms of investment (for example, land, buildings, equipment, or additional staff). In the current state of the art, such an application of the concept is fruitless, because it does not persuade decision makers one way or the other.

The second kind of decision involves choosing between training program A and training program B as alternative routes to training objectives that senior management has declared essential. Today, so many different means of achieving a given set of training objectives are available that the realistic choice is not just between programs A and B, but among A, B, C, D, and E. Here, application of the cost-effectiveness concept is both feasible and necessary, even though there is no established formula and each company must devise its own system.

Decision Making

The occasion for deciding among alternative programs may arise before training, when a program is part of an annual training plan proposed in support of the annual business strategic plan, or after training, when the returns on costs and results are in. Forecasting compels management to think through the choices; comparing the forecast with reality enables the organization to learn from experience.

Before any reasonable choice can be made, the objectives of the program must be specified in writing, so that there can be no doubt now or later as to: (1) which groups and individuals are to take part, (2) what improvements in their knowledge and skills are to be effected, and (3) the date by which the objectives need to be achieved.

When objectives are agreed on, a particular program to meet them will presumably be recommended in the training plan. It then falls on the CEO and senior associates to decide, first, how likely the program is to achieve its objectives; second, whether alternative programs can achieve the same objectives; third, whether the recommended program is more cost-effective than the alternatives; and fourth, whether the objectives can be met more cost-effectively by in-house resources or by the use of outside organizations. The pattern resembles the one that managers are supposed to follow when deciding to purchase a major piece of equipment.

Making such decisions is easier if management gets into the frame of mind of regarding training as itself a form of technology. Correctly speaking, it is. The original meaning of "technology," going back to the seventeenth century, was the systematic study of practical or industrial arts. Gradually "systematic study" evolved into "application of science." Not until the late nineteenth century did "technology" come to include tangible embodiments of study—that is, hardware and software. Today training and education have indeed become industrial arts, as amenable to systematic study as engineering of any kind, and a large industry of instructional designers, program developers, and equipment manufacturers floods the market with their products.

In judging how effective a particular program is likely to be, managers should ask:

- Is the content of the program sufficient to achieve the program objectives?
- Is the content only what is needed to achieve the program objectives?
- Does the program make correct assumptions about the current knowledge of learners?
- Does the program make use of the best available delivery systems?
- Does the design of the program make best use of the delivery system?
- Do program design and delivery take account of the latest knowledge about how adults learn?
- Is documentation of the program sufficient to ensure its maintenance and quality control?
- Does the program provide for measurement, evaluation, and validation from the beginning?

The quality of a program's content and design depends on how much attention is paid to needs analysis and instructional design. The more important the program, the more important it is that needs analysis and design be performed by the best available resources, whether inside or outside the company; but outsiders should not serve as subject matter experts unless no one in the company can do so. Audiovisual materials usually require specialists, because students have become accustomed to contemporary broadcast quality and are impatient with anything less.

Cost and effectiveness are closely entwined in the design and delivery of training. The more sophisticated the design and the delivery system (for example, classroom, computer-based, or interactive TV training), the greater the initial costs. On the other hand, some of the most effective delivery systems enable learning to take place at the work site, with minimal time away from the desk or shop. Since the cost of travel and lodging for students raises the price of training programs—indeed often far exceeds the cost of design and delivery of a major program—it may be more cost-effective to choose the more expensive model.

When judging the probability that a particular delivery system will fit the task envisaged for it, it is useful to ask:

- Does it suit the kind and degree of performance improvement being sought?
- How much does it cost?
- Is it easy to use? Does it require a lengthy setup, or complicated instruction for the student?
- Is it readily available when the student is ready?
- Is the system reliable? How much maintenance does it need?
- Can it be used under various training conditions?
- Does it hold the student's attention?

Identified and described here are some especially noteworthy programs that show how training and education can be made more cost-effective through the ingenious matching of design and delivery methods to shrewdly defined objectives.

IBM and the Systems Approach. Several years ago, concurrent with the establishment of a new corporate department of education, IBM pulled together its innovations in the training field and called them a "systems approach." Implementing the approach throughout the organization will take five to ten years, although some elements are already in use in some divisions.

The ever-increasing demand for readily available, low-cost, yet consistently high-quality education is the prime force behind the approach. Moving part of the training responsibility from the divisions back to the corporate headquarters was required by the desire to convert from central classroom education to site-based delivery. This move necessitated coordination of course development and delivery as well as planning of curricula. Also, there was much redundancy because many courses were given at more than one location. IBM's strategy is to centralize development and to decentralize delivery—tasks that are easier said than done.

Introduction of new delivery methods has widened the range of choices but also made course design, development, and delivery too complex for reliance on the talents of a single instructor. A team of highly trained specialists is needed. The systems approach breaks the training process into manageable steps and facilitates decision making and budget planning at each stage.

The approach consists of (1) detailed curriculum design, based on defined business requirements, (2) instructional design for each course, (3) course development led by interdisciplinary professional teams, (4) delivery through the most advanced techniques available, and (5) measurement and evaluation at every stage. The overall objective is to maximize the cost-effectiveness of training.

The goal is to ensure that each job has a matching but flexible curriculum for those points within an employee's career when training is needed: entry education for basic orientation, training on how to do a job, training to permit growth within the job, and advanced education to enable movement into a more responsible job. Curricula are based on people-performance requirements outlined in the corporate strategic plan. Detailed curricula now exist for many major categories of jobs.

Quality of instructional design is the primary determinant of quality of training, regardless of delivery methods. IBM's aim, to make every fifteen minutes of education outstanding, raises three questions: What motivates people to learn? How and why should learning objectives be determined? What makes lessons "stick" and be applied on the job? How can information be conveyed faster and more effectively? Instructional designers also design the workbooks and other materials used in the courses and provide remedial lessons as needed.

A major task is to develop education and training programs to facilitate the introduction of new products and services. IBM spokespersons believe that if executives are seeking a major directional change to support a product or service, the message on how to make that happen can be built into the educational system. Needs analysis is crucial: Who must be aware? What does the company want the employees to remember? What references must be available? What skills are required?

IBM has abandoned the traditional method of course development, in which an instructor spends a few days creating a course, because such courses often require months or years of costly amendment by other instructors. A development team now includes a project manager, instructional designers, professional writers, audiovisual specialists, print-layout experts, computer programmers, and authors. A typical project schedule might include ten phases: needs analysis, course design, development, validation before production, production, pilot classes, reproduction of materials, training of trainers, and evaluation and enhancement.

Until ten years ago, IBM relied solely on company professionals to design and develop courses. Today, it employs many outside educational development companies, depending on the volume of work. The larger the assignment, the more likely it is to use outsiders. Nonetheless, IBM aims to develop an in-house cadre of talented, well-trained specialists, to avoid total reliance on outsiders.

Delivery is the key to cost-effectiveness. The push to decentralize through on-site video-computer systems of interactive TV is relatively recent at IBM; 75 to 80 percent of all IBM training is via the traditional classroom. But decentralization is the wave of the future. Within the next ten years, half of IBM training will be delivered by student-driven, learning-center-based methods (for example, computer-based training, instructional TV with personal computer, and other self-study methods using workbooks or videos). Despite the steep up-front development costs of the new methods, some divisions have "off-loaded," or decentralized, 50 percent of their courses, cutting costs by 25 to 50 percent and saving millions by closing educational centers and eliminating travel and living expenses. IBM sees a potential for off-loading 50 to 75 percent of all student days.

The main advantage of off-loading student days is shown by IBM's rule-of-thumb calculations of the costs to transmit a given body of content via alternative delivery systems:

$50 a day. For self-study, computer-based, or interactive videodisk training, and the like, when an employee receives education on-site

$150 a day. For classroom education within commuting distance from home (includes $150 for cost of education facilities, instructors, administrators, and managers)

$300 a day. For classroom education at a central education center (includes the cost of travel to and from airports, plane fare, the cost of hotel, and meals)

According to many companies, the largest single item of training cost is the salary and benefits of the student while away from the job. However, objection has been raised that such a calculation amounts to double-counting; that is, since the student receives only one total of salary and benefits in the course of a year, regardless of how his or her time is divided between training and "work," it is misleading to superimpose the salary and benefits of training time. In other words, if a trainee earns $24,000 a year in salary and benefits but spends one month (one-twelfth) of that year in training, then charging the cost of that month as an extra would make it appear that he or she actually costs the employer $26,000 a year.

We suggest that more than one rule is needed. If an absent student has to be replaced by another employee who would not otherwise be on the payroll—which is often the case with "direct labor"—then the salary and benefits paid to the replacement are a valid additional cost. Any loss of output due to the replacement's inferior skill, and so on, should also be a valid cost.

Often, however, no one actually replaces the student during his or her absence at training. Another permanent employee or the student's supervisor may keep an eye on the student's work load and do whatever cannot wait, but no extra costs are actually incurred. In such a case, which is probably typical for white-collar workers, the only valid extra cost would be any loss of output due to the delay in processing nonurgent work.

Another advantage of off-loading is that some courses can be taught in one day rather than two, or one week rather than two. IBM has found that, in general, new delivery methods produce learning with equal effectiveness 25 percent faster than the traditional classroom.

As stated in Chapter Three, as continuous learning becomes the norm, the line between work and learning disappears. Learning becomes a part of the job. Nevertheless, the less time students require to absorb a given amount of learning, the more time they have to perform other valuable work. The same would hold for time saved through using a computer instead of slower techniques for doing the job.

Often self-study is combined with the classroom: basic information is learned in self-study, but application to job conditions needs practice in the classroom. For example, logical selling process is learned in self-study; selling IBM's most recent product is learned in the classroom. Another example: responding to customer service questions can be learned through self-study; practice can be acquired through role playing in the classroom. This combination makes the instructor's job more challenging because trainees are better informed before they reach the classroom. Therefore, IBM is developing a fifty-module program to improve the effectiveness of instructors, embodying the principle that "the instructor is an active manager of the learning process."

Manpower, Inc. It would be hard to find a more thorough application of the systems approach than in the training of word-processor operators by Manpower, Inc., the world's largest supplier of temporary workers.

As office automation becomes more complex, employers

find it does not pay to hire temporary workers unless they have been trained to operate their specific equipment. When standard office equipment consisted of an electric typewriter, a secretary or typist could move from one brand of machine to another with little loss of efficiency. Today, work stations and electronic typewriters vary so widely in operation that specific training is necessary. And training is expensive.

On the supply side, a large proportion of Manpower, Inc., workers are women returning to the work force after raising families. Many are overwhelmed by the thought of the new technology.

The company's turnover rate can be as much as 35 percent a year (which is typical of temporary-help firms); so training by means of the usual approaches, such as classroom sessions or vendor-supplied manuals, proved not to be cost- or time-effective. Charging employees for the training was ruled out on strategic grounds. Manpower's solution to training has been the development of the SKILLWARE system. Designed by Manpower's own staff specialists, SKILLWARE has proven to be a cost-effective method of training, as well as a highly efficient way of developing skilled operators. Currently, the company calculates that training costs for each employee (including costs for new equipment) exceed $100. Manpower hopes to lower that cost to $35 per employee. However, if major purchases of new equipment are made, costs may remain near the $100 level. The company estimates that even this amount would represent a tremendous savings over training that involves the use of teachers in classrooms.

For each model of office equipment (or software) there is a SKILLWARE disk-based computer program. The program leads the trainee step by step from disk insertion to document printout, on the actual machinery for which he or she is being trained, right in the local Manpower office. The disk uses operator-to-operator language rather than the usual "techno-speak," and it spices the instruction with enough humor to off-set fatigue. Self-paced, the program can be mastered in as little as six hours, or as long as two days. Because of the strong family resemblance between one disk and the others, mastery of Machine

A enables the operator to master Machine B more rapidly.

Trainees start and finish on their own schedules. No instructor is needed, but a facilitator is available to answer questions. At completion, the trainee receives the gift of a small, colorful, pocket-sized "Operator Support Manual," written in the same style as the disk itself. If time elapses between the end of training and the offer of a job on that particular machine, the trainee can use the manual to brush up at home or on the job. Trainees are also free to take a refresher course at the Manpower office.

SKILLWARE has helped to cement relations between Manpower and a number of its corporate clients. Three companies that have successfully applied SKILLWARE to help meet their unique training needs are Miller Brewing Company, Xerox Corporation, and Vista Chemical Company.

- Miller Brewing had installed IBM System/36 word-processing machines in its field sales offices to amplify and speed the flow of marketing information. Miller wished to provide training fast, without taking staff members away from their jobs. The plan called for IBM to run a two-and-a-half-day seminar at each office. As an experiment, it was decided that half of the offices would receive SKILLWARE training (free of charge) before the IBM training, in hopes of breaking through the field staff's resistance to office automation. A hot line for quick answers to questions connected the sales office with the local Manpower office. Miller reports that sales staff who began with the SKILLWARE training got much more out of the IBM training than those who did not.
- When Xerox brought out its Model 860 work stations in 1984, it was necessary for its sales force of 4,000 to learn to operate the equipment so that they could sell it effectively. Most were total novices when it came to using word processors. Like Miller, Xerox wanted to train its employees fast and without taking them out of the field. The training was conducted in three waves. First, a Manpower, Inc., team went (again, without charge) to Xerox's main training facility in Leesburg, Virginia, and trained twenty-eight Xerox

trainers as SKILLWARE facilitators. The twenty-eight returned to their respective regional offices and trained additional facilitators. Finally, the expanded force of facilitators administered SKILLWARE training to the entire 4,000. According to Xerox, the training helped lay the foundation for introducing new keyboards, document-management software, and word-processing software.

- Vista Chemical, unlike Miller and Xerox, was not a Manpower, Inc., client but became one as a result of a joint training effort. Vista had installed a large number of IBM 5520 work stations at its Houston headquarters. Although Manpower, Inc., considered the 5520 too expensive to install in its own local offices, it developed a SKILLWARE disk for the 5520 and made it available at no charge to Vista. Manpower is now the primary supplier of trained temps to Vista, which, in turn, donates computer time to the local Manpower office for training purposes.

Although Manpower, Inc., has chosen to stay out of the training business as such, SKILLWARE's success has opened some interesting leads. The company has developed and validated a hands-on test that measures an operator's ability to create an actual document on any word processor or any PC word-processing software in an office environment. The test also measures key clerical skills. Armed with the test results, the company not only can offer the operator brush-up modules, but also can match temporaries' skills precisely to a client's needs. Finally, Manpower is considering offering its clients a new category of temporary worker: the temporary trainer, who will facilitate SKILLWARE training for clients' permanent employees on client premises.

Travenol Laboratories, Inc. Poles apart in instructional design and delivery system from the Manpower, Inc., example, yet similarly cost-effective, is a training program developed by Travenol Laboratories, Inc., that provides a common language between production and maintenance managers for the operation of new technology.

Travenol Laboratories' plant in North Cove, North Carolina, manufactures and packages large parenteral solutions, such as the intravenous dextrose and water solutions used in hospitals. The plant has a large work force, including 160 in maintenance. It embodies a unique production technology and requires rigorous process standards. Much of the process is computer-controlled, and the equipment involves complex pneumatics, hydraulics, electronics, and computer logic. Process and environmental conditions are continuously monitored and adjusted to meet U.S. Food and Drug Administration requirements. Because the plant covers many acres, maintenance supervisors manage their workers like a large commando force with constant walkie-talkie contact.

Between 1979 and 1984, despite ups and downs of production at North Cove, demands for maintenance support steadily climbed, and maintenance staffing and costs climbed with them. Reorganization of the department and the addition of a few management positions helped improve controls and planning. They also facilitated cooperation between production and maintenance on longer-term projects. Maintenance supervisors, however, continued to function much as before. Having previously worked as mechanics or technicians, they still did mechanics' tasks on many occasions, were slow in cross-training their workers, fell behind on preventive maintenance, and largely ignored the new planning and costing systems.

In late 1984, a needs analysis survey persuaded the plant engineer that the sixteen maintenance supervisors should be trained in (1) diagnostic problem solving, (2) fundamentals of business and asset productivity, (3) defining practical skill requirements for maintenance crafts workers, and (4) improving maintenance work methods. He designated a three-man steering committee—the maintenance manager, the plant training director, and the administrative supervisor for maintenance planning—to take responsibility. The administrative supervisor served as program coordinator. Training began in March 1985.

Although the immediate objective was to train maintenance supervisors, the underlying concept was that maintenance performance should not be judged by maintenance costs or the amount of maintenance work performed, or even by the performance of the production function, but rather by how well maintenance helps the plant as a whole to maximize productivity in the use of all its resources. That criterion makes production and maintenance partners, rather than making one the servant of the other. The common language of the partners is the prosperity of the plant as a whole. Therefore, the starting subject for maintenance supervisory training was not maintenance productivity but fundamentals of business and asset productivity. Other subjects were keyed to that basic notion.

The training format was a series of high-involvement workshops in which a leader presented subject matter in conceptual form. Trainees then applied these concepts to real on-the-job projects. For example, a discussion of the impact of maintenance on gross assets and the productivity of capital investment was reinforced by exercises in diagnosing the causes of downtime and by identifying opportunities for improving the productivity of resources. A discussion of budgeting concepts was followed by exercises in using actual budgets and making investment decisions, and by the formulation of actual cost-reduction projects. A discussion of cross-training of crafts workers stressed the connection between skills, labor costs, and equipment uptime; it was followed by applications, such as identifying current bottlenecks due to a skill deficiency and recommending ways to improve skill inventory forms.

At the urging of the trainees, the workshops did not include role-playing exercises, and did not generate paperwork for the supervisors.

Each of the nine sessions ran about four hours, with the following agenda:

- Group discussion of current improvement projects and problems encountered in them, needs for information or support, and strategies for obtaining needed resources.
- Presentation of conceptual subject matter, conducted in a framework of group discussion and problem solving. The maintenance manager, the training director, and the consultant took turns as presenters.

- Trainees' plans for applying the course content during the two- to four-week interval before the next session.

Between sessions, the steering committee followed up with the trainees, providing help to those who needed it. The follow-up established continuity, reinforced the project work, and gave encouragement. Trainees' formal and informal comments to the steering committee were factored into plans for subsequent sessions.

The improvement projects on the applications side of the workshops were real, not simulated. About half were actually carried out on the job during the course of the program. The other half developed ideas for real improvements but did not reach fruition during the program. Improvements fell into five categories:

1. Reduction of costs associated with specific maintenance activities
2. Improvement of production equipment and processes
3. Changes in maintenance responsibilities and procedures
4. Improvement of training for maintenance workers
5. Changes in organization or personnel

The final workshop was supposed to have dealt with the extension of problem-solving methods into work simplification. In the course of the program, however, many supervisors told the steering committee that the most effective way to improve maintenance results would be to get production supervisors more actively involved. Accordingly, the subject of the final workshop was changed to the Production/Maintenance Relationship.

In preparing the workshop, a consultant surveyed twelve managers or supervisors from the production department and thirteen from maintenance, using interviews and questionnaires. All twenty-five took part in the workshop, which followed this agenda:

- The consultant presented the survey findings at length, highlighting differences of opinion between the departments.

- The consultant summarized the findings in the form of a cause-effect diagram, and outlined what he, as a neutral party, considered to be five core problems.
- Group discussion expanded and refined the outlines of the core problems.
- The group selected some of the joint problems as worthy of joint problem solving.
- The workshop concluded with planning for joint follow-up on the jointly selected problems.

Travenol considers that the training program achieved its objectives for three reasons. First, maintenance supervisors gradually changed their methods of management, increasing their reliance on financial and productivity information. Second, working relationships between production and maintenance improved. At the production department's request, maintenance managers held briefings for over 200 production employees regarding the technical functioning of production equipment. Production employees became more involved in the care and maintenance of their equipment. And third, direct cost savings from the projects, which constituted the applications side of the program, amounted to $250,000. Most savings took the form of reduced consumption of parts, materials, and supplies, or reduced costs of obtaining them.

Tennessee Eastman. Collaboration between the training department and the line managers of Tennessee Eastman's manufacturing plant in Kingsport, Tennessee—a sprawling facility that operates on four shifts—has produced a new approach to guide the design and delivery of training programs. In a plant where technology is continually being updated, this approach enhances both the rapid mastery of essential knowledge and skills and consistency of performance among manufacturing workers. The procedure, originally developed for the basic training of process operatives, has now found its way to clerical, sales, and other functions within the plant and to other work areas. Its critical elements are:

- *A team approach throughout.* The training team usually involves supervisors, technical experts, and professional trainers, but it always involves experienced operators selected for their ability to perform the tasks that are the subject of the training program. Operators are temporarily relieved of normal work duties and are paid a bonus during their service as course developers and instructors. All instructors go through a two-day, train-the-trainer workshop.
- *Agreed-upon target levels of work performance to be made possible by training.* Program objectives are set by (1) agreeing on the work unit's standards of performance for productivity, quality, and safety; (2) comparing the standards with actual performance levels; (3) determining how much of the difference can be traced to lack of knowledge or skills; and (4) setting performance standards the individual learner will be held to.
- *Detailed job and task analysis, to pinpoint needed skills and knowledge.* A detailed job analysis diagram is drawn for each program, concentrating on what the learner needs to know or do to achieve the performance objectives. Lesson plans, prepared in twenty-minute blocks, specify what to teach, how to teach it, and how to measure performance against target. Specific learning aids and delivery mechanisms are chosen by the training team. The training program must be approved by the supervisor and department head whose employees are to be trained. The department is responsible for keeping the program up to date.
- *Measurement of actual performance levels against targets during and after training.* Individual training records chart each learner's performance on the job. When the performance objective for a lesson plan is attained, the date and results are recorded. Thus the learner receives accurate feedback and reinforcement, and the instructor can direct his or her attention to learning problems.

The general rule at the Kingsport plant has been to train new hires before training incumbents. Often, however, incumbents, observing how effectively this systematic approach works with new hires, ask to be trained and take tests in order to find out whether training would benefit them. The test results usually result in training for the incumbents.

The next two chapters present some cost-effective design and delivery solutions for special training needs, ranging from those of graduate-level engineers at one extreme to those of "functional illiterates" at the other.

Recommendations

Recommendation 15. Senior management should require training proposals to include clear-cut information related to cost-effectiveness, including need, objectives, content, design, and delivery. Costs should be related to subject matter and performance-improvement goals. Comparative cost data should be required whenever possible.

Recommendation 16. Senior management should evaluate cost-effectiveness in terms of agreed-upon objectives—specifically whether the functional elements are shaped and combined in the manner best suited to the organization's needs. The key elements include project management, use of in-house versus outside talent, instructional design, course development, and delivery systems.

Recommendation 17. The effectiveness of a program should be measured by how fully and how durably the trainees have mastered the subject matter.

Recommendation 18. The most controversial—and potentially the largest—factor in measuring the cost of a program is whether the trainee's time spent in training should be considered a cost. Since training (assuming that its objectives are strategically necessary) is an essential part of every job, we recommend that it not be considered an added cost. On the other hand, management should count as a cost any additional expense incurred to cover the trainee's work while training is in progress.

Background Paper

Gurin, L. "Training, Technology, and Delivering 'People' Performance." Mar. 1986.

Case Studies

Casner-Lotto, J. "Achieving Cost Savings and Quality: IBM's Systems Approach to Education." June 1986.

Casner-Lotto, J. "Tennessee Eastman Company: Improving Productivity and Quality Through a Comprehensive Approach to Training." June 1986.

Hamburg, S. K. "Manpower Temporary Services: Keeping Ahead of the Competition." June 1986.

Scalpone, R. W. "Reducing Maintenance Cost at Travenol Laboratories, Inc., Through Supervisory Education and Involvement." June 1986.

6

Delivering Training
to Geographically Dispersed
Employees

To develop a high-quality training program for skilled employees, whether blue collar or white collar, is costly and time-consuming. When, as often happens, those who need the program are employed at numerous dispersed sites, it may be more cost-effective to bring the training to them than to bring them to a central point. The initiative for multisite delivery may come from one or more employers or from one or more program-developing institutions. Two-year colleges have carved out a growing market for services to skilled trades workers and technicians. The National Technological University (NTU) serves engineers and scientists.

Many community and junior colleges design and deliver training programs for full-time employees, often more cost-effectively than an employer could with in-house resources. Such programs are growing in number and diversity; they are flexible as to both site and time; they benefit the educational institution

The information in this chapter, unless otherwise referenced, is drawn from the background papers and case studies listed at the end of the chapter. Both papers and cases were commissioned by Work in America Institute in the course of its three-year policy study entitled "Training for New Technology."

as well as the employer; and they strengthen the economic development of the community as a whole.

The most recent line of development has been the organization of consortia of two-year colleges and employers, to market large-scale programs and maintain quality control for dispersed training operations. This chapter discusses some of the problems and pitfalls to be considered in organizing such consortia. It also describes in detail the NTU's imaginative use of high-tech communications for graduate-level education, which overcomes barriers of time and space and delivers the highest quality of instruction to geographically dispersed, full-time, engineer employees.

For engineers seeking advanced degrees or up-to-the-minute knowledge, instructional television via satellite is a more cost-effective delivery system than physical attendance at a university. NTU's methods are illustrated by the experiences of some of the university's principal corporate clients—Digital Equipment, Hewlett-Packard, Eastman Kodak, IBM, and Honeywell.

The Role of Community Colleges

The power of images and names deceives us into picturing big companies as big concentrations of people. They rarely are. Most of the work of any major organization goes on at a multiplicity of small to medium-sized shops, offices, or factories, often widely separated from one another as well as from the head office. Each work site may be no larger than an independent small or medium-sized enterprise in its neighborhood.

Since the operations performed at one work site may bear little resemblance to those at another in the same company, work sites may differ in their training needs as widely as they differ in geography. Accordingly, each work site normally administers most of its own training, with the exception of specifically managerial subjects or skills so company-specific, important, and widely needed that it is more cost-effective to conduct them at a central location.

By the same token, each work site has finite resources of

staff, space, equipment, and money available for training. One point it must therefore decide about any particular need is whether it is more cost-effective to conduct the training in-house or outside. More and more work sites have turned to community and junior colleges to run training programs for them.

A recent survey under the auspices of the American Association of Community and Junior Colleges (AACJC) found that 47 percent of all community colleges offered employee training programs for large private-sector employers. (Return rate on the survey was 63.2 percent; three-fourths of the respondents reported that they offered such programs.) Although success has been variable, the better colleges have provided services that are flexible as to both site and time, and economical.

According to Nell Eurich, in the *Corporate Classroom:* "Between 1980 and 1982 the [AACJC] and the Small Business Training Network linked 186 two-year colleges to district offices of the U.S. Small Business Administration to organize and deliver more than two million hours of short-term training in 47 states. Cooperation works for this segment of higher education and for vocational and technical institutes, but frequently with the handicaps of obsolete equipment and obsolete faculty who lack direct access to the latest techniques and developments in industry, which has always and naturally been ahead of classroom teachers" (Eurich, 1985, p. 16).

Colleges have evolved various arrangements for working with employers:

- Six hundred colleges have business-industry coordinators, who learn what services the employers need and tell them what the colleges can do to help.
- Some colleges hire and train industry people to execute the colleges' training assignments.
- Delta College, in Michigan, sends its faculty into GM Training Centers to instruct dealers' staff. In addition, eighteen faculty members are in GM facilities providing instruction to engineering and technical staff and to workers on the line.
- Bay de Noc College, in Wisconsin, pays local companies to provide technical training to students, while it provides

basic skills. Students take responsibility for finding employers who will train them. John Wood Community College, in Illinois, follows a similar policy.

Some employers, however, report problems in dealing with colleges:

- Often a college's administration manifests initiative in selling services to employers, but faculty appear reluctant.
- In one northeastern metropolitan area a dozen colleges compete for a limited training market. As a result of their noncooperation, the classes offered to employees are often so undersubscribed that they have to be canceled.
- Colleges and employers often fail to spend enough time in specifying what training needs to be done, and no one is pleased with the outcome.
- Evaluation of training gets insufficient attention. A dissatisfied employer votes with its feet, leaving the college ignorant of what should be done to improve its services.

Ordinarily a two-year college acts on its own when seeking out, accepting, and executing training assignments. Lately there have been cases of groups of colleges joining in consortia with one or more employers to supply large-scale training services, sometimes with financial assistance from public agencies. The problems of coordination are challenging, but some results have been impressive.

Los Angeles Community College District. For example, Los Angeles Community College District (LACCD) won one of the three 1985 Keeping America Working (KAW) College/Employer/Labor Partnership Awards for cooperative training programs with local employers.

LACCD—embracing Los Angeles Valley College (the sponsoring college), Los Angeles Southwest College, and East Los Angeles College—joined with Lockheed California Company, the International Association of Machinists and Aerospace Workers, and the Engineers and Scientists Guild in two pro-

grams to train laid-off and likely-to-be-displaced aerospace workers, with funding from California's Employment Training Panel
(ETP) in the amounts of $429,408 and $485,820. (Created by
legislation in 1983, ETP finances the training of displaced—or
about-to-be displaced—employees, to fill available jobs with
employers who have requested ETP's assistance. The panel's
activities are supported by a diversion of one-tenth of one percent of the state's unemployment insurance funds.) This investment in employee retraining came about because the threat of
imminent job loss, human resource loss, and tax revenue loss
got everyone's attention. Equally important was the investment
in the long-term future. The area economy is unable to keep
up with the demand for highly skilled technicians, and Lockheed
is cultivating its vineyards for the future.

The first initiative trained 144 machinists and machine
operators to operate computer numerical control (CNC). One
notable challenge facing this effort was the fifty-mile geographic
separation of two training sites at Lockheed and General Dynam-
ics, a problem solved by placing the $200,000 CNC lab in a
semitrailer. ETP was so pleased with the success of this operation that it provided support for another mobile lab and an additional $711,360 to continue the program through the first
quarter of 1986.

The second initiative was a program in computer-assisted
design (CAD), delivered by Los Angeles Valley Community
College. Lockheed supplemented the Employment Training
Panel funding with a contribution of $185,000 in software.
Again, the training succeeded so well that ETP invested a further $374,697 to continue the program through spring 1986,
and Lockheed has since donated two extra software sets.

Lockheed and the unions supported the CNC and CAD
training programs in other ways, too. They assisted Valley College in developing the curricula, helped specify the equipment
needed, backed the proposal for funding, recruited trainees, and
supplied, when needed, instructors who met credentialing requirements.

All the participating groups benefited from these retraining
programs. Industrywide, 468 workers will have received CNC

training, and 297 aerospace industry employees will have attended the CAD program. Lockheed and its fellow employers will have increased productivity and competitiveness while retraining workers in skill areas, thus preventing their displacement due to technological change.

State-of-the-art equipment valued at $834,257, used for training, remains the property of Valley College and will be accessible to students for years to come. In addition, Lockheed has made a three-year, $676,000 commitment to the revitalization of the engineering programs at East Los Angeles and Los Angeles Southwest colleges, which have largely minority student bodies. In fall 1983, Lockheed, in its continuing effort to recruit minorities into engineering, donated $27,000 in cash to restore engineering classes that were going to be eliminated due to budget cuts. Lockheed also pays for fees and texts for up to 400 minority students, funds tutors, provides guest lecturers to the colleges, opens its training facilities to the colleges' technical faculties, provides summer jobs, and awards scholarships to students of merit who transfer to four-year engineering schools. The three-year program is financed with cash donations from Lockheed totaling $133,000.

State Technical Institute at Knoxville, Tennessee. Since 1979, the State Technical Institute at Knoxville, Tennessee, has teamed with the Aluminum Company of America (ALCOA) to (1) train 275 apprentices in state-of-the-art industrial electrical maintenance, industrial mechanical maintenance, and machining; and (2) run a forty-hour train-the-trainer program for ALCOA personnel who then serve as instructors. The customized training is provided by eighteen colleges and sixteen ALCOA instructors at the plant site. In addition, ALCOA has invested more than $6,000,000 in the program and reimburses the Institute each month for all instructor and material costs.

The training is part of a quarter-billion-dollar modernization program designed to save 4,000 high-paying ALCOA jobs.

Technology Exchange Center. Another Los Angeles area model has been the Technology Exchange Center (TEC) in

Orange County, California. TEC, an independent nonprofit corporation, generates revenue by brokering and coordinating training resources for emerging labor needs in new and existing industries. Its board of directors is composed of chief executive officers—the majority from business, others from education and government. TEC has been especially helpful in serving the educational training needs of medium to small businesses.

Orange County has a high population density and a healthy economic growth curve, particularly in electronics and technical skills. Many of its businesses need expert skill development and training for their employees but are too small to support internal education departments. On the other hand, Orange County contains eight community colleges, located so that 95 percent of the county's residents live within ten miles of a college.

The task of TEC has been to forge a linkage between training-starved businesses and the college educational/training resources. First, TEC staff analyze the client's training needs; then they match the client with one of the eight colleges, based upon proximity and the programmatic expertise of each college. The TEC staff write the training contract and continue to manage it on behalf of the client.

General Motors Automotive Services Educational Program. General Motors has formed the largest reported consortium of two-year colleges to carry out a vast Automotive Services Educational Program (ASEP). ASEP provides up-to-the-minute training for technicians who will service GM automotive products, especially in dealers' repair shops. Previously, in the opinion of the company, college courses for automotive technicians were seven to ten years out of date, and high school courses fifteen years out of date, as a result of rapid advances in the industry. For example, between one and six computers are found under the hood of every new GM car or light truck; major new engines, braking systems, and transmissions are on the way; new computerized diagnostic devices have become essential to the job; and the company is aiming at the paperless repair shop, where each service mechanic will have a terminal and obtain parts by way of electronically directed conveyers.

The first school to institute ASEP was Delta College, in Michigan, in 1979. By December 1986, thirty-nine colleges all over the country had been enlisted. Ultimately, there will be fifty, putting ASEP within reach of every GM dealer in the United States. The colleges provide faculty, curriculum, classrooms, and administration. GM provides equipment and materials (including new cars, shop manuals, parts, and so on) plus free training for the faculty. GM starts new programs, identifies suitable colleges, enlists sponsoring dealers, helps to recruit students, ensures that course standards are met, and continuously updates the faculty.

The course consists of two years of rotating education and training, leading to an associate in arts degree. The college provides classroom training; the dealer provides on-the-job training. The student spends full time on campus for a period of five and one-half to eight weeks (depending on local course design), taking a full load of academic and technical subjects. That is followed by a similar period as a full-time paid service employee of a sponsoring GM dealer, in carefully supervised on-the-job training. The cycle is repeated six times over the two years.

The sponsoring dealer, although not bound to employ the student after graduation, has a strong interest in doing so because the graduate probably has management potential. The dealer has to pledge sponsorship for the full two years, furnish the student with a uniform, and pay wages for on-the-job training, but has no other financial burdens. The student is responsible for college tuition and housing, but a few dealers voluntarily share some of these costs too. Many dealers sponsor two students at a time, so that one will always be working in the shop. A few large dealers sponsor as many as six at a time.

GM, dealer, and college share in selecting students. Careful screening ensures that students are literate, are highly motivated, have good mechanical aptitude, and have demonstrated ability to complete the program.

The college must be one that already offers automotive technician courses as part of its curriculum. The college tests prospective students, and two administrators interview them. Most students are recent high school graduates, but many are experienced people who want to upgrade their knowledge and skills. Allegedly, ASEP students show more esprit than students in regular automotive technician courses, probably because they are employed during on-the-job training. Classes range in size from sixteen to thirty-two, but only half that number are on campus at any given time. Dropout rates are very low; those students who do drop out typically do so because they have landed full-time jobs.

While instructional programs differ in detail from college to college, all contain three elements: liberal arts (English, math, history, psychology, and communications/reasoning skills), automotive theory and practice, and practical training. Since the college grants credits for on-the-job training, the college's program coordinator has the duty to ensure that dealers provide training closely linked to what is learned on campus. The dealer also evaluates the student's performance as a basis for grading.

Average cost of tuition and books is $400 to $500 per semester for residents, which amounts to $2,400 to $3,000 for the six-semester course. Nonresidents usually are charged twice as much, but GM has worked out arrangements to soften the blow. For example, if there is a GM Training Center in the area, nonresidents sign up with the center, the center contracts with the college, and all the center's students receive resident status from the college. ASEP students must also purchase their own tools, which cost between $800 and $1,000—but so must all automotive technicians.

At GM's corporate level, ASEP is managed by the national college coordinator, who is ultimately responsible to the vice-president for customer and sales and service staff. Four regional coordinators work directly with the colleges.

Since more colleges apply for participation in ASEP than are chosen, GM can be selective. It demands demonstrated experience in running automotive technician programs up to journeyman level, attention to basic liberal arts, an administration open to experimentation, and a willingness to let GM have a hand in course design and faculty training.

In addition to its plan to expand ASEP to fifty colleges, GM is working toward a Faculty Development Institute: four colleges in different regions of the country will be designated to offer training in the latest GM technology to college faculty, both ASEP members and others.

It is reported that Ford and Chrysler are creating "look-alike" programs for community colleges to implement.

Mid-America Training Group. Another major consortium is the Mid-America Training Group—a group of midwestern colleges that markets itself as a training/retraining consortium. Its programs, administered by Triton College in Illinois, offer to provide training of high quality and consistency to companies based anywhere in the Great Lakes region. The consortium comprises Cuyahoga Community College, Ohio; Des Moines Area Community College, Iowa; Kellogg Community College, Michigan; Lorain County Community College, Ohio; Macomb Community College, Michigan; North Central Technical Institute, Wisconsin; Rock Valley College, Illinois; Sinclair Community College, Ohio; and Triton College, Illinois.

Cleveland Advanced Manufacturing Program. Cleveland's Cuyahoga Community College is also collaborating with Case Western Reserve University and Cleveland State University in the Cleveland Advanced Manufacturing Program (CAMP). The primary thrust of CAMP is spawning an academic-industrial partnership for innovation and economic development—a fusion of academic, private-sector, and public-sector resources to sponsor feasibility studies, research and development, and training. Founding business partners of CAMP are the Allen-Bradley Company; Cleveland Pneumatic Company; Eaton Corporation; General Electric Company; Parker Hannifin Corporation; Reliance Electric Company; TRW, Inc.; and White Consolidated Industries, Inc.

A critical component of this collaboration is a Unified Technologies Center to be opened at Cuyahoga Community College. This $20 million facility, with advanced technical equipment, will devote two-thirds of its programming to training in advanced manufacturing technologies; it will also offer training in telecommunications, biomedical technology, and business information services. Satellite transmission facilities and 400 computer learning stations, all housed in the center, will enhance its capacity to deliver instruction in computer-aided design and manufacturing, instrumentation and control, laser electro-optics, metrology and testing, microcomputers, and robotics.

Community colleges also take part in training consortia based on the inverse situation. That is, a group of employers discover that they have a shared need to train people for a particular occupation. Rather than enlarge their permanent staffs to create and execute the necessary training programs, they jointly engage a community college to do it for them. For example, Edmonds Community College, near Everett, Washington, helped organize a group of fifteen local electronics firms that had been pirating each other's employees because of severe skill shortages in the area. The college then began training to fit their needs. Also, in conjunction with Everett Community College, Edmonds operates a newly constructed Applied Technology Training Center that provides specialized training and continuing education in several rapidly developing technologies (Fields, 1987).

Bay State Skills Corporation. In Massachusetts, such projects are brokered and partially funded by the Bay State Skills Corporation (BSSC), a quasi-governmental agency established by the state legislature in 1981 with a board representing labor, industry, education, and government. One of its functions is to provide grants-in-aid to education and training institutions, matched from the private sector, for skills-training programs in occupational growth areas. Initiative for a grant may come from a company or group of companies, from an educational institution, or from unions. The application must demonstrate that prospects for employment after the training are favorable. Matching support can be financial or in kind; it usually exceeds BSSC's.

For example, four hospitals in western Massachusetts teamed up with Berkshire Community College in a twelve-month program to train sixteen entry-level people as respiratory

therapy technicians. BSSC granted $51,000. The college con-
ducted classroom and laboratory instruction; the hospitals provided clinical training, along with support in the form of personnel, equipment, materials, and supplies. Each institution had
a seat on the advisory committee, which developed the program
and oversaw recruitment, curriculum, program monitoring,
clinical training, and job placement.

Instructional Television for Technologists

For the U.S. economy to remain vital, a high percentage
of engineers in the workplace must continue their technical
education beyond the bachelor's level. However, largely because
of attractive industrial salaries, fewer than 30 percent of graduates with B.S. degrees in engineering now enter advanced
degree programs. Engineers in their forties, who were not exposed during their formal education to the technology that
dominates the current industrial world, are especially at risk;
but advanced education will also be important for today's young
engineers in years to come.

Of those engineers who do pursue further education, credit
courses appeal generally to the young. The average age of credit
enrollees is twenty-eight. However, the average age of technical
professionals is about thirty-nine. The experienced engineers
who make up the majority seek instruction in applications, in
the form of short courses with little theory, taught by leading
authorities.

An employer faced with these needs and preferences has
three broad alternatives:

1. Allow engineers, young and old, to obsolesce.
2. Send engineers to the university, and accept the cost of their
    time away from the workplace, plus the cost of travel and
    lodging.
3. Bring university courses to the workplace.

The first alternative is counterproductive, the second too
costly. But bringing university courses physically to the work-

place is rarely practical. First, due to the very diverse, rapidly changing interests of engineers seeking advanced education, only widely scattered small clusters of students are available for instruction at any time. Second, the students want to be taught by leading authorities, to ensure that the information received is up-to-the-minute and reliable. Third, a single university cannot meet the diverse demands.

Conceivably, courses might be brought in by way of interactive videodiscs or modern computer-aided instruction systems. But since class materials must be constantly updated to provide the most current information, they can rarely be reused—and this makes the production costs for advanced topics exorbitant.

A solution has been found. University courses are being brought to the workplace through the medium of instructional television (ITV). Engineering educators have pioneered the "candid classroom," that is, broadcasts of live classroom courses. The average enrollment at any particular workplace to receive broadcasts of candid classrooms for credit is four engineers, and the average instructor has students at eight to twelve sites. The performance of ITV adult students usually equals that of on-campus students who take the identical class, when comparable admission criteria are applied.

But ITV is not without limitations. First, as already noted, no single university can meet such diverse demands. Second, the cost of developing state-of-the-art courses for television is high and, for any format other than courses for older engineers, are even more costly to produce: top professors require sizable financial incentives to induce them to do the extra work.

ITV needs an efficient national distribution system to reach its potential. Ten years ago, the engineering colleges that operated regional instructional television systems formed a common goal: to increase the national effectiveness of continuing education of engineers. Two new institutions, the National Technological University (NTU) and the Association for Media-Based Continuing Education for Engineers (AMCEE), which coordinate credit and continuing education programs, now link engineering faculty to working engineers via a satellite delivery system.

Origins of ITV for Engineers. Engineering faculty at several colleges started in 1963 to evolve a simple but effective way to teach adult students at a distance via television: candid classroom, which remains a mainstay of ITV today. ITV instruction originates in regularly scheduled, on-campus courses. The classrooms are equipped to transmit student questions and discussions, as well as the lectures, to off-campus students at their job sites.

Although one studio classroom is like another, signal delivery systems for linkage to job sites vary. The first major system, established in 1964 at the University of Florida, used a leased two-way point-to-point microwave from the telephone company to link with several extension centers in central Florida. In 1969, Stanford University began transmitting to corporate classrooms in the San Francisco Bay Area, with a four-channel instructional television fixed service (ITFS) system that featured FM-talkback capability; ITFS has a broadcast radius of about thirty-five miles. In 1967, Colorado State University was the first to employ courier-carried videotape as a delivery system; tapes are returned, erased, and reused on a schedule.

Today, most microwave and ITFS receiving sites are equipped with video recorders to store the class for review or for making up missed sessions. By scheduling occasional visits and regular office hours for telephone consultations, faculty in regional systems have largely overcome the no-talk-back disadvantage of videotape. Newer systems use combinations of delivery methods to fit the needs of each geographic area.

Acceptance by both faculty and students has led to a rapid growth of regional ITV systems in engineering, from four in 1967 to over forty systems today. Two dozen major universities have awarded over 3,500 master's degrees to engineers who completed all their degree requirements as part-time ITV students.

Some hallmarks of good ITV practice have emerged:

- Small groups of engineers do best when they meet on a regular schedule, particularly if one participant serves as discussion leader.

- On-site tutors are beneficial, even if they meet only occasionally with the group.
- Active involvement of each participant in brief discussions, perhaps at ten- to twenty-minute intervals throughout a fifty-minute lecture, is strongly encouraged.
- Individual commitment to outside study and completion of problem assignments are vital to mastery.
- Interaction with the lecturer need not be live or face-to-face, but telephoned questions should be answered while the issue is still under active discussion on campus. Early tests using electronic mail and computer conferencing for interaction are encouraging because they offer the same flexibility and convenience as ITV itself.
- The employer must provide administrative support: textbooks need to arrive on time, equipment needs to be maintained, and conference rooms need to be set aside.

Employer sponsorship of all direct costs is almost universal. Employers differ, however, on how fully they integrate study into the jobs. Some allow time for classes as part of the work schedule and pay all costs of work/study directly to the university, but they require study and assignments to be done on the student's own time. Others—perhaps the majority—expect engineers to make up for class time or to view classes after work hours. The engineer is reimbursed for tuition and books at the successful conclusion of the course, as a fringe benefit.

A National System Emerges. In August 1974, representatives from two dozen colleges operating video-based programs attended a workshop with a sample of customers to discuss ways to improve continuing education service. Follow-up planning ensued and in April 1976 a nonprofit consortium, the Association for Media-Based Continuing Education for Engineers (AMCEE), was formed. Start-up support came from the National Science and Sloan foundations.

AMCEE members share information on customer needs and encourage the publication of short video courses for practicing engineers. The consortium serves as a marketing cooperative to reduce distribution costs. The first AMCEE catalogue in 1978 contained 172 courses from ten universities; the current catalogue lists over 500 courses from 33 schools and from the consortium itself.

AMCEE clients include AT&T, General Motors, Hewlett-Packard, Honeywell, Digital Equipment Corporation, Allied Corporation, IBM, McDonnell Douglas, NCR, RCA, Rockwell, Texas Instruments, and numerous government laboratories and agencies, including the Department of Defense.

By the early 1980s, the consortium was a clear success, but the regional systems were available to less than half the engineering work force. With the increasing affordability of satellite communications, AMCEE's board of directors saw the possibility of extending ITV coast-to-coast. In February 1982, it decided to investigate the feasibility of a national engineering college that would deliver programs through advanced telecommunications technologies and pledged $100,000 of consortium funds to the study. Fourteen industrial and Department of Defense sources added $370,000 to the planning effort. These sponsors also provided technical advice and met regularly over a two-year period to help shape the plan.

The National Technological University. The National Technological University (NTU) was established in Colorado as a separate nonprofit private educational corporation in January 1984, with the aim of awarding accredited master's degrees in selected fields. Approved courses are offered by its twenty-four universities, all members of AMCEE (see Table 1). The universities evaluate and record grades for students completing their courses, and transfer the records to the NTU registrar at the end of each term.

Each NTU-receiving site is operated by the student's employer, following NTU guidelines. With over 3,500 full-time engineering and computer science faculty members, rigorous, high-quality instructional programs are assured. Moreover, NTU conducts research in educational technology to ensure continued responsiveness to the needs of the students.

Table 1. Member Universities of AMCEE.

*Arizona State University	*Stanford University
Auburn University	*University of Alaska
*Boston University	*University of Arizona
*Colorado State University	*University of Florida
*Georgia Institute of Technology	*University of Idaho
GMI Engineering and	University of Illinois at
Management Institute	Urbana-Champaign
*Illinois Institute of Technology	*University of Kentucky
*Iowa State University	*University of Maryland
Massachusetts Institute of	*University of Massachusetts
Technology	University of Michigan
*Michigan Technological University	*University of Minnesota
*North Carolina State University	*University of Missouri at Rolla
*Northeastern University	University of Notre Dame
*Oklahoma State University	*University of South Carolina
Polytechnic Institute of New York	University of Southern California
*Purdue University	*University of Washington
*Southern Methodist University	*University of Wisconsin at Madison

*Participating in NTU
Source: Baldwin, 1986.

NTU's functions are to:

- Award accredited master's degrees to qualified individuals in selected disciplines
- Provide research seminars in each discipline
- Operate a modern telecommunications delivery system for convenient, flexible, on-site service
- Offer AMCEE noncredit short courses, seminars, and workshops to introduce newly advanced technology concepts to a broad range of technical professionals
- Establish a sophisticated satellite network infrastructure between industry and the university communities

At the beginning, NTU offered courses by video cassette only; more than 150 technical professionals signed on, at fourteen sponsoring sites of Eastman Kodak, Hewlett-Packard, IBM, GE, and NCR. Six universities taught fifteen courses of the computer engineering graduate program. In the fall/spring terms of 1984–85, seven universities delivered twenty-one courses to over 250 enrollees, including new sites sponsored by Digital Equipment Corporation and Motorola.

NTU ceased shipping cassettes by May 1985. On August 28, 1985, it began broadcasting two channels of full-motion, color ITV by satellite. Dual channel per transponder service puts NTU at the forefront of satellite transmission technology. Satellite delivery boosted participation dramatically: receiving sites more than doubled and enrollments in credit courses quadrupled. NTU is viable with as few as three to eight engineers at a site. Over fifty receiving sites were active in the spring 1986 term; ninety sites participated in the fall 1987 term.

Eventually, every NTU instructor will be able to teach on- and off-campus students simultaneously. Broadcasts originate from specially equipped ITV classrooms, each with several remote-control color cameras and audio microphones. The ITV signal can be beamed instantly from that campus to the satellite, enabling part-time students at their job sites to view the class live and, through telephone linkages, ask questions during the class session.

Demonstrations of this interaction through teleconferencing via satellite have been successful. Since NTU classes are designed to serve about fifty-five off-campus students on average, classroom interaction between teacher and off-campus students can be easily accommodated. When broadcasts of classes are delayed a few hours because of schedule conflicts, NTU provides time for recitation sessions by teleconferencing. If a student must miss a session, videotape machines allow him or her to view it at a later, more convenient time. Indeed, videotape is an essential part of all live ITV today, because it adds a time buffer, when needed, as well as an opportunity for review.

Surprisingly, live broadcasts do not elicit more NTU student participation than videotapes do. Employed engineers prefer not to risk appearing ignorant in public: they would rather phone the professor after the class or send electronic mail. When an engineer calls in "live" on a noncredit course, his or her name is not announced.

In early 1987, fifteen universities were equipped for real-time broadcasts: Colorado State, Georgia Institute of Technology, Illinois Institute of Technology, North Carolina State, Northeastern, Oklahoma State, Purdue, Southern Methodist, Alaska, Arizona, Maryland, Massachusetts, Minnesota, Missouri at Rolla, and South Carolina. A final addition to uplinking (transmitting) facilities, scheduled for 1987–1988, adds another ten stations. Universities not so equipped send a master videotape overnight to one of the schools with an uplink.

Although NTU employs the best available methodology, the three-hour time difference between the East and West coasts, and the fact that NTU has schools and clients in each of the four time zones, require more opportunities for teachers and students to communicate outside of classroom periods. Experiments to supplement telephone interaction with AT&T electronic mail service are under way, and enhanced computer conferencing will be tested over the next few years.

Each downlinking (receiving) site is equipped with a TV receive-only station, costing the sponsoring organization less than $10,000. Color monitors and several programmable half-inch VHS recorder/players complete the receiving station equipment, which is often located in small, multipurpose conference rooms at the corporate sites. In certain buildings and geographical areas, problems of installation and reception sometimes cause a significant increase of costs.

Each receiving site pays an access fee to join the NTU/AMCEE network. Some corporations pay a corporatewide fee, which allows all their U.S. locations to participate. In addition, enrollees are charged tuition and fees, whether they register for academic credit or for audit. The participating university sets the tuition for its courses, and the employer either pays this bill directly or reimburses the employee when the course is completed.

NTU currently offers programs leading to the Master of Science degree in five disciplines: computer engineering, computer science, engineering management, electrical engineering, and manufacturing systems engineering. The 1987–1988 NTU Bulletin contains 455 academic courses. New classes are added to the curricula each year, and some courses are revised or dropped.

Major corporate subscribers to NTU have informed Work in America Institute that the service has proved highly cost-effective:

- The experiences of Digital Equipment, Hewlett-Packard, and Eastman Kodak are described in the companion casebook *Successful Training Strategies: Twenty-Six Innovative Corporate Models* (Jossey-Bass, 1988).
- IBM, which sends engineers and programmers to universities to obtain technologies that the company expects to use in the future, finds NTU particularly valuable because when a project is suddenly moved from one part of the country to another (as often happens) and a couple of hundred people move with it, those who are studying with NTU lose no time whatever from their courses.

Consultants, selected from the instructors, are organized into graduate faculties; typically, there is one representative of each discipline from each participating institution. A graduate faculty is supported by four standing committees (curriculum, admission and academic standards, staffing, academic executive) and by a senior administrator at the NTU offices, who coordinates functions and activities. Each NTU graduate faculty conducts its affairs through two annual faculty meetings, correspondence, and teleconferences.

Matriculated students in approved degree programs are assigned to academic advisors who have access to student records through the interactive, computer-based record system maintained at NTU.

In May 1984, NTU applied for institutional accreditation to the Commission on Institutes of Higher Education of the North Central Association of Colleges and Schools. NTU was granted initial accreditation by the Commission in August 1987. In the same month, it graduated its second class of master's level students.

NTU also offers noncredit courses. For six hours a day, thirty hours a week, fifty weeks a year, NTU/AMCEE receiving sites can choose from a wide range of noncredit, continuing-education short courses and workshops, live or taped. Clients for whom videotape delivery works best can continue getting them from AMCEE as in the past. In addition, AMCEE is beginning to bring the twenty hours of annual technical seminars of the Institute of Electrical and Electronic Engineers to engineers via satellite.

Plans are also under way to develop thirty or more short courses for engineers on subjects related to but not strictly engineering; for example, technical management, project management, salary administration. Some short courses are presented by nontraditional faculty, adjuncts, and even people without university connections.

There is a growing movement for public receiving sites. A number of university campuses provide access to AMCEE programs for small companies that cannot afford a downlink. At AMCEE's facility at Georgia Tech, both the television studio and a nearby viewing room permit local students to take courses on campus. Other AMCEE universities plan similar arrangements.

In the first three months of operation, 900 participants enrolled in AMCEE satellite telecourses, partly because satellite delivery is more cost-effective than videotape. AMCEE clients pay a flat fee for courses on videotape, regardless of the number of people using it, but many have only two or three students for a given course. By contrast, satellite delivery costs only $15 to $25 per instructional hour per student, once a client has paid the network access fee.

Honeywell evaluates every program and reports uniform praise from the roughly 900 employees in the Minneapolis area who have taken NTU courses. This large number reflects the company's strong promotional efforts. Honeywell employees in Phoenix and Boston also receive the service. However, many sponsors made relatively little use of the ten to fifteen courses broadcast from videotapes each month. In late 1985, the AMCEE Board of Directors engaged NTU to make the noncredit programming more attractive.

Since April 1986, all AMCEE courses are offered live with ample time for interaction with the instructor. Top authorities are scheduled. And, to make planning and scheduling easier, AMCEE has developed three regular program series.

Ordering and billing have been simplified: sites have the option of ordering a course and paying a per-site fee or a per-person fee, which makes courses cost-effective for both small and large groups. Also, AMCEE now provides free publicity materials for site coordinators to spread the word about upcoming courses and events. As a consequence of these changes, participation has increased dramatically.

NTU has taken a series of actions that will enhance and expand its services to industry in years to come:

- During the next three years, NTU will experiment with (1) computer communications between students and teachers, (2) simple graphics capability as an add-on to asynchronous electronic networking, and (3) side-channel data transmission to students who use personal computers.

- A study is now under way with leading business and engineering faculty to develop a program leading to a master of science degree in management of technology. The goal is to launch the new offering for executives in fall 1988.

- By fall 1988, the NTU/AMCEE network will double its current channel output, with four channels of satellite ITV.

- NTU's Board of Trustees has pledged to use the satellite facilities to enhance relations between industry and the university community. Once industry sites have installed video sending sites, talented industry scientists will have the opportunity to contribute course material. In manufacturing systems engineering, computer-aided design, software systems engineering, and other fields where industry generally outpaces universities, industrial leaders could share advanced research results with on-campus graduate students and faculty. The first credit course was offered in spring 1986 by the chief engineer of Hewlett-Packard. IBM and others may also develop some courses soon. The resultant quality of instruction may well surpass what either academe or industry could do alone.

Background Papers

Baldwin, L. V. "The NTU/AMCEE Instructional Satellite Network." Mar. 1986.

McKenney, J. F. "Community Colleges: 'Land Grant' Colleges for an Information Age." Mar. 1986.

Case Studies

Gutchess, J. F. "A Cooperative Approach to Training for the Future: General Motors Automotive Services Educational Program." June 1986.

Hickey, J. V. "A Government-Education-Industry Partnership in Training: Bay State Skills Corporation." June 1986.

Stackel, L. "National Technological University: Learning by Satellite." June 1986.

7

Designing Programs to Train "Functional Illiterates" for New Technology

"Functional illiterates" are considered poor risks for technical training, but recent research offers an intelligent basis for redefining illiteracy and opens new options for training millions of current and potential employees whose talents would otherwise be wasted. The vast majority of these individuals should be classified as midlevel literates because they read well enough to be capable of becoming fully literate.

A new form of instructional design enables employers to train these so-called functional illiterates to handle new technology. Current methods require a long period of general literacy training before students are deemed ready to acquire technical skills. The new method interweaves sharply defined basic-skills training with technical-skills training and thus reaches the objectives faster, at lower cost, and with higher rates of student success.

This chapter describes cost-effective demonstrations of the design in three occupations: word processor operators, wastewater treatment plant operators, and electronic technicians.

The information in this chapter, unless otherwise referenced, is drawn from the background paper mentioned at the end of the chapter. It was commissioned by Work in America Institute in the course of its three-year policy study entitled "Training for New Technology."

172

Functional Illiterates Can Be Trained

According to employers, a large proportion of young adults, and some mature workers, cannot be trained for new technology because they lack the basic skills—reading, writing, listening, comprehension, and math. Since employers must have both new technology and properly trained employees, they usually take one or more of the following approaches:

- Hire young adults only if they demonstrate an acceptable degree of literacy.
- Demote or dismiss functionally illiterate employees and recruit more literate ones to replace them.
- Hire or retain functional illiterates, but put them through extensive remedial basic education before training them for new technology.

The first approach severely restricts the pool of available job applicants. The second and third are costly and time-consuming.

Recently, an alternative approach—a more cost-effective instructional design—has been developed. By integrating basic-skills training with technical training, and by ensuring that trainees are familiar with the content of written material before they read or write about it, researchers have (1) enabled functional illiterates to understand and successfully operate new technology, and (2) shortened the overall training time while increasing the trainees' success rate.

The Perceived Lack of Basic Skills. The problem, as employers see it, is twofold:

1. The number of young adults (eighteen to twenty-four years old) available for employment is decreasing, while job openings are increasing.
2. The basic academic skills of many young adults and mature workers are insufficient for handling new technology.

U.S. Bureau of the Census (1983) figures show that the

United States has reached the peak of a twenty-year growth in the number of eighteen- to twenty-four-year-olds available for employment. In 1981, more than thirty million individuals were in this age group. By 1995, there will be only twenty-four million, a decrease of 22 percent.

Business and industry compete with the military for the 44 percent of young people who do not attend college. The military, it is estimated, will have to increase its share of high school graduates from one in eight today to one in three by 1995, to maintain current strength and quality figures.

Unfortunately, a high school diploma no longer proves that the holder possesses high school levels of basic skills. Figure 1 shows the estimated reading grade levels of a nationally representative sample of youth eighteen through twenty-three years of age, with different numbers of years of education. Seventy-five percent of the sample had completed high school. Those whose formal education ended with the high school diploma had a median reading level of 9.6, which means they had the reading skills of a student in the sixth month of the ninth grade.

Young adults with nine to eleven years of education, numbering 8.3 million in 1980, had a median reading grade level of 7.6 (seventh grade, sixth month). Three-quarters of a million young adults had only 6–8 years of education and a median reading level of grade 5.4 (fifth grade, fourth month).

Thus, if industry loses high school graduates to both higher education and the military, and must increasingly draw upon youth with less than a high school education, it will encounter more and more youth with only midlevel literacy skills.

Another concern for human resource departments and equal opportunity programs is that black and Hispanic minority members score well below the national median on reading skills. (See the right side of Figure 1, showing profiles for blacks and whites. Hispanics fall in between.)

Women also demonstrate scores on the Armed Services Vocational Aptitude Battery (ASVAB) that suggest difficulties in gaining access to, and training for, technological fields. Figure 2 is arranged so that scores on ASVAB subtests covering technological content areas are represented toward the left, and

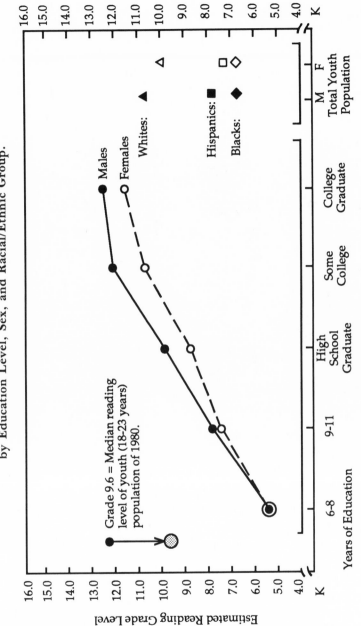

Figure 1. Estimated Reading Grade Levels for 1980 Youth Population by Education Level, Sex, and Racial/Ethnic Group.

Source: Office of the Assistant Secretary of Defense, 1982, pp. 84–85.

Figure 2. Armed Services Aptitude Test Scores for Whites and Blacks
(Youth Population 18–23 Years of Age in 1982).

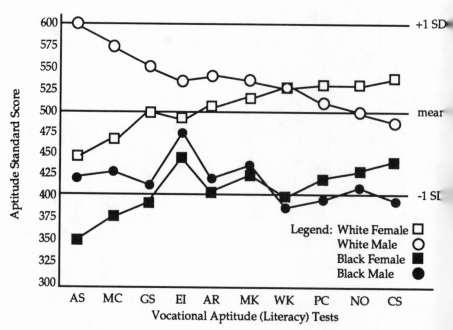

Tests: AS = Auto & Shop Information   MK = Mathematics Knowledge
        MC = Mechanical Comprehension   WK = Word Knowledge
        GS = General Science   PC = Paragraph Comprehension
        EI = Electronics Information   NO = Numerical Operations
        AR = Arithmetic Reasoning   CS = Coding Speed

Source: Sticht, 1986.

scores on verbal (reading) and quantitative (arithmetic) subtests
are represented toward the right. Women perform better than
men of both racial groups on coding speed (rapid matching of
numbers to words) and numerical operations (rapidly adding,
subtracting, multiplying, and dividing).

Within ethnic groups, men and women performed equally
well on the verbal subtests, word knowledge and paragraph
comprehension (these are parallel to the vocabulary and com-

prehension subtests found in most standardized reading tests). On the tests of technological knowledge, however, men far surpass women—for example, in auto shop information, white men score 100 points above the mean of 500, and white women 50 points below the mean. This gender gap in technological literacy (all tests are paper-and-pencil tests requiring reading) is also found among blacks and Hispanics.

On the ASVAB, blacks score about 100 points lower than whites in tests of both general literacy and technological literacy, and Hispanics about 50 points below whites.

These aptitude data imply that women and minorities will have a hard time gaining access to jobs in, and to job training or retraining programs for, technological fields demanding a great deal of previous knowledge in mechanical, scientific, or mathematical areas. Minorities will also have a hard time gaining access to, and successfully completing, training programs that rely extensively on the collegiate model—education consisting of lectures, textbook assignments (or other communication technologies that require high-volume, graphic symbolic learning), and paper-and-pencil tests.

Midlevel and Technical Training. Although millions of young adults and mature workers score low on tests for basic skills and have been demeaned as functionally illiterate, it does not follow that they cannot learn to handle new technology until they make up the basic skill deficits. In fact, they often surpass more literate people in mastering technical skills.

1. Most of the people alleged to be functionally illiterate neither are nor consider themselves to be so. A series of studies sponsored by the Department of Defense permit comparisons of the reading skills of the young adult population, based on various aptitude, intelligence, and standardized reading tests spanning the past forty-five years. They show that if the spectrum of literacy is divided into three levels— low, middle, and high—and if midlevel literacy is defined as reading ability in the range from grade 5.0 to grade 9.9 (corresponding roughly to IQs from 70, the borderline

normal, to 106), then 47 percent of young adults should be classed as midlevel literates. Forty-eight percent are high-level. Only 5 percent fall into low-level (Sticht, 1975; Sticht, 1985; Sticht, Hooke, and Caylor, 1981; U.S. Department of the Army, 1965).

As far as business and industry are concerned, most of the literacy problems they encounter will have to do with the 47 percent thus classified as midlevel literates. Despite the popular impression that midlevel literates are word-blind incompetents barely able to cope in our complex society, the crucial fact is that these people can read.

From the trainer's standpoint, what midlevel literates lack is skill in the processing of knowledge and information (that is, analysis, reasoning, language). That is why they find it difficult to absorb large amounts of information quickly, when it is presented in complex textbooks or manuals and taught by the collegiate model of assigned readings, lectures, and paper-and-pencil tests.

2. Branding midlevel literates as functionally illiterate not only slanders them—it stacks the cards against them, as military history shows. In military parlance, "low aptitude" means functional illiteracy. Large numbers of low-aptitude youth entered military service on three occasions in the past forty years: during World War II; during the Vietnam War, as part of Project 100,000; and from 1976 to 1980 when, through a procedural mistake in assessing mental aptitude, the military admitted hundreds of thousands of recruits who would otherwise have been excluded. Analysis of these experiences shows that:

- There has been a consistent bias against personnel designated as "low aptitude." When low-aptitude men in World War II were administratively redesignated as higher-aptitude, commanders stopped complaining about too many low-aptitude soldiers. The announcement, during Vietnam, of Project 100,000 as a War on Poverty program for the military was met by blistering criticism, which persists to the present time. It is still referred to as "the infamous effort" of a generation ago. When large numbers of low-aptitude personnel were mistakenly and unknowingly brought into the military in 1976–1980, no public outcry occurred, even after the error was disclosed.

- Although on all three occasions the lower-aptitude personnel had somewhat higher attrition rates and lower levels of job proficiency, and achieved less rank than higher-aptitude personnel, the differences were small. The low-aptitude personnel did 80 to 100 percent as well as the average aptitude groups on these various indicators of performance.

- In 1983, some 8,200 of the Project 100,000 personnel had achieved career status in the military and were still on active duty. As a group, their years of education had increased, the aptitude scores had risen, and they were working in middle management and supervisory roles in occupations that make higher cognitive demands than the job assignments of Project 100,000 personnel as a group.

- When Project 100,000 veterans were compared to a nonveteran group of similar background, they were found to have earned more per hour, suffered less unemployment, achieved more education, and had higher enrollments in education or training programs. Fully 68 percent of Project 100,000 veterans had used the GI Bill.

3. The fact that midlevel literacy is associated with midlevel intelligence and aptitude scores suggests that basic-skills deficiencies in the group will not be overcome without considerable time and effort. Past programs that tried to upgrade literacy skills rapidly have not been very successful (Ryan and Furlong, 1975). To add a year of literacy growth, a typical grade school child must learn about 1,000 new words and read about 1,000,000 words. It is reasonable to assume that an adult must do the same.

On the other hand, programs designed to develop

literacy rapidly in a specific domain have been far more successful (Sticht, 1985). Such programs integrate the teaching of basic skills with job-technical skills.

4. A higher level of general literacy does not denote a higher level of ability to read and comprehend technical material, except when the reader is already familiar with the content of the material. For example, many highly literate women (as well as men) do poorly with technical materials about which they are poorly informed (for example, concerning automobile maintenance). Obversely, a relatively low level of basic skills may suffice for a reader highly familiar with the contents.

    In a recent research project, U.S. Navy personnel who took the new Functional Reading Assessment tests were divided into quartiles based on their knowledge scores on the Navy Knowledge subtest, which measures background knowledge about the Navy. Then each quartile's reading skills were measured, applying the same formula of reading difficulty to the tests. In addition, the officially prescribed Flesch-Kincaid formula to measure reading difficulty was applied to the same passages (Sticht and others, 1986).

    Figure 3 displays the results. The solid line at the top, labeled Flesch-Kincaid, shows that an estimated reading grade level of 11.3 is needed to comprehend the passages when background knowledge is not considered. The left-hand bar graph shows a similar estimated reading level for people with very little background knowledge as measured by the Navy Knowledge test. However, as background knowledge increases, the estimated reading-grade level needed to comprehend the passages drops rapidly until, at the highest level of background knowledge, a 6.0 reading-grade level of general literacy suffices.

5. The standard approach to technical training of education follows the collegiate model, with lectures and assignments in textbooks or other media requiring a high degree of skill in symbol manipulation and paper-and-pencil tests. This model aggravates the midlevel literate's difficulties in learning, because it demands the possession of the very skills that are lacking.

Figure 3. Background Knowledge Level.

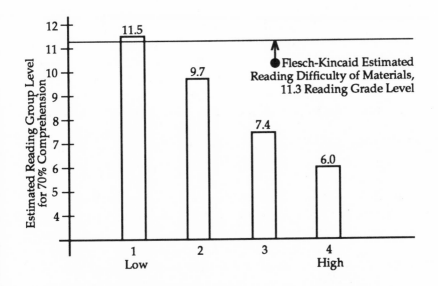

Source: Sticht, 1986.

A different instructional design is needed. "Repeatedly, studies in the military have indicated that . . . where significant improvements in useful competence have been demonstrated, say in performing military-life reading tasks, the instruction has not been academically oriented, but rather the contents, materials, and tasks have been developed to incorporate the functional concepts and practices of military life, training, and job requirements. This has been true from World War II to the present" (Sticht, Armstrong, Hickey, and Caylor, 1986, p. 4).

A New Instructional Design for Midlevel Literates. Based on the foregoing data, researchers have worked out a set of design principles for training midlevel literates:

1. Let students know what they are to learn and why, in such a way that they can understand the purpose of the training or education in their lives.

2. Develop new knowledge on the basis of knowledge that the student already has on entry to the program.
3. Develop new lessons on the basis of old lessons, so that the new learning builds on prior knowledge.
4. Integrate instruction in basic skills—such as reading, writing, and arithmetic—into the technical training or academic content area courses, to permit students to better negotiate the requirements for these skills in the program at hand and to permit them to transfer such skills to other, related settings.
5. Derive objectives from an analysis of the knowledge and skill demands of the situations for which the course is supposed to be providing human resources.
6. Utilize in the course—to the extent feasible—contexts, tasks, materials, and procedures taken from the setting for which people are being trained and educated.

Principles 1 through 4 guided the training programs of Project 100,000. The basis ideas behind principles 5 and 6 were also recommended by the designers of Project 100,000 but never implemented by the military.

Within the past few years, however, several programs, each embodying all six principles, have been successfully designed and executed. Three examples follow. The first two, for word processors and for wastewater treatment plant operators, are the work of Professor Larry Mikulecky and collaborators at Indiana University (Sticht and Mikulecky, 1985). The third, a prototype program for electronics technicians, was developed by Thomas Sticht and colleagues (Sticht, Armstrong, Hickey, and Caylor, 1986).

Training Word-Processor Operators (Sticht and Mikulecky, 1985). During 1981 and 1982 a survey of businesses involved with the Chicago-area Private Industry Council revealed the need for trained word-processor operators. Positions paying over $20,000 per year were going unfilled. Although administrators of the Comprehensive Employment and Training Act (CETA) program were interested in training CETA-eligible individuals for such jobs, they had little experience in cooperative efforts with business; so a private consulting corporation proposed to develop a word-processing training program for CETA-eligible applicants—a program that would integrate basic-skills training with job training and use performance levels of employed word-processor operators as criteria.

The general literacy level required to do well as a word-processor operator is fairly high (tenth grade to thirteenth grade level). Therefore, success in the training program was dependent, in part, on trainees being able to attain that level in the relatively short period of fourteen to twenty weeks. To select trainees most likely to succeed from among the thousands of potential applicants, a series of literacy screening exercises was developed from actual job materials. Currently employed secretaries and word-processor operators took the screening exercises so that performance levels could be set.

The first level of screening tests was constructed from representative samples of business correspondence and word-processing manuals used on the job. Trainees who scored more than two reading-grade levels below the average practicing operator were screened out of the program.

A second level of literacy screening involved spotting and correcting errors on actual job correspondence involving forms and business reports. Norms were based on the performance of the average secretary or word-processor operator. Potential trainees had to identify and correct errors on a piece of printed material. When they had done their best, the test giver showed them what they had missed and how to make additional corrections. Following this, a similar task was given to determine their rate of learning. Acceptance into the training program signified performance slightly below that of employed secretaries, or the ability to learn quickly. Those accepted were midlevel literates reading at eighth-grade level and above.

All trainees selected were CETA eligible (that is, economically disadvantaged, unemployed or underemployed, and identified as having difficulties in entering or advancing in private-sector employment). One hundred trainees were selected to enter the program in three waves of thirty-plus students.

Thirty percent of the trainees were male; 70 percent, female. Eighty percent were between the ages of twenty-two and forty-four. Seventy-nine percent were black; 15 percent, Hispanic; 5 percent, Caucasian; and 1 percent, Asian. Half of the applicants had some secretarial or clerical experience; a few had no work experience at all.

Trainees were paid to attend forty hours of training per week. Each day was divided among language training, typing and word-processing training, work-habits training, and individual study time. Three full-time teachers (a reading specialist, a word-processing specialist, and a business specialist) worked with students throughout the day.

Assignments integrated language and machine skills. Much of the work simulated actual job demands. Students composed business communication, much of it handwritten as a rough draft, with editing notations; other students edited and later produced it in final form on word-processing equipment. The job-simulation training that integrated language and machine experience ranged from 5 percent of assignments the first week to nearly 100 percent in the final weeks. Class assignments replicated the time constraints present in business performance. Though much of the work was for individual performance, some required teamwork, which again replicated workplace conditions.

Trainees used up-to-date word-processing equipment and were aware of the industry standards they had to meet. Integrated training in language, work habits, and machine use gave them focused practice to meet those standards.

Over 70 percent of trainees found employment as word-processor operators during the project. The time needed for trainees to reach job-level competence varied. The earliest trainees found employment after only fourteen weeks of training. The average time the trainees took to reach the preset industry standards was twenty weeks, but a few took nearly twenty-eight weeks.

Training Wastewater Treatment Workers (Sticht and Mikulecky, 1985). An urban municipality recently opened a wastewater treatment plant, incorporating several technical innovations. Workers had needed little technical training to work in the old treatment plant, but now they would have to use super-cooled oxygen and nitrogen, dangerous chlorine gases, and computer-aided monitoring of environments for microorganisms.

Before they could be transferred, the workers had to learn (1) how the new process and equipment functioned, (2) safety precautions when working with particularly dangerous gases, and (3) how to maintain the microorganisms essential to waste-water treatment. Ignorant mistakes could cause loss of life, plant shutdowns, and replacement of equipment and organisms. The unstated implication of the training program was that workers unable to be retrained adequately would face demotion or un-employment.

To avoid these alternatives, the municipality contracted with an engineering firm to provide technical retraining. The firm, relying on its previous experience in retraining engineers and upgrading technicians, developed a technical curriculum and arranged for workers to be paid for attending full days of classes at a centrally located, converted elementary school. Trainers were under pressure to meet retraining goals with a minimal loss of worker time on the job. The learning format was two full weeks of classes, followed by two weeks of on-the-job training, alternating until the employee had attended all ten two-week training modules.

It soon became apparent that the usual technical retrain-ing procedures were not working for a large percentage of the trainees. Many read below eighth-grade level, several read below third-grade level, and many had little or no familiarity with the concepts covered in the brief, high-powered technical classes. Classroom training materials, on the other hand, ranged in dif-ficulty from eleventh-grade to college level and included heavy use of graphs, charts, and schematics. On-the-job explanatory material was nearly as difficult.

The engineering consulting firm, therefore, engaged a university consultant and a university-trained reading specialist to develop a basic skills component and to integrate the use of microcomputers to provide more individual practice and feed-back to the trainees.

Workers with literacy problems spent three additional afternoons a week with the reading specialist, concentrating on occupationally related basic skills. The specialist also taught content-reading techniques to the engineers who ran the morning classes.

The reading specialist estimated that 80 percent of the trainees with literacy problems were extremely anxious about appearing ignorant or retarded. Most had experienced difficulty in public school; over a quarter had had unhappy experiences in adult basic-education classes. When the specialist tried to diagnose basic-skills problems in an efficient, clinical manner, trainees refused to return. Rapport and trust had to be created. The specialist increasingly relied on careful observation of how trainees performed during learning sessions.

The major academic goal was to help trainees master technical vocabulary, concepts, and materials. Special study guides, arranged by the reading specialist, broke assignments into manageable tasks. Trainees received special help in interpreting graphs and schematic diagrams. About forty-five minutes of each ninety-minute session were allocated to oral feedback and questioning on what they had read from manuals or work material. For the remainder of the time, they read materials whose purpose the specialist had clearly explained.

In some classes, the specialist managed to rewrite or redesign training materials to make them less difficult. Students were asked to read general material no harder than they could handle independently. Simple rewrite tests and handouts were used to lower difficulty levels; in many cases, difficulty was reduced 40 percent without noticeable loss of content. The average mastery level of students whose instructors used rewritten materials improved significantly over the others. However, reducing the difficulty of materials to below the sixth-grade level proved both taxing and counterproductive. Students reading below that level did not grasp the concepts, even when simply expressed.

As a result, nearly half the students who took special basic-skills training passed their technical class post-tests. According to the technical instructors and the reading specialist, fewer than

5 percent of those students would have passed without special attention. Of the students who attended, 70 percent were able to summarize materials in their own words by the end of the training. Students who received special basic-skills training actually retained learning better than students who had only attended technical classes.

Gains in general reading ability were less encouraging. Only 10 percent of students taking special training increased their ability to read general material or new material for which the teacher had given them no direction or purpose. Those who made the most significant gains in job and general reading ability invested five or more hours per week in reading suitably difficult outside material.

Training Electronics Technicians (Sticht, Armstrong, Hickey, and Caylor, 1986). Admission into technological training programs is often contingent on proof of ability in reading or mathematics. One electronics training program in Southern California requires students to score not lower than the ninth-grade level on a standardized reading test. Applicants who do not reach minimum levels are encouraged to enroll in remedial basic education, with the assurance that "when further evaluation indicates that they can comprehend the vocational training, they will be admitted."

Having to take remedial education deters adults from seeking technical training, because they need the extra time to earn a living. To overcome that problem, the Ford Foundation sponsored a project to demonstrate how basic and technical skills training could be integrated in a complex technical field. The outcome was the Functional Context Training Electronics Technicians (FCT/ET) course schematized in Figure 4.

At entry into the FCT/ET course, students are given information about jobs for electronics technicians (ETs) and further training they may wish to consider after the program. The ET's role in operating, maintaining, and repairing equipment is stressed. Students are told that they will learn how to think about equipment in a systematic way, and that they will learn by using common, everyday electrical devices they most

Figure 4. Overview of an Electronic Technician's Functional Context Training Course.

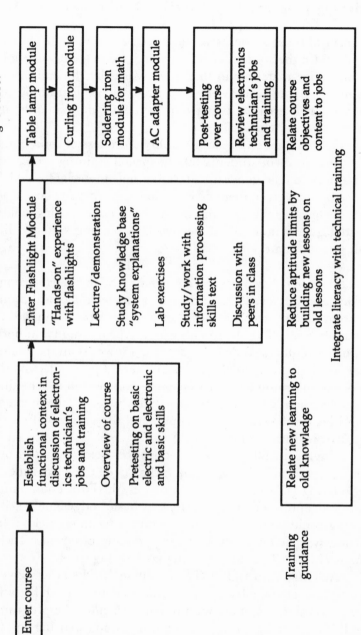

Enter course

Establish functional context in discussion of electronics technician's jobs and training

Overview of course

Pretesting on basic electric and electronic and basic skills

Enter Flashlight Module

"Hands-on" experience with flashlights

Lecture/demonstration

Study knowledge base "system explanations"

Lab exercises

Study/work with information processing skills text

Discussion with peers in class

Table lamp module

Curling iron module

Soldering iron module for math

AC adapter module

Post-testing over course

Review electronics technician's jobs and training

Relate course objectives and content to jobs

Training guidance

Relate new learning to old knowledge

Reduce aptitude limits by building new lessons on old lessons

Integrate literacy with technical training

Source: Sticht, 1986.

likely have used in their day-to-day lives: a flashlight, a table lamp, a curling iron, and an AC adapter used to recharge or replace the batteries of portable radios and tape players. These appliances were selected because they are familiar to women as well as men, and because they facilitate introduction to basic electric and electronic concepts and procedures.

In consideration of the problems that lower-aptitude, less-literate students might encounter, the designers planned the contents and sequence of the course to move from concrete to abstract, from specific to general, from practice to theory, and from the familiar to the unfamiliar. The text, therefore, uses direct, expository prose, avoiding analogies and metaphors that might require knowledge not possessed by the students or provided in the course.

A book on information-processing skills covers the basic literacy skills needed to read training and job-related materials in the electronics field. Exercises in this book help students process the information found in the course textbook. Simple worksheets explain and offer practice in reading-to-do and reading-to-learn tasks (Sticht and others, 1986). Reading-to-do tasks involve looking up information (such as repair specifications in a technical manual) and remembering it just long enough to apply it: tasks such as extracting information from documents; using tables of contents, indexes, and glossaries; and searching or scanning text, tables, and graphs to locate information. Reading-to-learn tasks involve reading information and storing it for the long term as part of one's knowledge base for later use, as when studying for a test or learning to use a piece of equipment. Specific tasks include rereading something until it is understood; asking oneself questions about material; transforming information by paraphrasing and summarizing, block diagramming, or pictorializing; and focusing attention for rereading by highlighting or underlining and so on. Reading specialists usually teach such activities to improve reading comprehension.

Comprehension of reading in electronics is abetted by beginning the course with the study of concrete objects (electrical devices such as flashlights and hair dryers) and with information already known to the students. Readings build on this prior knowledge to expand the students' knowledge base in electronics technology. By coupling the improvement in content knowledge with instruction in strategies for reading-to-do and reading-to-learn, it is anticipated that students will develop more generally useful literacy skills and increase their overall employability.

Ability in mathematics is also required for entry into technology training programs. A technician who troubleshoots electrical devices requires many different mathematical skills. For example, when testing flashlight batteries with a multimeter, one must understand fractions to read the scale, and decimals to adjust scale readings. The frequency and amplitude of a waveform on the oscilloscope screen cannot be read without a solid grasp of concepts, including scientific notation. In the textbook, students are introduced to mathematical concepts and their application; then they practice the skills from worksheets in the information-processing skills book.

Students in the center's electronics course ranged in age from nineteen to fifty-five. Most had no formal training or experience in electronics. All took the vocabulary and paragraph comprehension components of the Test of Adult Basic Education. As a result of initial screening, most of the participants in this pilot test were at the high end of midlevel literacy (ninth to tenth grade). Although the FCT/ET course is ultimately intended for students of much lower literacy, the use of the experimental curriculum to improve the performance of the current population of students at the center was considered a reasonable first test.

The pilot test indicated that it is indeed feasible to integrate basic skills instruction into technical skills training. Despite some minor logistical problems, the course was delivered as it had been constructed. The electrical devices (flashlights, hair dryers, and so forth) had been, as it turned out, well chosen. Examining and testing the devices they had to read about appeared to motivate the students: they were surprised and pleased to use the multitimers on the very first day of class. All said they preferred the experimental curriculum's mathematics instruction to their regular math class. Two students, whose math pretest scores were below those of the others and who found regular "electronics math" difficult and frustrating, stated emphatically that they preferred learning math concepts in the context of application.

There was no formal data gathering, but the students clearly evidenced that they had learned both basic electric and electronic skills and basic skills. They answered quiz questions correctly and demonstrated the skills covered. All were able to use the multimeter to measure voltage and resistance values.

The administrators of the center and the instructor whose class was used for the tryout were enthusiastic about the approach and volunteered the center as a site for future implementation and evaluation of a complete FCT/ET course.

Background Paper

Sticht, T. G. "Job Skills and Basic Skills: Training 'Midlevel Literates' for Work with New Technologies." Mar. 1986.

8

The Connection Between Continuous Learning and Employment Security

Continuous learning thrives best in an atmosphere of employment security. As a general rule, employers that invest most heavily in employee learning also make the greatest efforts to provide employment security in order to protect their investment. Conversely, employers that provide little employment security invest a minimum in employee learning.

The reasons are straightforward. An employer that provides employment security has to regard its employees as permanent assets, whose abilities must be maintained and improved; and turnover among such employees tends to be very low. An employer that regards its employees as disposable creates a self-fulfilling prophecy: employees leave as soon as something better comes along, so there is no point in making them valuable to another employer.

However, the relationship between learning and security is twofold. Investment in learning strengthens the competitiveness of an employer and increases its ability to provide employment

The information in this chapter, unless otherwise referenced, is drawn from the background papers and case studies listed at the end of the chapter. Both papers and cases were commissioned by Work in America Institute in the course of its three-year policy study entitled "Training for New Technology."

security. At the same time, the existence of employment security motivates employees to seek learning that will be useful to the employer and to make better use of the learning opportunities that are offered.

The incentive for learning is, of course, only one reason—though a strong one—for a policy of employment security.

When our report speaks of employment security, it does not refer to a "no-layoff policy." In broad terms, it means not laying employees off (temporary) or dismissing them (permanent) until all practical alternatives have been exhausted; and, when dismissal is unavoidable, it means helping them find suitable jobs in other firms.

In a previous national policy report, *Employment Security in a Free Economy*, we argued that employers should adopt employment security as a part of corporate strategy—not as a favor to employees, but because increasing security can improve the economic performance of the company without diminishing the employer's freedom to manage (Rosow and Zager, 1984). The dominant feature of our economy today and for the foreseeable future is continuous, rapid change: changing markets, products, technologies, skills, and competitive threats. Continuous change inevitably unsettles an organization, but organizations whose employees are free of anxiety about remaining employed have the best hope of keeping their equilibrium and gaining strength from change.

Employment security encourages cooperation by freeing employees to accept management-proposed changes, contribute ideas for improving performance and productivity, maintain an optimal pace of work, give up job-protective restrictive practices, agree to perform tasks outside their normal classification, accept necessary inconveniences, and volunteer for and profit from training.

In addition, employment security brings the employer such practical benefits as greater flexibility in the use of employees; greater trust among managers, supervisors, and workers; ability to move rapidly when a downturn ends; and reduction in the cost of turnover.

Instead of trying to define what employment security ought to mean in an abstract sense, we have asked ourselves what kinds of promises by employers actually stimulate employees to give their best efforts under conditions of continuous change. Case after case demonstrates that workers are extremely realistic (unless the employer has lulled them into false expectations) about an employer's ability to shield them from the winds of economic change. When an employer is in genuine trouble, they consider it fair (although painful) that they should suffer hardship, provided that the rest of the organization shares equitably. But they see no reason why they should suffer when the employer introduces changes that lead to displacement, such as productivity improvements and technological changes. Employers that offer guarantees in line with these views and persuade employees that they can and will honor the guarantees can count on employee cooperation under all circumstances.

The same factors that favor employment security also underlie the need for continuous learning. As described in Chapter Three, continuous learning is characterized by the following statements:

- Learning is an everyday part of every job. The line between job performance and learning disappears.
- Employees, in addition to mastering the skills specific to their immediate tasks, are required to learn the skills of others in their work unit. They are also required to understand the relationship between their work unit and the organization as a whole, and to be familiar with the operation and goals of the business.
- Active, free-form interaction among employees, team, trainers, and managers is encouraged and institutionalized.
- Employees are required to transmit their job knowledge to, as well as learn from, co-workers.

The late 1980s, when wholesale layoffs and dismissals seem to be the order of the day, may strike readers as the wrong time to be advocating employment security. Although some large companies are reported to be taking these painful measures precisely because they want to get into position to make deliverable promises of security later on to those employees who remain, the great majority reject employment security as a practical policy. When they introduce new technology, they do not train their employees to operate it; they fire those whose jobs have become obsolete and hire new people whom they believe to be equipped with the necessary skills.

Many employers assume that firing and hiring are more economical than retraining in terms of quantifiable costs. In fact, the assumption is usually no more than an assumption, unchecked by arithmetic. A deeper fallacy is the assumption that costs are not tangible unless they can be quantified. In case after case, employers discover—too late—that in the process of getting rid of employees who lack necessary new skills, they have lost other equally essential assets: loyalty, stored know-how and experience, flexibility, perpetuation of the corporate culture, institutional memory.

The fire-hire policy also underestimates the flexibility of current employees and the strength of the incentives for them to learn new skills—for example, the likelihood that higher skills will lead to higher pay and more interesting work.

Those who reject employment security in principle usually attack it as unworkable. This chapter is therefore devoted to exploring how the policy actually works. In each of the supporting cases learning or retraining is an element, although not always the central element.

Three aspects are reviewed: the cost-effectiveness of retraining for new technology, as against hiring already-trained outsiders; managing the movement of employees from old to new jobs; and enhancing the success rate of retrainees by bringing them into contact with the new work unit as early as possible.

Fire-and-Hire

In a 1984 survey, more than 300 senior human resource executives at *Fortune* 1,500 companies were asked how their companies dealt with workers whose skills had become obsolete. Forty-four percent replied that their companies were "most likely to hire new employees with the required skill.'' Forty percent said that workers with obsolete skills were switched into new positions requiring no additional skills. But 36 percent said their companies consistently moved employees into new positions that required additional training, and the figure was higher—57 percent—for companies that have been influenced a great deal by technological changes (''Replace or Retrain?'' 1984).

These figures present a flattering picture of the economy as a whole: the human resource policies of *Fortune* 1,500 companies are far more enlightened than the rest.

Recently, California's Employment Training Panel's (ETP) policy of retraining currently employed people whose jobs are in jeopardy because of new technology was criticized on two grounds: (1) that it should apply only to those who have actually received a notice of layoff, and (2) that employers would have provided such retraining even if ETP had not subsidized it. The agency replied as follows:

Unfortunately, the Panel's experience in developing 400 training projects with thousands of employees all over California is not consistent with the . . . optimistic view of the capabilities and intentions of the vast majority of California employers. The Panel has seen no evidence that the type and level of training that is provided with Panel support would have been provided without that support. On the contrary, layoffs continue to be an all too frequent fact of life in California in both service and manufacturing sectors, even during the current economic expansion. Business and labor have sought out Panel assistance to act in advance to prevent such layoffs. The Panel has found that training is not high on the list of priorities of many California businesses. Cost cutting, improving the bottom line, and impressing the securities analysts by cutting personnel—even if that means layoffs—too often are at the top of the list. Panel support provides a practical alternative to layoffs by helping to change the priorities [Duscha, 1986].

Since employment security is widely regarded as a powerful morale booster, one must conclude that employers normally resort to fire-and-hire in preference to retraining because they judge that the former is less costly and difficult than the latter. One looks in vain, however, for evidence that employers have actually done any calculations to warrant their preference. It is a fair guess that even employers who practice employment security make the same assumption but accept the supposed extra cost as justified by the long-term value of the policy.

The fact is, no one can say confidently which option, as a general proposition, is the less costly in strict accounting terms. Each situation may lead to a different answer. Employers owe it to themselves, if not to their employees, to check the facts and analyze the alternatives before they decide to fire and hire. The following approach is offered as a starting point for employers willing to test the general assumption.

In any given workplace, some positions will have overlapping requirements; that is, certain skills are needed in more than one job. The training needs of moving from job A to job B are those additional skills required in job B but not in job A. Training requirements of moving from any job to another job can be determined by comparing the skills of each job category and highlighting the differences. For most large employers, this information is readily available in position descriptions.

Training requirements can be viewed as a collection of training segments. The costs of each segment are defined as the sum of the costs of formal classroom training, on-the-job training, proficiency acquisition (learning-curve costs), and the loaded wage of the trainee. A total training cost of $35 per hour of training is used in this example. Once the costs of each training segment have been identified, a total cost matrix (see Table 2) can be developed.

In Table 2, assume that blue-collar jobs A, B, C, and D have certain elements of skill and knowledge in common. Jobs A, B, and C are existing jobs. Jobs A and B are becoming redundant; demand for job C is static. Job D has recently been made necessary by the introduction of new technology. Table 2 lists all the training segments required by each job and the number of hours for each segment. An arbitrary (but not farfetched) cost of $35 (which includes formal classroom, on-the-job training, and learning-curve costs plus loaded wage of trainee)

Table 2. Training Costs.*

Training Segment and Hours		Job A	Job B	Job C	Job D
Plant orientation	4	$ 140	$ 140	$ 140	$ 140
Environmental risks	4	140	140	140	140
Soldering	40	1,400	1,400	0	0
Wire winding	40	0	1,400	1,400	1,400
Harness layout	80	0	2,800	2,800	2,800
Test equipment operations	120	0	0	0	4,200
Air tool operations	64	0	0	2,240	2,240
Schematics reading	80	0	0	0	2,800
Quality control	40	0	1,400	0	1,400
Total		$1,680	$7,280	$6,720	$15,120

*These costs are based on analysis of actual costs in a number of companies. They illustrate a cost-accounting approach that can be adapted to other situations.
Source: Ward, 1986.

has been assigned as the cost per hour of training, regardless of subject matter. The totals show the costs of training an employee for each job, from scratch.

The figure of $35 per hour as the cost of training is, we stress, arbitrary; each employer needs to work out its own figure. However, $35 per hour is not so far from reality as to vitiate the exercise. For example, the ETP trained almost 37,000 people in California between January 1, 1984, and June 30, 1986, at an average cost of $3,096. Since each trainee received an average of 422 hours of training, formal training expenses alone cost $7.34 per hour. If we add $10.00 per hour for wages, plus $3.00 per hour (30 percent of wages) for benefits, the gross cost of formal training comes to $20.34 per hour. Much of the difference between $35.00 and $20.34 would be filled by the subsequent costs of on-the-job training and the learning curve.

But we are not interested in the cost of training from scratch. We want to know (1) how much it would cost to train the occupant of a redundant job (A or B) to fill job D; (2) how

Table 3. Costs of Retraining Versus Costs of Hiring.

	Job A	*Job B*	*Job C*	*Job D*
Job A	$ 0	$5,600	$6,440	$14,840
Job B	0	0	2,240	9,240
Job C	1,400	2,800	0	8,400
Job D	1,400	1,400	0	0
Hires	$1,680	$4,480	$3,080	$ 4,480

Source: Ward, 1986.

much it would cost to hire someone already fully trained for D; and (3) how much it would cost to fire the occupant of job A or B. Another possibility (4) is that someone from job C might be trained to perform job D, while someone from job A or B is trained to fill the vacancy in job C, and the position vacated by the retrained A or B is closed down.

Table 3, derived from Table 2, shows how much it would cost to provide the incremental training needed by an occupant of job A, B, C, or D in order to become a fully qualified occupant of any of the other jobs in that quartet. For example, a holder of job B would need no additional training to qualify for job A, but would need $2,240 in training to qualify for job C, and $9,240 in training for job D.

In Table 3, the line marked "Hires" shows the staffing and administrative costs, plus a certain amount of training costs, incurred for new hires. A skilled recruit may possess many, but rarely all, of the skills required for a complex job. The costs are probably understated because they disregard the less-than-full contribution a new employee makes during the one to six months it takes to adjust to new procedures, tools and equipment, supervision, work pace, quality demands, and plant culture. The more complex the job, the higher the start-up costs.

Thus, it would cost $14,840 to train an occupant of job A to fill D, or $9,240 to train an occupant of job B. It would cost $4,480 to hire someone fully trained from outside to fill a D spot. It would cost $8,400 to train someone from C to fill a D spot, plus $2,240 to train a B to replace the C, totaling $10,640.

Although Table 3 tells how much it costs to hire a skilled worker, it does not tell the cost of firing an occupant of job A or B. However, a previous calculation has estimated the direct cost of dismissal in the real world at approximately $8,900 for a semiskilled worker. This includes severance, unemployment compensation, loss of production value, and so on. It does not include the unquantifiable costs due to injuring the organization and the morale of those who remain. Each employer must make its own estimates.

Thus, in filling job D, the employer has the following options:

- Retrain (and do not replace) an occupant of B, at a cost of $9,240.
- Retrain an occupant of C, at a cost of $8,400, and retrain an occupant of B to replace the individual moved from C, at a cost of $2,240, for a total cost of $10,640.
- Hire someone from outside, at a cost of $4,480, and dismiss an occupant of A or B, at a cost of $8,900, for a total of $13,380. In such a case, even an employer who considered employment security a frill would almost certainly go for one of the retraining options.

We do not mean to imply that the calculation will always favor retraining—only that the cost of retraining is often much less, and the cost of hiring and firing is much more, than generally believed. The more senior the employees, the more they command in severance pay, pensions, and unemployment benefits, and therefore the more strongly the balance leans toward retraining.

The hard choices come when the cost of retraining exceeds the cost of fire-and-hire by a relatively small proportion of the total expense involved. Then the employer must decide how much weight to give the "soft" benefits that flow from employment security.

The experience of California's ETP gives us some clues to the actual costs of successful retraining. In principal, any large employer should be able to do even better, because ETP, as an outsider, must pay to overcome many obstacles that would not impede an employer dealing with its own employees.

California's Employment Training Panel (Gutchess, 1985). Although few employers calculate the costs of retraining versus the costs of firing and hiring, an offer of government funds often tips the balance toward retraining. California's ETP has subsidized hundreds of retraining projects for employees whose jobs were considered to be in jeopardy due to new technology or other causes. These projects were in addition to 2,000 or more for the retraining of unemployed people. Businesses in such industries as construction, telecommunications, autos, computers, electronics, food processing, aerospace, and agriculture have taken part. Between January 1, 1984, and June 30, 1986, ETP paid out $113.9 million to retrain 36,803 people.

The seven-member ETP that administers the fund is entirely drawn from the private sector. Appointed by the governor and leaders of the legislature, the panel includes representatives of business, labor, and the general public. In addition to taking people off the unemployment rolls by retraining and putting them back to work, the panel has adopted a twin goal to stimulate the state's economic development. Training support provided by the panel has helped troubled industries to retool and survive and has convinced other healthy businesses that might have moved out of the state to stay and expand in California. According to ETP, support is given when business is unable to find an adequate number of appropriately trained workers.

The program differs from traditional vocational training programs in two major respects. First, training is financed by diverting $55 million a year that otherwise would have gone into the unemployment insurance (UI) system. California is the first state to use UI funds in this manner. Second, all training is directed toward specific jobs, and there must be a commitment on the part of the employer to hire the trainees. Furthermore, the panel pays employers or other trainers only if the trainees go to work.

Because of federal restrictions on the use of UI funds for training, the state legislation first reduced the UI tax paid by

positive-reserve employers (those who have experienced little
or no unemployment and have, therefore, underutilized their
UI account) and then imposed a new state tax, to be collected
with the UI tax, on the same employers. There was little concern about eroding the UI fund in California because at the time
the legislation was enacted, there was a surplus in the fund. Nor
did employers object, since the program did not involve any
additional taxes for them. In effect, a portion of the tax that
private-sector employers pay to support the federal/state UI system was set aside in a separate fund for training and retraining.

In many cases, the cost of training is shared between the
state and the employer or other groups involved in training.
However, the financing arrangements—depending on the number of trainees, the complexity of skills to be taught, and other
factors—vary widely.

Performance-based contracts with employers or other
groups designate the number of people to be trained, the types
of jobs to be filled, and the company or companies that will hire
these trainees. Contracts can last up to two years or be as short
as six months. To be paid for training costs, employers must
certify that the trainees have been hired and have remained on
the job for at least ninety days. The panel does not pay any
of the wages of trainees.

Another requirement of the program is that training be for
"good, steady jobs that pay a decent wage and keep people from
cycling back onto the unemployment rolls." From the very start,
staff members were instructed to work directly with business and
labor and with public and private training agencies in developing training programs in high-demand and expanding fields.

Many of the positions are in high-technology businesses,
but even more are in traditional manufacturing industries where
there are frequent high-technology applications. Blue-collar
workers learn new technologies in their changing industries instead of facing unemployment. Projects include training in the
use of computerized numerical controls for machine tools, computer-assisted manufacturing systems, automated manufacturing
equipment, and high-technology specialties for electrical and

sheet-metal contractors. In other instances, training has been provided for businesses that have undergone extensive modernization and need additional workers, such as a recently reopened portion of a lumber mill that hired workers and trained them on the job in plywood-manufacturing skills.

White-collar workers are also learning new skills to adapt to changing technologies. Some of the projects supported by the panel have taught computer-assisted drafting, automated bookkeeping, and word processing to office workers, and electronics to business-machine repair people who fix computerized equipment.

Several retraining projects have been targeted to the needs of special groups, including farm workers, construction workers, women, minorities, and veterans.

In large measure, input from employers and labor unions determines the structure and operation of specific training projects. Employers—and unions, when appropriate—have the opportunity to determine who will be trained, what the training will consist of, and what the standards are for completion. Organized labor has taken an active interest in the California program, serving as the catalyst for developing about one-third of the panel's training projects. Many of the training projects have kept union members working and have reemployed others who had lost their jobs.

Xerox Reprographics Business Group. An instance in which the employer did calculate the costs of fire-and-hire against the costs of retraining, and then decided in favor of retraining, occurred in Xerox's Reprographics Business Group, in Webster, New York, now part of the Business Products & Systems Group, with worldwide operations. The case is especially noteworthy because it involved retraining professional specialists to fill altogether different professional specialist positions, a feat usually considered impractical. Xerox's Critical Skills Training Program has been carried out not once but three times, each time with better results than before. By March 1987, more than forty employees had made the transition.

In late 1982 and early 1983, severe competitive pressure compelled Xerox to change its products, processes, organization, and staffing. The Reprographics Business Group (RBG), which operates the company's copier business, faced two particular staffing problems. The product's increased technological complexity required skilled professionals in computer engineering, electronic engineering, and computer science, skills for which the market was tight. At the same time, RBG's need for the skills of many of its current professionals—experienced engineers, chemists, physicists, and others—was diminishing.

At first it appeared that RBG would either have to relocate people with these surplus skills, or, if worse came to worst, dismiss them and hire people with the new specialties. Although Xerox does not formally guarantee employment security to its professional/technical staff, its unwritten policy has been to dismiss only if all other practical alternatives fail.

Then it occurred to RBG managers that a third course of action, retraining, might allow them to avoid both the dislocation of current employees and the recruiting of scarce new skills. Despite the lack of precedent to guide such a program, either in Xerox or elsewhere, a preliminary estimate indicated that it would be cost-effective. They decided to take the risk, based on the company's long experience of courses for professional updating and career expansion. An established relationship with Rochester Institute of Technology (RIT), which had carried out many professional/technical training programs for Xerox (sometimes with RIT staff people on company premises), bolstered their confidence.

A task force, including the heads of the divisions that would receive the people who had completed the program (Electronics, Xerox Systems, Reprographics Manufacturing, and RBG), plus the manager of human resource management and representatives of RIT, assumed responsibility for designing and overseeing the program. The close involvement of the receiving divisions gave concrete expression to their interest in the outcome.

Engineering managers specified the skills and knowledge

the trainees would have to possess at completion to fulfill the program's objectives:

- Understanding of computer and microprocessor concepts and technology
- Specialized knowledge of software operating systems and languages
- Knowledge of hardware (for example, digital design, hardware interfacing)
- Programming experience with at least two languages
- Ability to contribute to the design, debugging, and documentation of microprocessor-based solutions to engineering problems
- Sufficient background and understanding to handle follow-on courses in electronics and computer engineering

The task force designed a curriculum of formidable proportions: seventeen courses, with a class load of sixteen hours weekly during each quarter for three-quarters of the year (RIT operates twelve months a year and divides the year into quarters). All courses were held at the RIT campus in classes attended only by Critical Skills Training enrollees. Twelve courses were customized to RBG's requirements.

How should candidates be selected for such a stringent curriculum? The task force announced the program through regular company communication channels, offering employees a chance to change career direction and prepare for opportunities in new high-tech growth fields. One hundred or so employees applied. Most applicants were in fields where they felt future opportunities would be limited. Most were able and highly motivated.

Applicants completed a simple form and submitted personnel data. Interviews by management members of the task force served as the principal means of determining motivation, which, in view of the intensive study, classwork, and homework required, was deemed highly important.

Of the twenty-nine applicants finally selected for the first program, to begin in the fall of 1983, people with bachelor of science degrees in mechanical engineering predominated. Others had degrees in chemistry, physics, and mathematics.

Trainees received full pay and benefits throughout the program. In addition, Xerox provided each trainee with a computer terminal at home and paid the phone charges for linking the terminal to RIT's mainframe computer. To relieve anxieties about employment security, enrollees were assured that if they had to drop out of the program, they could return to their old jobs, and that those who graduated would be immune to dismissal or demotion for two years.

The costs of the program—tuition, computers and linkage, salary and benefits, administration, equipment, course development—were charged against RBG's training department, using funds that would otherwise have been allocated to relocation, redeployment, or dismissal of surplus employees. No costs were charged to either the work units from which the trainees were drawn or those to which they went after training.

The outcome of the first program fulfilled the company's hopes, except for the number of dropouts. Only eighteen of the original twenty-nine graduated, but the eighteen drew high praise from the managers who received them.

At the conclusion of the first program, the task force adopted several important improvements:

- *Curriculum design.* To lighten the academic burden on the trainees, the program was lengthened to twelve months.
- *Selection.* To smooth reentry at graduation, each trainee would be selected—before training—by the department to which he or she was headed.
- *Dropout prevention.* Since analysis showed that many trainees dropped out due to a lack of aptitude for mathematics or programming, aptitude tests for these subjects were added to the selection process.

Analysis also showed that trainees' test scores in mathematics and programming were reliable predictors of success in the related academic courses. Therefore, applicants for the second and third programs were offered the opportunity to take a three-week, fourteen-hour math refresher course (open to all employees) before undergoing the math test or interviews. Trainees unfamiliar with computers took a preliminary four-week, twenty-four-hour course, "Introduction to Computing," taught in-house.

Because the curriculum cuts sharply into the time a trainee can spend with spouse and children, families are invited to a special orientation and to occasional social events.

Counseling and tutoring are made available to help trainees meet the demands of class schedules and homework. In addition, each trainee was assigned a mentor from his or her new department. The mentor observes the trainee's progress and keeps him or her abreast of current projects in the new organization, thereby helping the trainee find the right niche.

The program changes achieved their aim: only one trainee dropped out of the second program, which began in March 1984; none has yet dropped out of the third round, currently in session, except for a few who are suffering health problems unrelated to the training.

The original task force still holds quarterly meetings to evaluate, guide, and support the program. Its findings have been impressive:

- Reentry has been problem free for trainees and their new work units. The receiving managers have given the graduates excellent ratings at each of the follow-up evaluations (six months, twelve months, and twenty-four months). Trainees rate themselves more modestly but express satisfaction with the career change. Many of them have received promotions.
- The program is highly regarded by other Xerox employees.
- Xerox has found the program cost-effective. Although unit costs vary with the size of the training group, they have been in line with the costs of available alternatives. To relocate a professional/technical employee in such a far-flung company can be very expensive. To dismiss one is also costly, since the company allows a redundant employee six months at full pay to find another job, plus severance pay and bene-

fits. Moreover, it must be borne in mind that hiring a new employee with the needed skills is also costly: the employee must be recruited, trained, and then supported for the six months it takes to become fully productive.

Other cases also challenge the assumption that fire-and-hire is an obvious choice. For example:

> *Hewlett-Packard* has retrained redundant blue-collar workers to fill emerging office jobs of the following kinds: electronic data-processing support, computer operator, administrative support, telemarketing operator, secretary, and field-and-factory order-processing support. The course takes three months—most of it at a community college, some at the company's Office Learning Center. Additional courses are given to those in telemarketing and computer operations. Trainees earn fourteen units of college credit, applicable toward a degree. The cost of training is about $2,200 per trainee, exclusive of salary.
>
> *General Electric* converted an old plant in Fort Wayne, Indiana, into a "postindustrial" facility—whose new products and processes were far more technologically sophisticated than the old—and staffed it with its own displaced employees. Yet, for the two main categories of workers, the amount of retraining needed prior to job assignment proved quite modest. The less skilled group received eleven days of mostly on-the-job training. The more skilled group received nine days in the classroom and three on the job.
>
> *General Motors'* assembly plant in Wilmington, Delaware, was thoroughly retooled to build an advanced new car at a cost running into hundreds of millions of dollars. The bulk of its workers—the semiskilled—needed only two weeks of technical retraining, plus a shorter period of "social" retraining to prepare for working as members of teams. Maintenance craft employees received a much more extensive course, but probably

no more than would have been needed by any outsiders who could have been recruited (if recruitment were allowed) to replace them.

Managing Redeployment

A policy of employment security carries with it the task of managing the steady movement of employees out of redundant jobs and into jobs that have come into demand inside or outside the firm. Otherwise the employer faces mounting costs and the danger of carrying surplus people on the payroll, in addition to the costs and turmoil of hiring new employees. Uncontrolled, these costs jeopardize the policy of employment security, the viability of the firm, or both.

Managing the redeployment of people is not accomplished by merely stating goals and urging managers to pay heed. Specific responsibilities have to be assigned to individual managers, and specific routines for anticipating, planning, and implementing moves must be instituted. In a large organization, these arrangements will be put into place at site level, division level, and corporate level.

Retraining is and will continue to be an essential step in the process. The following cases illustrate concrete methods that companies (and unions) have devised to ensure that retraining serves the purpose of employment security.

At General Electric, Fort Wayne, a corporate planning review led to the decision to place a new higher-tech facility in the Rust Belt rather than at a neutral site. At Packard Electric, the union accepted joint responsibility with the employer for managing redeployment. At Pacific Bell, management and union jointly managed retraining with the aid of company-supplied information about future needs. At Pacific Northwest Bell, a computer system helped salaried personnel apply and train for jobs that promised a better future within the firm.

General Electric, Fort Wayne, Indiana. A multidivisional company has more room to maneuver than a smaller company in managing redeployment: obvious possibilities lie in transferring employees or work from one part of the firm to another. But the corollary is that someone or, more likely, some department at corporate level continually monitors the situation and sees to it that the most complete information is brought to bear on decisions. General Electric's (GE) foresight spelled the difference between jobs and despair for hundreds of displaced GE employees in Fort Wayne, Indiana.

In 1973, GE's labor force in Fort Wayne was close to 8,000, and demand for its products (electric motors and transformers) was strong. By 1980, the force had declined to 5,200. In 1983, it was down to 3,100 employees who had an average company service of twenty years. One thousand employees were on layoff, several hundred more were slated for layoff in the near future, and half of one large plant was mothballed for lack of business.

In that same year, GE's prosperous Aircraft Engine Business Group, based in Evandale, Ohio, was seeking space to relocate the work units that manufacture engine controls (known as Aircraft Engine Electronic Controls Department, or AEECD). Although it had tentatively decided to house them in an empty building in Florida, a facilities review at corporate level suggested that Fort Wayne, where further work-force reductions loomed, might be a better alternative. However, inasmuch as the products, manufacturing processes, and organization of work would differ markedly from those of GE's existing plants in Fort Wayne, the move would be feasible only if (1) the union—the International Union of Electrical Workers (IUE)—would agree to a new kind of contract for the new plant, and (2) local and state government agencies would offset some of the labor cost differential between Fort Wayne and Florida. Both conditions were met.

IUE agreed that special contractual terms at AEECD were justified because its members there were to work in teams, in contrast to the traditional form of organization in the old plants. Teams would take full responsibility for quality and production; they would meet weekly to be updated on product status, manufacturing techniques, and business results. These new terms were adopted:

1. There would be a separate supplement to the Fort Wayne contract just for AEECD.
2. AEECD workers would be selected first from those slated for layoff at the old plants and second from those on the recall list, in order of seniority.
3. A selectee's refusal to transfer to AEECD would not jeopardize his or her seniority for recall to the old plants.
4. AEECD workers would be promoted only from within, and their replacements would be selected from the same pool as themselves.
5. AEECD employees would be isolated from the bumping procedure at other plants.
6. Pay would be based on measured day work instead of the incentive plan in effect at the old plants.
7. Job classifications would be broad and few; cross-training would be part of the job for everyone.

Local and state governments came through with substantial help:

- The state and the city, working through regional and local Private Industry Councils, offset a large part of GE's retraining costs.
- GE earned tax credits because the plant was in an Urban Enterprise Zone.
- The city reduced property taxes on the new facilities and equipment.

Once the decision was made, AEECD moved into the empty half of a small electric motor factory and completely refurbished it. Quiet carpeting went in over noisy concrete and woodblock. The two halves of the building were sealed off from each other by a wall.

Training began months before the conversion of the plant was completed. The courses were developed by IVY Tech, a state vocational/technical college, in cooperation with AEECD personnel from Evandale.

AEECD's work is primarily assembly and testing. Electronic circuit boards are assembled from purchased components; boards are assembled into modules; modules are assembled into finished units; finished units are tested against the temperature extremes and vibration characteristic of operating conditions. Since parts are small and color-coded, employees need dexterity and excellent color vision.

Despite the major technological differences between the new plant and the old, employees needed only a modest amount of retraining. Compared with the cost of laying off hundreds of employees with twenty-plus years of seniority, the retraining option looks like a clear bargain.

Two basic programs were given: one for assemblers, and a more difficult one for assembler-solderers. Each of these jobs includes a number of related skills. The assemblers' course took eleven days, most of it on the job. The assembler-solderers' course took twelve days—nine in the classroom and three on the job. Successful completion of either course led to immediate job assignment, followed by additional on-the-job training. Employees, including those who qualify as testers, also took a two-day team-building course. All training took place on company time at full pay.

GE now encourages these workers, through tuition refunds, to take further electronics courses at IVY Tech. Numerous employees have sought advancement in the plant by attending after-hours classes in electrical fundamentals (an eleven-week course) or in testing (fourteen weeks).

Packard Electric Division of General Motors. A growing phenomenon in U.S. industry is joint employer-union management of aspects of the business in which the hourly workers have a direct and vital stake. For unions to carry out their part of the bargain, they must have access to any pertinent corporate information. Employers are therefore providing them with data about costs and future plans that, in the past, were often withheld from supervisors and junior managers. At GM's Packard Electric division, some of the most sensitive subjects are now jointly managed: control of work-force levels, terms of employment, and redeployment and the attendant training.

In partnership with their employer, workers at Packard Electric in Warren, Ohio, are engaged in a long-term struggle to save their plants and their employment from intense foreign and domestic competition. Through their union, Local 717 of the IUE, they share fully with management the responsibility of making tough decisions on work-force levels, deployment, and the training necessitated by that struggle.

Packard Electric, with 30,000 employees in six countries, supplies a great variety of components for autos and trucks all over the world. In Warren alone the division has nineteen plants and 9,000 hourly workers, represented by IUE. The struggle began in the 1970s, when Packard began moving final-assembly work to Mississippi and then Mexico to reduce labor costs. Several years of bitter conflict ensued: the company could not persuade the workers that survival was indeed at stake; the union could not persuade the employer that employment security in the devastated "Steel Valley" was a fight-and-die issue. Finally, in 1984, the parties achieved mutual understanding and agreement, embodied in a strategic decision: all high-labor, low-tech assembly jobs would be moved gradually from Warren to Mexico, while at the same time high-tech, low-labor operations would be moved to Warren.

The contract therefore provided that:

- Any full-time employee with seniority antedating January 1, 1982, and remaining capable of the job would have employment and income security until normal retirement (subject to certain agreed-upon escapes). All other employees, full-time or otherwise, have to accept less security and lower pay.
- Quality of working life (QWL) and other forms of joint programs would be encouraged.
- The parties would work together to improve competitiveness.
- The parties would seek to increase employment opportunities in Warren by (1) training, (2) reassigning employees and work, and (3) pursuing new business.

In support of the agreement, the parties established a joint management-union structure in Warren to direct QWL activities and to determine, based on annual and long-term business plans, the hiring and training needs of the plants. A joint board, consisting of members of the division's senior operations managers, the director of labor relations, and Local 717's chairman and president, administers all aspects of the security agreement; among other duties it assigns products to the plants and decides what their work force and training requirements will be.

A comparable joint board at each plant, consisting of the plant's top management and union people, decides the plant's specific training needs. The plant boards arrange for planning, developing, and carrying out the training. They also initiate and carry out proposals to improve operational effectiveness or to resolve problems, working through a structure of over forty internal staff people from union and management ranks.

Suggestions for training activities may originate anywhere in the organization but must receive approval from the appropriate joint committee. Each curriculum is developed by a design team, plantwide or divisionwide, according to the intended audience. A typical team includes a manufacturing supervisor, an engineering supervisor, an hourly worker, a union committeeman, an industrial engineer, and the senior administrator of the Skills Development Center. QWL specialists attend as facilitators. Instructional teams comprise representatives of management and union.

The division's Skills Development Center administers all divisionwide programs to train both supervisory and hourly employees for the new high-tech equipment being introduced, such as plastic injection insert molding machines. Teams from the center also train employees at the plants if requested by the plants. Other jointly developed and implemented courses teach statistical process control, problem solving, and subjects related to the QWL process.

Because of the division's reliance on joint management-union action, the parties have stressed training in the social skills that promote group problem solving and conflict resolution. After only two years, the Packard Electric/IUE employment security initiative has already led to the successful introduction of and training for new technology as well as to higher morale, lower absenteeism, and improved productivity.

Pacific Bell. Since divestiture in 1984, Pacific Bell—a subsidiary of Pacific Telesis, serving the state of California—has reduced its hourly work force by 20,000 with only 500 actual layoffs. By contract, the company and the Communications Workers of America (CWA) have established a policy of employment security along with joint mechanisms for training and retraining in support of that policy. A Training Advisory Board (TAB), comprising four union and three company representatives, advises on curricula and courses, evaluates programs, and encourages employees to participate.

To assess the need for training that will enable new jobs to be filled and obsolete jobs ended without causing displacement, the TAB draws on two sources of information:

1. *Technological change reports, issued quarterly by the company.* These reports forecast new systems and technological changes, their expected impact on the work force, and the projected beginning and completion dates of each change. The time horizon—as much as three or four years out—is long enough to plan and implement the necessary skills training. For example, a 1983 technological change report forecast that loop assignment (the job of determining where cables are routed) would be converted from a manual to a largely automated task and that the conversion would go on through 1988 (subsequently extended to 1989). Supervisors at loop assignment centers now know precisely when job cutbacks will occur. With this information, the TAB developed pretraining as well as on-the-job training programs. As a result, the number of jobholders in this specialty was reduced solely through attrition and reassignment, with no layoffs.
2. *Reports from local common interest forums.* In each major geographical area of California, a joint forum, headed by the company's local vice-president and the local union president, meets regularly to discuss operating changes that will have an impact on the work force—for example, office closings, technological changes, and so on. The forum considers possible force reductions and how to cope with them and transmits its findings to the TAB.

The parties have developed a system that keeps workers up to date on declining and rising job opportunities, and then provides training for those who volunteer to move.

- A weekly updated program shows the availability of jobs by geographic area, department, title, salary, and so on. Uptrends and downtrends are forecast for each management group. This service is offered at Career Directions Centers (CDCs) at ten locations in the state and should soon be offered at all job sites.
- CDCs contain reference libraries with information about career planning, job exploration, and the workings of the company's transfer and upgrade plan.
- Customized computer programs help employees determine skill requirements for specific jobs and assess their aptitudes for those skills. Individual career counseling will be available to help employees identify goals, make development plans, and select appropriate training courses. The Retraining Department is preparing a matrix that tells employees what basic courses are required for certain technical and skilled jobs.
- When the company identifies an area of job growth (for example, it recently forecast that 400 to 600 service representative jobs would open up each year until 1990), it works with community colleges and the CWA to develop curricula for pretraining courses. The names of those who complete the courses go into the file, ready when the time comes.
- With or without consultation, employees decide which courses to take for advancement or higher-skilled jobs.
- Employees can take virtually all off-the-job training at no cost, but on their own time. Degree-level courses may be given at community colleges, via correspondence, and through personal computers. Employees can also get instruction in test-taking techniques.
- Employees interested in jobs outside the company receive outplacement services.

Pacific Northwest Bell. Managing the redeployment of the work force for the purpose of employment security is so at odds with U.S. tradition that efforts to develop the necessary systems must overcome great inertia. It makes sense, then, to begin with a rough-and-ready method that works tolerably well rather than a sophisticated design that never gets off the ground. Pacific Northwest Bell (PNB) took such a pragmatic course and now, having demonstrated moderate success, is expanding and refining the system.

PNB, which, as a unit of US West, serves Idaho, Oregon, and Washington, has set itself the goal of maintaining employment security while its overall work force diminishes, technology advances, and individual skills expand. Within these conditions, it aims to make managers' careers more attractive by opening up, and making managers more aware of, new opportunities for mobility. The mechanism is a Job Skills Bank, inaugurated in 1985 and still evolving.

The idea was tested first in 1984, in the Finance and Comptrollers department, where many managers had asked for more information about career paths and more chances to put their untapped abilities to work. Favorable response to the test encouraged PNB to open the bank to all 4,000 managers in the system.

The basic concept of the Job Skills Bank is simple:

- Each management employee who wishes to enter the bank fills out, with the help of a handbook, a detailed profile of skills, experiences, and preferences. The profile goes into the computer and is updated annually.
- When a management job opens, the personnel administrator must submit a job vacancy form, filled out according to the same handbook codes.
- The bank's computer notifies registered employees (and their supervisors) of all job vacancies for which they appear to be qualified.
- If an employee is interested in a vacancy, he or she must discuss it with his or her current supervisor. Only the supervisor may nominate the employee for the vacancy. However, personnel administrators of the departments with vacancies are also notified which employees are available to fill the vacancies.

According to PNB, the success of the bank requires two conditions:

1. Precise coding of skills both in the applicant's profile and in the job vacancy notice. Employee participation in the bank has been high except in the engineering and technical departments, where mismatches due to imprecise coding have concerned both sides. The bank staff is working to refine coding methods to show skill proficiency levels more accurately. They are also integrating PNB's bank with those of two sister companies—Mountain Bell and Northwest Bell—which will greatly expand the opportunities for both applicants and internal recruiters.
2. Cooperation on the part of the applicant's supervisor. Because some supervisors have tried to hang on to valued employees, consideration is being given to permitting direct contact between an interested employee and a manager with a vacancy.

In addition to matching people and vacancies, the Job Skills Bank has proved useful in identifying employees for special projects or promotion and in estimating local skills surpluses and deficits. It is expected to be helpful also in staffing new business ventures the company may undertake.

Managing Redeployment Outside the Firm

As noted earlier, American workers are realistic about the ability of an employer to provide employment security. They do not expect airtight protection of their jobs against economic vicissitudes, but they do expect the employer to give as much consideration to their misfortune as to its own. They view the employer's active help in obtaining a suitable job outside the firm as a fulfillment of that expectation. At Columbia, Maryland, GE has done just that and has been repaid in kind.

The Columbia case is not unique, but it points up the value of actively managing the redeployment of employees to jobs outside the firm. The basic concept springs from the practice of outplacement, which originated as a means of removing unwanted managers without incurring guilt. The practice was later applied to lower-level employees made redundant by total or partial plant shutdowns. Eventually both employees and employers realized that outplacement should be viewed positively as a means of preserving continuity of employment when economic forces necessitate dismissals. Major labor-management agreements in the telecommunications and auto industries now provide for jointly managing the retraining and placement of workers for jobs in other firms.

The scope of preparation for outside jobs may be as narrow as job-search training or as broad as college education to acquire a new profession. Typically, the retraining is provided by a community college or similar institution, rather than being offered in-house. What matters is that the employer takes responsibility to assist displaced workers until they find new employment. At GE's Columbia plant, the training was keyed to a detailed analysis of the local labor market.

General Electric at Columbia, Maryland. Battered by Korean and Japanese competition, GE's major appliance plant in Columbia, Maryland, is now winding down all microwave manufacturing and phasing out 900 jobs, half of its work force. The company's action was preceded by lengthy notice and accompanied by generous layoff compensation and benefits. Displaced workers, for want of suitable opportunities within the company, are being retrained for jobs in the area.

Retraining is managed by a Re-Employment Center at the Columbia work site, funded jointly by GE, the state of Maryland, and the federal government.

Most of the displaced are semiskilled hourly assembly workers, with long service at GE. A few with soldering skills that meet military specifications are expected to find comparable jobs with military contractors nearby, but prospects for the others are dim unless they can be retrained.

The center's director, who had previously directed the county's Department of Employment and Training and thus knew the area well, made it an early priority to assess the local labor market and determine where current job opportunities existed and where they would exist in the future. The center didn't want to steer people to jobs where they might be laid off again in a few years. With the aid of studies conducted by state and county agencies, the center predicted that the most promising job markets would be in medical services, food services, hotel management, auto mechanics, word processing, computer programming, and other computer-related work.

To prepare displaced workers for new occupations, the center provides job-search training, frequent reports on job and training opportunities, remedial education, and community college courses tailored to the conditions of the local job market. The community colleges' experience in cooperative employment/education programs helps retrainees to build bridges to the new occupations, for example, through internships with employers.

Some contracts between the center and colleges make part of the fee contingent on placement related to the training, or placement at or above a stated pay level.

The center reports good progress to date. Of the 750 hourly workers laid off, 100 took early retirement; about 275 have been placed in new jobs; 300 are taking skills training. According to Maryland officials, the proportion of displaced workers in training is remarkably high, and this is attributed to the quality of the counseling they have received at the center.

GE, which has an outstanding record for managing reductions in force so as to cause the least injury to employees and communities, also judges the success of a reduction by its effect on the employees who remain. At Columbia, the company reports, the continuing operations have maintained, and even improved, the high levels of performance that prevailed before.

Context Learning

Reliable knowledge and skills related to the operating processes of the work unit are essential, whether the processes are physical, chemical, biological, or informational, but they are only a part of what employees must know in order to do an acceptable job. Employees must also understand in some detail how the work unit actually operates, its specific objectives, the

kinds of problems that arise, how people in the unit share responsibility, where to turn for help, what sort of performance the
supervisor expects of employees, and how the unit interacts with
other parts of the firm (especially its internal customers).

Normally, these contextual matters are learned on the job,
after the employee joins the work unit. However, when a significant proportion of retraining consists of classroom or other off-
the-job instruction, and when this instruction takes place before
joining the work unit (which is the usual case), its effectiveness
may be seriously impaired. As noted in Chapter Seven, the ability to acquire new knowledge through reading and lectures is
directly related to the learner's familiarity with the subject matter
of the new knowledge.

Familiarity with the work-unit context enables a retrainee
to acquire new knowledge and skills faster and more easily
because he or she sees how they can be put to use on the job.
And if the retrainee is actually assigned to the new job before
instruction begins, the retrainee wants to put them to use to
ensure success on the job.

To achieve the highest possible success rate in retraining
employees for new occupations within the firm, employers are
paying closer attention to contextual learning. In large multidivisional firms, a transfer from one division to another may present learning problems as severe as those of a transfer from one
firm to another.

Hewlett-Packard. We have already noted how the Xerox
Critical Skills Training Program sought to make training voluntary, to screen for motivation as well as intellectual capacity,
to ease familial tensions caused by retraining, to provide mentors from the "hiring" departments, and to involve supervisors
from "hiring" and "originating" departments. Some of these
procedures, and a number of others, are incorporated in a recent Hewlett-Packard (HP) program that retrains blue-collar
workers from surplus occupations to fill white-collar jobs in areas
of new demand.

As a result of the rapid changes rocking the computer and
electronics industries, HP finds that fewer people are needed

to manufacture and assemble products and more people are needed to fill the increasingly sophisticated technological jobs in the office. Since HP does not lay people off except as a last resort (only two instances since 1939), it has chosen to deal with the growing job mismatch through retraining. All retraining is given at the employee's request but on company time. The company provides guidance and covers all costs.

A pilot program for divisions in the San Francisco Bay Area began in June 1986. Five of the divisions expected declines in manufacturing; the other five expected to hire people for office and computer work. A core set of skills was designed to fill jobs in the six categories of greatest demand in the Bay Area: electronic data-processing support, computer operator, administrative support, telemarketing operator, secretary, and field and factory order-processing support. The thirty-five pilot trainees received core academic training, over a period of three months, in math, English, typing, office procedures, time management, and introduction to computers. Trainees spent one full day and four afternoons each week at a community college, in addition to taking introductory and advanced computer classes at HP's Office Learning Center. Employees headed for telemarketing or computer operations took specialized courses after the three-month program.

HP tried to assign trainees to new positions as soon as the training began, but that was not always feasible. Most were transferred while the program was in progress. If reassignments were delayed, the sending unit was pressed to remove the trainee from production work during the training program and to assign new job responsibilities similar to those of the eventual new job. In either event, a career mentor immediately went to work with the trainee, linking classroom and job. The mentor came from the division to which the trainee was attached; if the trainee transferred during the program, a new mentor was appointed from the hiring division. If a full-time position was not available by the end of the retraining program, the trainee was placed in a temporary assignment in the chosen career field until a permanent match was made.

The trainee's current supervisor and the personnel department helped the trainee with job-search instruction during and after the program. Trainees' resumes and transfer requests, directed to divisions with current openings, were screened by hiring supervisors before interviews took place.

By September 1986, most retrainees had been placed in their new positions, with enthusiastic feedback from hiring supervisors and department managers. The program is expected to become companywide, but each region will be free to adapt the guidelines to its special conditions.

To strengthen the trainee's motivation to learn and the relevant manager's motivation to help, HP emphasized the element of choice on both sides of the transaction. For example, in eliciting applications the following steps were taken:

- Notices of the program were posted.
- Personnel managers in divisions with excess production jobs described the program to interested employees and discussed long-term market changes affecting the work force and the urgent need for retraining.
- In panel discussions, people from the major career tracks described their jobs and answered questions.
- Interested employees toured the divisions with job openings.
- Candidates reviewed generic job profiles of the six career tracks.
- First priority was given to candidates whose jobs were no longer needed. Second priority went to those whose jobs were scheduled to be phased out within the coming year.
- After screening, applicants were interviewed and rated for expressed interest in career change, willingness to be retrained, demonstrated dependability, initiative, flexibility, teamwork, and ability to communicate orally and in writing.

Upon acceptance, candidate and company signed an agreement outlining the responsibilities of the individuals involved on both sides. The trainee agreed to complete on-the-job training assigned by the career mentor, and to keep supervisors and program coordinators informed about the trainee's progress. The trainee's current supervisor agreed to adjust work schedules and responsibilities, to facilitate retraining and job placement. For example, if the trainee transferred to a new job during the training period, the supervisor worked closely with the "hiring" supervisor to smooth the transition. The hiring supervisor agreed to give the trainee detailed information about the new job and to work with the trainee's career mentor to get the most out of on-the-job training. The program coordinators of the sending and hiring units agreed to oversee the program, work closely with the supervisors and career mentors, and discuss training progress with the trainee.

Since many pilot trainees had not been in a classroom for years, they were instructed about the community college system, effective learning and study techniques, test taking, career planning, and interpersonal relations. They toured the community college and met instructors and other college officials.

The college and the company shared responsibility for counseling, career advice, and tutoring.

According to HP, training worked best for those who were placed in their new jobs early in the program. Early placement increased the motivation of the trainees and also elicited rapid support from the supervisors and program coordinators of the hiring organizations. The trainees quickly became familiar with the new work environment and were thus able to put more of the substance of the training into proper context.

Context Learning for External Placement

While the Hewlett-Packard and Xerox experiences are concerned with retraining for new occupations within the firm, even greater attention to context learning is needed in the case of outplacements, since the shock of transition is greater. In a previous work, *Employment Security in a Free Economy,* we stated, "The strongest motivator and morale builder for retraining is knowing that the curriculum is essential to a job that one is about to undertake. It follows that the best use of retraining money is probably to help displaced workers get new jobs and then pay the new employers to retrain them" (Rosow and Zager, 1984).

As a step in this direction, when employees were displaced by the partial closure of GE's plant in Columbia, Maryland, some took a word-processing course at Howard Community

College. The college placed them in internships with local employers so that they could "adjust to the office environment, sharpen their skills, and build up their confidence." Employers providing internships are not required to pay their interns, but many did, and many offered their interns continuing employment.

Other steps are worth considering:

- The employee's previous supervisor can maintain contact with the hiring supervisor.
- The new supervisor should be involved in the employee's training, both on the job and off.

Recommendations

Recommendation 19. Employers should give serious consideration to the continuous learning/employment security connection as a strategy for the long-term survival and growth of the enterprise.

Recommendation 20. Employers should give as broad a guarantee of employment security as they can manage, to strengthen work-force receptivity to the continuous change and continuous learning that competition demands. At the least, they should guarantee that no program for introducing new technology into the workplace will cause employees to lose employment or income.

Recommendation 21. Employers should evaluate the costs of retraining career employees as compared with the visible and hidden costs of separation and replacement with new, trained outsiders. Often the costs of retraining (combined with the advantage of stability of the work force) may be lower, and the costs of dismissal or retirement and the hiring of new people may be higher, than appears on the surface.

Recommendation 22. To promote employment security, which is key to high productivity, employers should assign responsibilities and establish routines to (1) anticipate the obsolescence of current jobs and the emergence of new jobs, (2) identify current employees who can be advantageously retrained for the emerging jobs, (3) provide employees with early opportunities to volunteer for education and training, and (4) ensure that employees are ready to enter the new jobs when needed. Where there is a union, it should be involved in these activities insofar as they apply to employees in the bargaining unit.

Recommendation 23. When an employer invites an employee to be retrained, it should ensure that the employee becomes fully acquainted, as early as possible, with the new position, work unit, and supervisor, whether the position is within or outside the firm. Such acquaintance maximizes the trainee's ability to learn and to apply the new skills.

Recommendation 24. Employers should anticipate unavoidable displacements or forced dismissals as far ahead as possible and use the lead time to develop market-oriented retraining and outplacement programs. Economic supports should be built into the programs to reinforce employment security.

Background Papers

Feurey, C. (Committee for Economic Development). "Pacific Northwest Bell and Pacific Bell: Two Approaches to Employment Security." Aug. 1986.
*Morano, R. (Xerox Corporation), and Leonardi, J. (Rochester Institute of Technology). "Xerox's Critical Skills Training Program: A Commitment to Retraining Pays Off." Aug. 1986.
Ward, D. L. (GTE Communication Systems). "Hiring Versus Training: A Case Perspective." Aug. 1986.

*This background paper can also be found as a case study in the companion volume, *Successful Training Strategies: Twenty-Six Innovative Corporate Models,* edited by J. Casner-Lotto (San Francisco: Jossey-Bass, 1988).

Case Studies

Casner-Lotto, J. "Hewlett-Packard's Partnerships for New Careers." Dec. 1986.

Feurey, C. "Pacific Northwest Bell's Job Skills Bank." Dec. 1986.

Hemmens, K. C. "Linking Training with Job and Income Security: The Packard Electric Experience." Dec. 1986.

Hickey, J. V. "Brightening the Prospects of Displaced Workers: General Electric Company's Columbia, Maryland Re-Employment Center." Dec. 1986.

Smith, P. S. "General Electric, Fort Wayne, Indiana: High Tech Comes to the Rust Belt." Dec. 1986.

9

Summary of
Guidelines for Action

The central theme of this report is that training for new technology is becoming an issue of survival for American companies, demanding active intervention by the highest levels of management and (where appropriate) unions. What forms should intervention take?

Since training is but one of the many claims on limited corporate resources and must be spent to best advantage, employers will have several objectives: that training strategy be an inherent part of overall corporate strategy; that all employees who have to deal with new technology acquire the necessary skills and knowledge and that training be accepted as an integral feature of every job; that employees learn as much as possible from the manufacturers of new technology; that formal training programs produce the greatest amount of learning per dollar and per training hour; and that employees be retained by the company long enough for training to produce its money's worth.

Coordinating Training Strategy and Corporate Strategy. The primary objective is that employees acquire all the skills and knowledge they need, but only what they need. What do they really need? Whatever is essential to formulate and fulfill a successful corporate strategy. Certain skills and knowledge are needed to determine what products and services the company

228

should produce, and what kinds of technology should be used to produce them; other skills and knowledge are needed in order to apply new technologies most profitably.

Those who determine corporate strategy must calculate whether the organization is capable of acquiring strategically necessary skills and knowledge on schedule. In leading companies, therefore, a senior officer in charge of training takes part in formulating strategy. That individual can also advise whether a more ambitious strategy would be feasible from the standpoint of training, and can help subsequently to communicate the strategy to all parts of the organization.

Communication of the strategy is vital. Trainees and their supervisors take training seriously only when they believe it will further the company's prosperity and their own. If they do not understand the skill and learning requirements of the corporate strategy, they cannot make valid decisions on how to achieve strategic goals.

Ultimately, it is the CEO's responsibility to see that the training requirements of corporate strategy are met. The key points to be monitored are program priorities, program objectives, and program outcomes.

Continuous Learning. Difficult as it may be for Americans to believe, at some large work sites—factories as well as offices—rank-and-file employees look forward to coming to work and feel genuinely excited about their jobs. When asked why they like the job so much, one of the most frequent replies is "We learn something new every day." In such workplaces, opportunities are continually presented for learning new skills. Employees are motivated to take advantage of these opportunities by the chance for self-development and professional growth as well as for the sheer enjoyment of learning.

In today's fiercely competitive world, learning something new each day has also become an economic imperative. Employers can attain these mutually supportive ends by involving all employees in all aspects of teaching and learning skills for new technology. Management and employees (and their unions) should team up to analyze needs, develop curricula, design training materials, instruct, and evaluate results. The case studies analyzed for this report show that such teams can perform these functions proficiently, creatively, and enthusiastically.

To prevent learning from being overwhelmed by the press of day-to-day problems, the employer should make it known that learning is as much a part of the job as any other activity and should recognize achievements in teaching or learning. In addition, permanent mechanisms are needed to keep the process running at optimum level.

For example, a train-the-trainer policy creates a cadre of "content experts" as instructors with heightened ability to analyze and transmit important skills and knowledge. Members of semiautonomous work teams share responsibility for teaching and learning. The more formal system of learning-by-objectives requires employee and supervisor to meet periodically and agree on the new skills and knowledge the employee will acquire in order to reach key performance goals. Continuous learning centers enable and encourage employees to teach their peers innovative applications of new technology. Transfer of knowledge and novel applications of software are accelerated and become routine.

Since unions have a stake in their members' careers and the employer's prosperity, they have often urged employers to allow them a responsible role in training. Union involvement in training, where permitted, has proved to be beneficial to the employer. In fact, unions that have actively participated in the training process have made valuable contributions and have encouraged more employee participation and learning.

A Partnership in Learning. Due to the traditional arm's-length relationship between users of new technology and manufacturers, users are unable to take advantage of manufacturers' wealth of skill and knowledge; manufacturers, on the other hand, fall short of satisfying their customers and lose precious insights into how they might strengthen their market positions. The situation cries out for a partnership in learning.

Manufacturers should take the initiative in changing the relationship, since they hold most of the cards. To begin with, both parties must stop picturing their transaction as merely the sale and purchase of a piece of new technology. The purchaser's real, though usually unexpressed, purpose is to incorporate the new technology into a profitably operating business, and it will not be satisfied until that objective is attained. Selling a good product is necessary but not enough. Offering training along with the product is better, but still not enough. Getting the purchaser to understand the real objective and to pay for it may be the hardest part of a sale, but ignoring it hurts both parties.

Major purchasers occasionally have demanded—and obtained—better-than-usual training from the manufacturer as part of the deal. However, this rarely induces the manufacturer to do what it should—that is, develop a permanent, full-fledged, market-oriented training capability for every purchaser.

A partnership in learning should be marked by joint planning and realization of the learning opportunities that present themselves at every stage of the relationship, from the drafting of the contract through full achievement of steady-state operation. Plans for formal training need the longest lead time: an effective program includes not only the techniques of operating, troubleshooting, and maintaining, but also the scientific and technological principles on which the new technology is based, as well as hands-on experience—all to be completed by the time the new technology is installed.

The manufacturer should also advise the user about the probably impact of the new technology on organization, decision making, job design, work rules, and communications. Although the user's organization development consultants can provide some guidance, the manufacturer is more likely to have observed the equipment in actual use.

Integrated systems raise special obstacles to the establishment of a partnership in learning: components are supplied by numerous vendors, and no one vendor has a mastery of all the disciplines involved. The user needs the aid of an organization that can provide both a strong training capability, based on experience in manufacturing or assembling integrated systems, and access to the various technical disciplines. If the lead vendor can furnish this aid, fine. Otherwise, the user must resort to a third party.

Cost-Effective Design and Delivery. The latest techniques in design and delivery of training so dazzle the eye that an observer can easily lose sight of their cost-effectiveness—not cost-effectiveness in general, but that of a particular training program in meeting the objectives of a particular organization in a particular situation. Something that works wonderfully for a companywide program in IBM may be totally inappropriate for a small insurance-processing office. With so many different training jobs to be done, and so many techniques to choose from, employers should establish a regular routine to review the cost-effectiveness of proposed programs.

The effectiveness of a training program should be judged by how well trainees learn what they were supposed to learn. The decision of what they were supposed to learn is a separate matter, flowing from corporate strategy.

In assessing the dollar costs of a progam, employers should not consider trainee salaries and benefits as an added cost (because training is as essential as any other part of the job) unless additional expenses are actually incurred to cover the employee's other work while in training. However, the amount of time an employee spends in acquiring a particular skill is a significant variable.

When a program is proposed, the employer should ask whether the specified learning objectives—that is, the number, level, and location of trainees and the skills and knowledge to be acquired—could not be gained at lower cost and/or less consumption of trainee time. To answer this question, the employer should compare the proposed project management, instructional design, course development, and delivery systems with the principal available alternatives. Cost and effectiveness should be compared again after the program has been completed, to modify procedures for assessing proposals.

Linking Continuous Learning and Employment Security. The decision to invest time and money in training for new technology implies that an employer expects trainees to remain within the company to amortize the investment. However, if that expectation is not clearly communicated to the organization, employees' motivation to learn and apply this knowledge will be diminished by worries about continued employment. Still, most employers cannot bring themselves to make a commitment to employment security because they fear that the eventual cost of delivering on it might damage the company. They wrongly believe that the only effective commitment is a so-called no-layoff policy.

American workers do not expect airtight guarantees; every no-layoff policy has an escape clause. What employees want is assurance that layoffs or dismissals will not take place until all practical alternatives have been tried. Employers can afford to give this assurance and are well served when they do. They should also promise to help employees find suitable jobs elsewhere when layoffs or dismissals cannot be avoided. As a minimum, they should guarantee that new technology or new processes introduced in the workplace will not cause loss of income or employment. Otherwise, employees are encouraged to oppose change, resist learning, and restrict efficiency.

Employment is often jeopardized by the need to *re*train people for new technology. Retraining is not a precise word: it may mean acquiring the skill to run a new piece of equipment that changes a fraction of the job (for example, a secretary learns to use a word processor); it may mean learning to do the whole job differently because new technology has fundamentally altered the way work is done (for example, a newspaper compositor learns to paste up computer printouts); it may mean learning a totally different occupation because the previous one has become redundant (for example, a chemist becomes a computer scientist). The broader the change, the more the employer is tempted to dismiss current employees and replace them with people already trained for the new technology. This temptation should be resisted. A fire-hire policy not only demoralizes the rest of the organization; it often proves to be the more expensive option, once the dollar-and-cents costs of dismissal and replacement are calculated.

Sometimes fire-hire seems the only viable alternative because the employer has run out of time for retraining. Such a situation must be recognized for what it is: a failure to plan.

Employers should establish procedures for anticipating technological changes, their implications for new jobs, and the availability of employees in positions that are becoming surplus. With such information, it is practical to plan training programs that will match people to job openings as the need arises.

Although technology is, and always has been, one of the most dynamic forces in economic development, its products and processes are, in themselves, inanimate. They can be brought to life only through human skills, knowledge, and experience— the results of organized teaching and learning. That is why training is vital to every business. As one change rapidly follows another in processes, equipment, products, and services, learning in the workplace has to become continuous, lifelong, and, ultimately, critical to strategic investment plans.

For American companies in general, therefore, training for new technology will be a matter of survival. For those with vision and leadership, it will provide a competitive edge.

References

Baldwin, L. V. "The NTU/AMCEE Instructional Satellite Network." Unpublished paper commissioned by Work in America Institute, Mar. 1986.

Beam, A., and Lewis, G. "The IBM/DEC Wars: It's 'The Year of the Customer.'" *Business Week,* Mar. 30, 1987, pp. 86–88.

Bikson, T. K., Stasz, C., and Mankin, D. A. *Computer-Mediated Work: Individual and Organizational Impact in One Corporate Headquarters.* Santa Monica, Calif.: Rand Corporation, 1985.

Cook, K. "Marketing the 'Lowdown on High Tech.'" *Working Woman,* May 1987, pp. 74–75.

Duscha, S. "Response to Issues Raised by the Legislative Analyst." Paper addressed to the California State Legislature, Sacramento, Calif., Apr. 25, 1986.

Eurich, N. P. *Corporate Classrooms: The Learning Business.* Princeton, N.J.: Carnegie Foundation for the Advancement of Teaching, 1985.

Feder, B. J. "The Woes of a Robot Peddler." *New York Times,* Aug. 16, 1987, sec. 3, p. 1.

Fields, C. M. "Many Aggressive Community Colleges Focusing on Training Workers for Fast-Growing Fields." *The Chronicle of Higher Education,* 1987, *30,* 21.

235

236 References

Gutchess, J. F. *Employment Security in Action: Strategies That Work.* Pergamon Press/Work in America Institute Series. New York: Pergamon Press, 1985.

Hampton, W. J. "General Motors' Little Engine That Could." *Business Week,* Aug. 3, 1987, p. 88.

Harris, C. L. "IBM Finds a Substitute Teacher for Minicomputer Buyers." *Business Week,* Feb. 23, 1987, p. 122G.

Office of the Assistant Secretary of Defense. *Profile of American Youth.* Washington, D.C.: U.S. Department of Defense, Mar. 1982.

"Replace or Retrain?" *Bulletin to Management* (Bureau of National Affairs), Nov. 29, 1984, p. 8.

Rosow, J. M., and Zager, R. *Employment Security in a Free Economy.* A Work in America Institute Policy Study. New York: Pergamon Press, 1984.

Ryan, T., and Furlong, W. "Literacy Programs, the Armed Forces, and Penal Institutions." In J. Carroll and J. Chall (eds.), *Toward a Literate Society.* New York: McGraw-Hill, 1975.

Sabel, C. F. *Work and Politics: The Division of Labor in Industry.* New York: Cambridge University Press, 1982.

Skinner, W. *Manufacturing: The Formidable Competitive Weapon.* New York: John Wiley, 1985.

Sticht, T. G. *Reading for Working: A Functional Literacy Anthology.* Alexandria, Va.: Human Resources Research Organization, 1975.

Sticht, T. G. "Understanding Readers and Their Uses of Texts." In R. Waller and T. Duffy (eds.), *Designing Usable Texts.* Orlando, Fla.: Academic Press, 1985.

Sticht, T. G. "Job Skills and Basic Skills: Training 'Midlevel Literates' for Work with New Technologies." Unpublished paper commissioned by Work in America Institute, Mar. 1986.

Sticht, T. G., Armstrong, W., Hickey, D., and Caylor, J. *Cast-Off Youth: Policy and Training Methods from the Military Experience.* San Diego, Calif.: Applied Behavioral and Cognitive Sciences, 1986.

Sticht, T. G., Hooke, L., and Caylor, J. *Literacy, Oracy, and Vocational Aptitude as Predictors of Attrition and Promotion.* Washington, D.C.: Office of the Assistant Secretary of Defense (Manpower, Reserve Affairs, and Logistics), 1981.

Sticht, T. G., and Mikulecky, L. *Job-Related Basic Skills: Cases and Conclusions.* Columbus, Ohio: National Center for Research in Vocational Education, ERIC Clearinghouse on Adult, Career, and Vocational Education, 1985.

Sticht, T. G., and others. *Teachers, Books, Computers, and Peers: Integrated Communications Technologies for Adult Literacy Development.* Washington, D.C.: U.S. Department of Defense, 1986.

Uchitelle, L. "Industry Reluctant to Spend." *New York Times,* Apr. 20, 1987, Business Day section, p. 1.

U.S. Bureau of the Census. *Statistical Abstract of the United States.* 104th ed. Washington, D.C.: Bureau of the Census, 1983.

U.S. Department of the Army. *Marginal Man and Military Service.* Washington, D.C.: U.S. Department of the Army, 1965.

Ward, D. L. "Hiring Versus Training: A Case Perspective." Unpublished paper commissioned by Work in America Institute, Aug. 1986.

Index

A

Allen-Bradley, 100; and Caterpillar Inc., 119-122
Allied Corporation, 164
Aluminum Company of America (ALCOA), and State Technical Institute, 154
Amatrol, and Miller Brewing Company, 122-125
American Association of Community and Junior Colleges (AACJC), 151
American Society for Training and Development (ASTD), training expenditure estimate, 28-31
American Transtech, 46-48, 68
Appraisal: performance, 44; potential, 44
Armed Services Vocational Aptitude Battery (ASVAB), 174, 176-177
Armstrong, W., 181, 182, 187, 236
Arthur Andersen and Company, 31
Association for Media-Based Continuing Education for Engineers (AMCEE), 161, 163-164; clients of, 164; member universities of, 165; and NTU, 169-170
AT&T, 46-47, 81-82, 164

B

Baldwin, L. V., 165, 235
Bay de Noc College, 151-152
Bay State Skills Corporation, 159-160
Beam, A., 96, 235
BellSouth, 48
Bell System, 31, 47, 80, 87
Berkshire Community College, 159-160
Bikson, T. K., 101, 235
Budgets, and training, 11, 28-34

C

Carnegie, A., 62
Carnegie-Mellon University, 104
Caterpillar Inc., 40, 42, 118; and Allen-Bradley, 119-122
Caylor, J., 181, 182, 187, 236
Change(s), affecting corporations, 26-28
Cleveland Advanced Manufacturing Program (CAMP), 158-159
Colorado State University, 162
Columbia University, 32
Communications Workers of America: and AT&T, 81-82; and Pacific Bell, 82-84, 215